POWER PLAYS

ENERGY OPTIONS IN THE AGE OF PEAK OIL

Robert Rapier

Apress®

Power Plays: Energy Options in the Age of Peak Oil

ISBN-13 (pbk): 978-1-4302-4086-0

ISBN-13 (electronic): 978-1-4302-4087-7

Trademarked names may appear in this book. Rather than use a trademark symbol with every occurrence of a trademarked name, we use the names only in an editorial fashion and to the benefit of the trademark owner, with no intention of infringement of the trademark.

Distributed to the book trade worldwide by Springer-Verlag New York, Inc., 233 Spring Street, 6th Floor, New York, NY 10013. Phone 1-800-SPRINGER, fax 201-348-4505, e-mail orders-ny@springer-sbm.com, or visit http://www.springeronline.com.

For information on translations, please contact us by e-mail at info@apress.com, or visit http://www.apress.com.

Apress and friends of ED books may be purchased in bulk for academic, corporate, or promotional use. eBook versions and licenses are also available for most titles. For more information, reference our Special Bulk Sales–eBook Licensing web page at http://www.apress.com/info/bulksales. To place an order, email your request to support@apress.com.

For my family.
You are the reason I write.

Contents

About the Author

Robert Rapier works in the energy industry and writes and speaks about issues involving energy and the environment. He is Chief Technology Officer and Executive Vice President at Merica International, a forestry and renewable energy company involved in a variety of projects around the world. Robert has 20 years of international engineering experience in the chemicals, oil and gas, and renewable energy industries, and holds several patents related to his work. He has worked in the areas of oil refining, natural gas production, synthetic fuels, ethanol production, butanol production, and various biomass to energy projects. Robert is also the author of the R-Squared Energy Column at *Consumer Energy Report*, where he serves as Managing Editor. His articles on energy and sustainability have appeared in numerous media outlets, including the *Washington Post, Christian Science Monitor*, and *Forbes*.

Acknowledgments

Writing for an audience is rarely a solo event. It certainly was not for this book, and I would like to acknowledge some of the people whose help and support made this book possible.

I want to acknowledge the patience and support of my family as I wrote, isolated from them for long stretches at a time. To my wife Sandy, daughter Courtney, and sons Peyton and Luke—now we can go on a vacation.

I want to thank my publisher Apress, and my editor Jeff Olson, for believing in me enough to seek me out to write this book. I had long considered writing a book about energy, and Jeff's encouragement and confidence in me was a strong motivator in helping me to complete it. The valuable feedback that he and other editors at Apress provided on the text has made this a much stronger book, and has helped me become a better writer.

Nobody has helped improve my writing in recent years more than Sam Avro, the founder and editor in chief of *Consumer Energy Report*, where my regular energy column—R-Squared Energy[1]—is hosted. Besides offering critical feedback on my weekly column, Sam puts in long hours to make sure the site is running smoothly. In addition, Sam made many helpful suggestions on the topics and text covered by this book.

I am grateful to Greg Geyer for reaching out to his network of contacts on my behalf. I received valuable input from several people as a result of Greg's efforts, including Jeremy Gilbert on the "Peak Oil" and "Energy Production" chapters, and Steve Andrews, who jogged my memory on California's attempts to roll out methanol as a gasoline alternative.

Thank you to Alan Drake for the valuable contributions toward the chapter on oil-free transportation. His passion for electric rail inspires hope in a future that enables mobility with a fraction of today's fossil fuel consumption.

A special thanks to my good friend Jerry Unruh, who reviewed the chapter on global warming and made a number of helpful comments and suggestions. I know that Jerry would have preferred that I make a strong case for the need to urgently combat global warming, but the purpose of the chapter is really to help readers on both sides of the issue better understand the controversy.

---

[1] www.consumerenergyreport.com/columns/rsquared/

I would have never been in the position to write this book without the inspiration I have received from readers of R-Squared Energy as well as readers of *The Oil Drum*.[2] The constructive feedback is what has kept me writing all of these years. I solicited feedback from both sets of readers at various points during the process of writing this book, and the comments were invaluable in ensuring that major topics weren't overlooked, and that many minor details were clear and technically accurate. But the feedback also made me realize that I could not cover all topics to everyone's satisfaction. My apologies if there is something that you strongly feel should have been covered but is not.

A big thank you goes to all my friends and family back in my hometown of Hugo, Oklahoma. So many of you have been very supportive throughout this process, and provided inspiration when I was feeling drained. Now that the book is published, I can break free for a visit back home.

Finally, thanks to all of my colleagues at Merica International for providing a sounding board, and for helping me with a specific word or phrase when I was struggling. I want to especially thank Michael and Jeannette Saalfeld for convincing me to come to Hawaii to work in 2009. You have done so much for my family and me, and this book would not have been possible without your support.

---

[2] www.theoildrum.com

Preface

At various times over the past five years, I have seriously considered writing a comprehensive book about energy. My primary motivation for writing about energy is a sincere belief that many of our current global energy policies entail unacceptable trade-offs and threaten future generations. As a result, I feel compelled to engage people on the topic of energy, with the hope that these discussions can gradually help influence energy policy in a positive way.

To be clear, this is not a book about peak oil. There are plenty of those that cover both sides of that issue. This book is about the many energy options we have, and the many trade-offs we make as a result of our energy choices. The topic of peak oil is certainly covered, but I think my take on peak oil is a bit different from that of most people.

The topic of energy is wide and deep. As a result, it is impossible to cover all topics to everyone's satisfaction. My goals for this book are to pique your interest in a wide range of energy topics, encourage you to start thinking about energy in a different way, help you to more clearly understand our energy trade-offs, and to share with you interesting bits of energy trivia. I will tackle many polarizing topics—such as nuclear power and climate change—but hopefully in a nonpolarizing fashion.

Every reader is going to find points of agreement and points of disagreement in the book. I consider myself a reasonable person, and sometimes reasonable people disagree. We all view the world through a set of lenses influenced by our individual experiences, and those lenses frame our beliefs. The lenses come in many different forms, and to really understand a person's arguments, it helps to try to view the issue through their lenses. Some people believe we are entering the early stages of an unprecedented energy emergency, while others believe we are on the cusp of an era of abundant and clean energy. In order to effectively dialogue with such disparate groups of people, I want to understand what has shaped their views.

My lenses dictate what I write, as well as why I write. This book will go into depth about why I believe some of the things I believe, but there are three very broad beliefs that influence my writing:

1. We must transition away from fossil fuels with a sense of urgency, for reasons discussed in this book.

2. To achieve this transition, we need to develop systems and services with a much lower fossil fuel dependency—while ensuring that we have adequate energy supplies during the transition.

3. During the transition process, we must take care of our air, water, and especially our topsoil to preserve our ability to feed the population.

During my career, I have worked in the chemical industry, the oil industry, and the renewable energy industry. I have lived in many places—Oklahoma, Texas, Germany, Montana, Scotland, the Netherlands, and now Hawaii. These jobs and these places helped shape my perspectives on energy. I am a chemical engineer, but before going into engineering I received my bachelor's degree in chemistry, and then spent two years working on a PhD in chemistry. That training as a scientist helped to instill in me the understanding that scientific conclusions are tentative and always subject to revision as additional data come in. I therefore realize the importance of keeping open the option that any particular position of mine is wrong—and I have tried to maintain that perspective during my career, and while writing about energy.

But acknowledging that one could be wrong has to go hand in hand with the consequences of being wrong. Therefore, when I advocate for a specific course of action, I strive to understand the consequences if that action is based on beliefs that are ultimately wrong. I try to constantly keep that in mind as I write.

My goal is to write objectively. In order to be successful, I constantly find myself trying to view the world through another person's lenses. But as you read this book, you will see the world through my lenses.

All About Energy

Dependence and Disconnect

All our knowledge has its origins in our perceptions.

—Leonardo da Vinci

Over the past 250 years, energy has driven an enormous expansion of the global population, and it has dramatically changed the way we live. Beginning in the second half of the 18th century, the Industrial Revolution—enabled by cheap and ample supplies of coal—brought about many new inventions, large-scale industrial production, and jobs for many. The world's per capita income and population both began to grow rapidly.

The first half of the 20th century saw the rise of automobiles and airplanes—enabled by growing global production of petroleum. As the 20th century progressed, we began to heat our homes with natural gas, and during the 1960s and 1970s nuclear power became a major source of electricity.

As energy usage became a bigger part of our daily lives, the world built a structural dependency upon fossil fuels such as petroleum and coal, because no other source of energy was as cheap, convenient, and available at such a large scale. Globalized trade became possible in a way that would have been unimaginable without the fossil fuels used to fuel the global supply chain.

However, this dependency came with risks, as well as trade-offs. As countries became more dependent on oil, for instance, their economies were much more sensitive to fluctuations in oil prices. Environments were sometimes contaminated by the coal, oil, or nuclear power that provided most of our electricity and fuel.

But we made these trade-offs because people have an insatiable appetite for energy. We enjoy the conveniences—and sometimes vital necessities like food, medicines, and clean water—that have helped drive enormous increases in life expectancy, global population, and prosperity (for many).

The exploitation of energy has created a great deal of wealth, but that wealth has been unevenly distributed. It has created tyrants and victims of tyranny. Some countries have managed the wealth created from exporting energy to benefit all of their citizens (e.g., Norway), but in other countries the wealth is concentrated in the hands of a small group of people, with little to no benefit to the public at large.

Energy has many faces. The utilization of energy can save lives, and the desire for energy can cost lives. Energy can pollute, and energy can be utilized to clean up pollution. Energy is something most of us can't live without. But it is imperative that we become well informed about energy options if we are to make sound energy choices for the future.

The Perfect Drug?

In the early 1980s, American rock singer Huey Lewis wrote the song "I Want a New Drug." His perfect drug would be "One that won't spill, One that don't cost too much, Or come in a pill." He wanted a drug that made him feel good, without any of the consequences that are often associated with drug usage.

That magical drug is analogous to what the world wants for our energy supplies. We want energy that is cheap, reliable, and convenient. We want it to be safe, renewable, and have no serious environmental or economic consequences.

Unfortunately, there are presently no energy sources like this that are capable of powering modern society. We are therefore left with trade-offs where we accept only some of the criteria.

Most of us spend little time thinking about the implications of our energy usage. When we pull into a gas station and fill our tank, we are preoccupied with other thoughts. The price of gasoline might capture our attention for a bit, but beyond that we rarely stop to consider the implications of this regular ritual of filling our tank, multiplied millions of times around the world. We are making trade-offs in the name of cheap energy, whether or not we realize it.

Likewise, when we turn on a light switch, we rarely give it a second thought, but there are real implications from our electricity usage. Over 40% of the electricity produced in the world comes from coal.[i] A coal-fired power plant providing electricity for a continuously burning 100-watt incandescent light bulb requires over 700 pounds of coal a year and generates about a ton of air emissions like carbon dioxide, sulfur dioxide, and nitrogen oxides. This is a largely hidden trade-off we make for having the lights come on when we want them to come on—and without having to spend a fortune for lighting.

"Cheap" and "reliable" have always been near the top of the list of consumers' energy priorities. But the Fukushima Daiichi nuclear power plant disaster in Japan in 2011 and the Deepwater Horizon oil spill in the Gulf of Mexico in 2010 are but two examples of the sometimes-hidden trade-offs—in this case, environmental damage—that are made in the name of cheap and reliable energy.

Development of renewable energy also requires us to make trade-offs. Producing energy from wind kills bats and birds,[ii] generating hydropower can interfere with fish migration patterns and has put some species on the endangered list,[iii] and producing biofuels can create competition between food and fuel, driving up prices of both.

In short, there are no perfect energy solutions.

Many externalities—that is, many hidden societal and environmental costs and risks—are incurred as a result of the energy choices we make. But the basis of a sound energy policy should start with an understanding of what those trade-offs may be (namely environmental, economic, and political), followed by evaluating the risks, and then making informed choices on our energy usage.

Energy and the Global Economy

The energy embedded primarily in coal helped fuel the Industrial Revolution beginning in the 18th century. During the 20th century, oil enabled the rapid growth of a global transportation network.

Energy was crucial in the development of economies across Europe and North America, and it is now crucial in the growth of economies in developing nations such as China and India. However, developed countries that have a relatively high per-capita use of imported energy are more susceptible to economic slowdown in times of rising energy prices.

History has demonstrated many times that sharply rising energy prices can stall economic growth. In 1973, various members of the Organization of Petroleum Exporting Countries (OPEC) initiated an oil embargo against the United States and certain U.S. allies. U.S. oil production was already in decline, and the U.S. was unable to make up for the supply shortage brought about by the embargo. This resulted in a supply/demand imbalance. Oil prices quadrupled in a very short period of time, contributing to a deep global recession.

This event drove home the point that oil security in the U.S. was increase-ingly based on trade with other countries. Beginning in the early 1970s, the combination of the decline of U.S. production and the growth of demand in the U.S. resulted in continuous growth of oil imports into the U.S., often from countries whose interests ran counter to those of the U.S.

The global economy was rocked by a second oil shock in the late 1970s and early 1980s. Revolution in Iran and a subsequent invasion of Iran by neighboring Iraq in 1980 caused regional oil production to plummet. Globally, oil production fell by around 10%, and crude oil prices doubled in a short period of time to $35 per barrel. Again, the fast escalation of oil prices contributed to a recession in much of the developed world.

The recession that began for most developed countries in 2008 or 2009 also coincided with a time of rising oil prices.[1] After the price of West Texas Intermediate fell to less than $11 per barrel in 1998, oil prices began a ten-year climb that carried U.S. crude prices above $100 per barrel for the first time ever in January 2008.

From 2001 through 2008, each subsequent year saw a higher annual average price than the previous year. Global oil prices quadrupled, going from $26 a

[1] Sharply higher oil prices were but one aspect of the recession beginning in 2008. Irresponsible decisions by the global financial industry are widely considered to be the precipitating event. But James Hamilton, professor of economics at the University of California-San Diego, published a paper in 2009 in which he concluded "the economic downturn of 2007–08 should be added to the list of recessions to which oil prices appear to have made a material contribution."

barrel in 2001 to $99.75 in 2008. This had a negative impact on a number of industries. The airline[iv] and automobile[v] industries were especially hard hit, both of which experienced an increasing number of bankruptcies as oil prices increased.

Thus, the price of energy has a strong influence on the overall global economy. But as prices rise or fall, some countries are winners and some are losers.

Energy and Politics

Political relationships between an energy importer and an energy exporter are sometimes poor, but trade continues because each country needs what the other offers. For example, the U.S. wants oil and Venezuela wants dollars, so despite present political hostilities between the two countries, Venezuela is one of the largest suppliers of oil to the U.S. Likewise, Europe is dependent on Russia for gas supplies, and therefore often makes political concessions to Russia as a result.

As energy prices rise, money and power are transferred from the importing nations to the exporting nations. Russia is at present the world's largest producer of oil, and it has benefited from an enormous influx of cash for oil, as well as the natural gas it supplies to Europe. Other major oil-exporting countries, such as Saudi Arabia (the top oil exporter), have also greatly increased their financial and political stature in the world, particularly as emerging economies such as India and China rapidly accelerate their imports of oil from these exporters.

Oil has been used as a political weapon both by and against countries that depend on oil exports for funding their governments. OPEC's 1973 embargo of oil to the U.S. and Western Europe was a political response by oil exporters to the West's support of Israel during the Yom Kippur War. On the other side of the coin, in 2012 the European Union agreed to an embargo of oil imports from Iran as a part of sanctions against Iran's nuclear program. Since 80% of Iran's oil revenue is from exports, the embargo has the potential to hit Iran's economy hard. But in a tight global oil market, Iran may find plenty of willing buyers for their crude oil in India and China especially if the embargo drives up global oil prices.

Major oil-producing countries have sometimes found themselves subject to military intervention for reasons that boil down to a desire for access to their oil. This was basically the situation during Iraq's 1990 invasion of Kuwait. So even though countries with rich oil resources possess a powerful political tool that can and has been wielded against oil-importing countries, they are also put at risk of military conflict because of those resources.

Beyond the geopolitics, the price of energy is often a politically charged domestic issue. In some countries—especially those that are oil exporters—governments subsidize the price of fuel. In the U.S., a cornerstone of energy policy has long been to provide energy for consumers at the lowest possible price. When prices rise, political finger-pointing and posturing ensue because nobody wants to be blamed for driving up energy costs. The Right blames the Left for blocking domestic oil exploration, and the Left blames the Right for protecting the oil companies and for blocking taxpayer support for alternative energy.

Political parties are so sensitive about energy—and oil prices especially—because rising energy prices have such a direct impact on personal budgets. After all, most of our lives are highly dependent on energy, and we become very unhappy with politicians when those prices rise.

Energy and You

The basic necessities are generally defined as food, water, shelter, and clothing. However, for much of the world's population, energy is just as much a fundamental necessity as the food we eat.

In fact, our food is mass-produced using energy—natural gas for fertilizers, petroleum for herbicides and pesticides, and fuel for trucks and tractors. Water is purified using energy to pump and filter it, and the chemicals used to treat the water are produced from petroleum.

Petroleum-based fibers like nylon, polyester, spandex, and acrylic are used to make our clothing, as well as carpets and curtains in our homes. And large tracts of the world would be uninhabitable without the energy used to heat and cool homes.

We are perhaps most familiar with our use of energy to fuel the global transportation system. Not only does energy provide a level of mobility unprecedented in human history, the fuel for these trucks, ships, and airplanes enables the global supply chain that moves goods and produce from around the world into your local stores.

Electricity—which is itself produced from coal, natural gas, nuclear power, hydropower, geothermal sources, etc.—provides lighting, heating, and cooling. Electricity brings us entertainment and information—sometimes crucial—in the form of the television and the Internet, and it is the backbone of the global communications system.

In addition to the aforementioned uses, petroleum provides us with plastics, synthetic rubber, detergents, medicines, and paints. Toothbrushes, combs, sunglasses, cosmetics, aspirin, tires, DVDs, basketballs, and umbrellas are just a few of the things in our daily lives that are generally petroleum-based.

This explains why higher energy prices have such an impact on personal budgets. While we notice it more so at the gasoline pump, higher oil prices cost consumers in the form of higher prices for almost everything we purchase.

But misconceptions about the energy we use abound.

Energy Misconceptions

Everyone knows that most U.S. oil imports come from Saudi Arabia, that France is the world leader for nuclear power, that Iceland leads in geothermal power, and that Brazil is a country that essentially runs on renewable energy. Actually, none of these things is true, but they are all very popular misconceptions.

This book will explore and correct many misconceptions that people have about energy. Despite the immense importance of energy in our lives, people remain woefully uninformed and misinformed about energy issues. And uninformed people can't make intelligent choices about our energy options for the future. This book will help inform people about the energy embedded in their lives, and discuss the trade-offs we make for the energy we use. It will cover the politics of energy, look into the science of global warming, and detail possible energy alternatives for the years ahead.

Why You Should Care

Among other subjects, this book will explore the following:

1. Why is the world so dependent on fossil fuels, and why has energy independence remained such an elusive goal for so many countries?

2. Just what are our major sources of energy? How extensive is our usage of fossil fuels? What are the prospects for a renewable revolution to make fossil fuels obsolete?

3. Is the debate over global warming futile?

4. What is peak oil? What are the major misconceptions surrounding peak oil? Does the size of the resource base have any bearing on the potential consequences of peak oil?

5. What role will nuclear power play in the years ahead? Are fail-safe designs possible?

6. Is hydraulic fracturing ("fracking") the key to unlocking long-term supplies of cheap natural gas? Are we likely to contaminate our drinking water in the process?

7. With so many companies announcing technical breakthroughs to solve our energy crisis, how can someone determine which breakthroughs have real potential, and which are essentially hype?

8. Why have oil prices increased so dramatically over the past decade?

9. What are the major threats to energy security in the developed nations?

10. What are the best options for replacing oil in our transportation systems?

I will argue in this book that resource scarcity is likely to change the balance of power in the world, and that without proper planning, rising energy costs threaten to wreak havoc on nations that depend heavily on imported energy. Yet many will cling to the belief that technological advances will offer up replacements for the vast amounts of oil and coal we use.

Resource depletion will be a grave threat to the environment. But environmental considerations will continue to be overshadowed by economic considerations as countries seek the cheapest possible forms of energy.

Energy plays a critically important role in our lives. Depletion of energy sources threatens our quality of life and that of future generations. It is therefore imperative for people to be well informed about the implications of the energy we use and the energy policies we adopt.

Presently, the majority of the world's energy comes from nonrenewable sources. Further, the energy needs of developing nations will increase as living standards improve. These two factors have profound implications on nations that are heavily dependent on imported energy. Failure to be informed about energy issues will result in failure to recognize and act accordingly to threats posed by resource depletion and much higher energy costs.

This book will explore these threats in detail. It will also attempt to explore controversial issues in an objective fashion.

But let's first have a look at our major sources of energy.

References

i U.S. Energy Information Administration (EIA), DOE/EIA-0484(2011), *International Energy Outlook 2011*, September 2011, 87, http://www.eia.gov /forecasts/ieo/pdf/0484(2011).pdf.

ii Umair Irfan, "Bats and Birds Face Serious Threats from Growth of Wind Energy," *New York Times*, August 8, 2011, http://www.nytimes.com/cwire /2011/08/08/08climatewire-bats-and-birds-face-serious-threats-from-gro-10511.html?pagewanted=1.

iii Mike Sale and Chuck Coutant interview, "Hydropower: Licensed to Protect the Environment," *Oak Ridge National Laboratory Review* 26, nos. 3 & 4 (Summer/Fall 1993): 2–19, http://www.ornl.gov/info/ornlreview/rev26-34/text/hydmain.html.

iv David Goldman, "Bankruptcies Loom for Airlines," *CNNMoney.com*, July 15, 2008, http://money.cnn.com/2008/07/15/news/economy/airlines/

v Mike Spector, "Plunging SUV Prices Can Make Them a Bargain," *Fort Worth Star-Telegram*, June 8, 2008, http://www.star-telegram.com/2008/06/08 /689112/plunging-suv-prices-can-make-them.html.

Fossil Fuels and Nuclear Power

Powering Modern Civilization

Since 1850, burning of fossil fuels, coal, oil and natural gas has increased 100 times to produce energy as the world has industrialized to serve the world's more than 6 billion and growing population.

—John Olver, U.S. Congressman

The energy sources discussed in this chapter literally power modern civilization. The world's transportation system—automobiles, trucks, airplanes, and ships—relies almost exclusively on fuel derived from oil. Coal, natural gas, and nuclear power produce three-quarters of the world's electricity. Almost every modern country in the world is dependent on these energy sources, and most countries are heavily dependent. Let's take a closer look at the energy sources that most of us rely on every day.

Forms of Energy

The fossil fuel energy sources we use every day come in many different forms. Some of those forms are obvious to us, such as the fuel we put in our cars, or the natural gas we may use for heating and cooking. But energy sources are also used in many ways that are far less obvious to us. For instance, coal is used to produce carbon fibers that are used in everything from mountain bikes to laptops. Petroleum is used to make plastics found in everything from water bottles to DVDs. Natural gas is important in the manufacture of fertilizer and is therefore an important contributor to food production.

The energy that we consume can be classified as primary energy or secondary energy. *Primary energy* is energy that has not been subjected to a transformation process. It may be nonrenewable energy, such as the fossil fuels discussed in this chapter, or it may be renewable, such as hydropower or biomass, which will be discussed in Chapter 3. *Secondary energy* refers to primary energy sources that have undergone a conversion process, such as electricity or hydrogen.

Primary Energy

Primary energy is used directly for heat and power. Fuel wood is an example of primary energy that is used in most of the developing world for heating and cooking. Liquid fuels are used to fuel our transportation systems, and coal is used to provide over 40% of the world's electricity.[i] Natural gas provides another 20% of global electricity.

■ **Did you know?** In 2010, 87% of the world's commercially traded fuels were petroleum, coal, or natural gas.

Electromagnetic energy is another form of primary energy, covering the spectrum from very short-wavelength gamma rays and X-rays through ultraviolet rays, visible radiation, microwaves, and radiofrequency waves.

Energy from nuclear fission is a primary energy source that generates much of the earth's internal heat, and is the basis for nuclear power plants that provided 14% of the world's electricity in 2010. Nuclear fusion powers the sun, which in turn drives many of the energy systems on earth (e.g., solar power, wind power, and biomass result from solar energy striking the earth). Fossil fuels are primary energy sources that were formed from ancient biomass, and thus can be thought of as fossilized sunshine.

Secondary Energy

Secondary energy has undergone an energy conversion process. Forms of secondary energy are sometimes referred to as *energy carriers*. Two common examples are electricity and hydrogen, which are produced from primary energy sources.

Electricity Production

Electricity is the most common form of secondary energy. Electricity may be thought of in the same way as the steam that drove the steam engines of the 19th century, or the hydrogen that powers hydrogen fuel cells. Each of these energy carriers is produced via a primary energy source such as coal, natural gas, hydropower, wind power, or direct solar capture (see Figure 2-1).

Electricity is usually produced when a primary energy source is used to move a conductor through a magnetic field. The primary energy source can be used to produce steam, for example, which can be passed through a turbine. Inside the turbine are magnets that are moved past an electrical conductor such as a copper wire. This induces a current, which is electricity. In a motor, the opposite happens: instead of a force moving the magnets and producing electricity, the electricity moves the magnets and produces a force.

There are other ways to make electricity, such as with a solar panel or an electrostatic conductor. Further, even though electricity is an energy carrier, it could also qualify as a primary source of energy. An example of that would be if the energy from a lightning discharge could be harnessed.

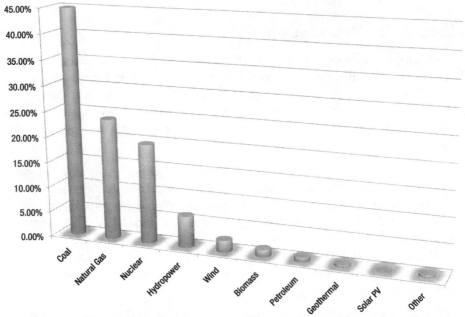

Figure 2-1. Fossil fuels and nuclear power accounted for 88% of U.S. net electric power generation in 2010. (Data source: Energy Information Administration)

Hydrogen Production

Elemental hydrogen (H_2) exists naturally on earth only in trace amounts, because it readily reacts with other materials. Hydrogen can be produced by breaking down water into hydrogen and oxygen via extreme heat or electrolysis, but the vast majority of the world's commercial hydrogen is produced from hydrocarbons such as methane.[1] Hydrogen has been envisioned as a possible clean fuel of the future, but today it is primarily used to produce fuels and chemicals in refineries and chemical plants.

---

[1] Methane is the largest component of natural gas.

Nonrenewable Primary Energy Sources

Nonrenewable primary energy sources have long been critical for the functioning of modern society. This section introduces the four major nonrenewable primary energy sources—petroleum, coal, natural gas, and nuclear power—and provides a brief history of modern civilization's increasing dependence on these energy sources. (Renewable primary energy sources will be covered in the next chapter.)

Petroleum

Petroleum, or crude oil, was formed from the remains of microscopic animal and plant life that accumulated on sea floors. Sediments piled up over these remains, and the pressure of the sediments and the heat inside the earth gradually converted them into a complex mixture of chemicals that we know today as petroleum.

Did you know?   The La Brea Tar Pits in California are formed from petroleum that has seeped to the earth's surface.

Humans have been using petroleum as an energy source for thousands of years. The earliest recorded usage of petroleum took place over four thousand years ago in ancient Babylon, where it was used as a binder in the construction of buildings. Eventually petroleum began to be used for lighting, and by the 9th century refined petroleum was being used in kerosene lamps in the Middle East. Petroleum could be collected in some locations from oil pits similar to the La Brea Tar Pits in California, but the Chinese are reported to have drilled for oil as early as 347 A.D.

The modern age of petroleum began in the mid-19th century when several commercial oil wells were drilled in Europe and North America. The industry was initially driven by demand for kerosene, used in oil lamps. Prior to the development of kerosene for use in lamps, whale oil was commonly used for this purpose. But kerosene quickly gained in popularity with consumers, demand for whale oil plummeted, and this was a major factor leading to the decline of the whaling industry.

The late 19th century brought the invention of the automobile. Gasoline, a highly volatile and initially undesirable byproduct of kerosene distillation, was found to be a very good fuel for the internal combustion engine. Diesel, a heavier petroleum fraction,[2] soon found a place as the preferred fuel for the diesel engine.[3]

The rapid growth in the early 20th century of affordable automobiles was largely aided by major oil discoveries around the world. In the United States, demand for Henry Ford's Model T grew rapidly, and major oil discoveries in Texas, Oklahoma, and California provided the fuel for these cars, which enabled a level of personal mobility that had never been experienced in human history.

▨ **Did you know?**   It was initially envisioned that both Henry Ford's Model T cars and the diesel engine would be fueled by biofuels.

Oil helped to enable the Green Revolution[4] by serving as the raw material for many pesticides and herbicides, and it powered the trucks and tractors that were used to plant and harvest the crops. The global population grew rapidly due to an abundance of food, and this in turn helped increase the demand for oil.

In the past 50 years, global oil production has nearly tripled—from less than 30 million barrels per day (bpd) in the early 1960s[ii] to approximately 87 million bpd[5] in 2010[iii] (see Figure 2-2). U.S. oil production began to decline in the early 1970s, but global oil production continued to expand at a rate that ensured a comfortable cushion of excess global capacity.

---

[2] As petroleum is heated, numerous chemicals are extracted. Over a certain boiling range, the product that is collected is defined as the chemically complex mixture we know as gasoline. At a higher boiling range, the product is diesel. These are different petroleum fractions.

[3] Ironically, both engines were first run on biofuels. Henry Ford first ran the Model T on ethanol and gasoline, and he envisioned that ethanol might become the fuel of the future. Rudolph Diesel first ran his engines on peanut oil.

[4] The Green Revolution refers to a series of agricultural advances beginning in the 1940's that enormously increased crop yields over ensuing decades.

[5] Oil production reported here is "all liquids" production. This includes not only crude oil, but also natural gas plant liquids and refinery processing gains.

Did you know? The largest domed stadium in the world is that of the Dallas Cowboys in Arlington, Texas. The amount of oil consumed globally each day would nearly fill five stadiums of this size.

As countries began to experience oil production peaks, many of them became ever more reliant on oil-exporting countries. A common misconception is that the 1970 oil production peak in the United States turned the U.S. into an oil importer. In fact, by the time oil production peaked in the U.S., petroleum demand had reached 14.7 million bpd and the U.S. was already importing over 3 million net bpd.[iv] The U.S. first became a net importer of petroleum in 1949.[v]

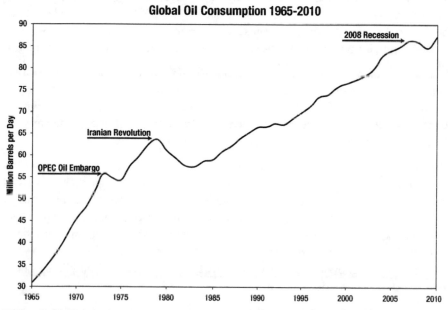

Figure 2-2. Global oil consumption over the past 45 years (Data source: *BP Statistical Review of World Energy 2011*)

Declining production following the production peak in the U.S. did cause a rapid escalation in the dependence on oil imports. By 1976, U.S. net oil imports of petroleum and petroleum products had reached 7 million bpd, and by 2004 the U.S. imported more than 10 million net bpd—almost half of total demand.

Did you know? The United States became a net importer of oil in 1949, 21 years before U.S. oil production peaked.

However, the U.S. remains a leading producer of crude oil, ranking third in the world in 2010 production[6] at 7.5 million bpd. The world's leading producer of oil in 2010 was the Russian Federation at 10.3 million bpd, barely edging out long-time leader Saudi Arabia's 10.0 million bpd. Rounding out the top five were Iran at 4.2 million bpd and China at 4.1 million bpd. Collectively, the Organization of Petroleum Exporting Countries (OPEC) provided 41.5% of global supplies.

Three of the top five oil producers are also among the top five oil consumers. The U.S. consumed the most oil in 2010 at 19.1 million bpd. China was the world's second largest consumer at 9.1 million bpd. Rounding out the top five consumers were Japan at 4.4 million bpd, India at 3.3 million bpd, and the Russian Federation at 3.2 million bpd.

During the 20th century, the world became heavily reliant on petroleum as a primary source of energy and as a feedstock for the petrochemical industry because it was relatively cheap, convenient, and energy-dense (i.e., oil has a high energy content per gallon compared to most alternatives).

Oil has been a blessing for many people around the world, but many also consider it a curse. I recently saw a protestor holding a sign that said, "Oil Kills." This is certainly true. Many people have died in order to supply oil, to protect oil supplies, or as a result of oil-related pollution. On the other hand, oil was used to create the sign the person was holding. He may have reached the protest via an automobile fueled by oil. He had certainly eaten foods that were grown and delivered with the aid of oil, and had likely taken medicine that was made from oil.

Thus, the question is not whether oil kills or whether it improves our standard of living. The question is whether it provides a net benefit to society. But when considering that net benefit, we must also weigh the risks of continued dependence on a depleting resource. These questions will be explored in later chapters.

---

[6] Data source: *BP Statistical Review of World Energy 2011*. Includes crude oil, shale oil, oil sands, and natural gas liquids.

Coal

While petroleum was formed from microscopic plant and animal life in the sea, coal was formed from the remains of more complex plant matter such as trees in swampy areas. As the plant matter accumulated, it first formed peat. If enough material accumulated on top of the peat, the heat and pressure slowly transformed the peat into coal.

Coal was reportedly first used for smelting copper in 1000 B.C. China, but it came of age during the Industrial Revolution. As countries began to industrialize, coal served many purposes, but perhaps most importantly it served as the fuel for steam engines that spurred the development of machinery used for manufacturing, as well as the rapid growth of the railroad industry.

As coal fueled industrialization, demand for it steadily increased. The Industrial Revolution created huge numbers of jobs, and as a result income and living standards improved and populations began to grow at unprecedented rates.

As incomes grew, so did demand for manufactured goods. In many cases these goods were produced in factories with coal-powered steam engine and coal furnaces, and demand for coal continued to grow.

One of the earliest uses of the steam engine was to pump water from coal mines, thus increasing the efficiency of coal mining. As the steam engine gained in popularity, and the Industrial Revolution expanded, coal carved out a large share of global energy consumption that extends to present day (see Figure 2-3).

In the second half of the 19th century, coal found a new use as a source of power for electric generators. The electrical-generation industry grew rapidly, and coal became the fuel of choice for electricity production. Even though oil overtook coal around the middle of the 20th century as the most widely used energy source, growth in coal consumption has remained strong. Today coal remains the most utilized source for electricity production, supplying 42% of the world's electricity.

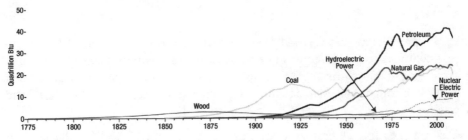

Figure 2-3. After overtaking wood in the late 19th century, coal became the predominant source of energy in the U.S. until 1950. (Source: *EIA Annual Energy Review 2009*)

China is by far the largest producer and consumer of coal. In 2010, China produced 3.2 billion metric tons of coal, which accounted for 48% of the global total. The United States was the second largest producer in 2010, with 985 million metric tons (mmt) produced (15% of the global total). Rounding out the top five coal producers were India with 570 mmt, Australia with 413 mmt, and the Russian Federation with 301 mmt. In total, the European Union (EU) produced 536 mmt of coal.

Did you know? China produces and consumes nearly half of the world's annual coal supply.

China was responsible for 48% of the world's total coal consumption in 2010, followed by the United States (15%), India (8%), Japan (3.5%), and the Russian Federation (2.6%). The EU consumes 8% of the world's coal.

While growth in the usage of coal in developed nations has been flat to negative over the past decade, consumption of coal in the Asia Pacific region has nearly doubled. This growth has been primarily driven by the economic development of India and China.

Because coal has a higher carbon content per unit of energy than oil or natural gas, it emits the most carbon dioxide when used to produce electricity. The U.S. Environmental Protection Agency (EPA) estimates that, per megawatt hour of electricity produced, coal emits 35% more carbon dioxide than does petroleum,[7] and 98% more than natural gas.[vi]

---

[7] The EPA estimates of carbon dioxide emissions per megawatt hour of electricity are 1,135 pounds when natural gas is the power source, 1,672 pounds for oil, and 2,249 pounds for coal.

Natural Gas

Natural gas is primarily composed of methane, the simplest hydrocarbon. Containing four hydrogen atoms for each carbon atom, natural gas when combusted produces two molecules of water and one molecule of carbon dioxide. For this reason, natural gas is generally considered the cleanest of the fossil fuels.

Natural gas is frequently found within coal and oil formations, as it forms under similar conditions and from the same types of organic matter. As a result, natural gas explosions are a frequent hazard for coal miners.

For many early civilizations, natural gas was the source of myth and mystery. Lightning sometimes ignited natural gas seeping from the ground. This "fire from the earth" was often believed to be of divine origin, and played a role in the religions of several early civilizations.

The Chinese made the first recorded practical use of natural gas in about 500 B.C. After routing natural gas through crude bamboo pipes, it was used for cooking, heating brine for extraction of salt, and as a source of lighting.

The commercialization of natural gas began in the Industrial Age as fuel for lamps. The emergence of electric lighting soon displaced natural gas, but the invention of the Bunsen burner in 1855 demonstrated that natural gas could be used for cooking and heating.

Global natural gas consumption grew slowly until the end of World War II, when improved pipeline construction techniques enabled reliable pipeline networks to be built. This began a strong growth period in natural gas consumption that continues to the present day.

In recent years, the United States and the Russian Federation have traded places as the world's top producer of natural gas. The shale gas revolution in the U.S.—which will be discussed in a later chapter—has significantly boosted natural gas production in the U.S. In 2010, the U.S. was the largest natural gas producer at 59 billion cubic feet per day (bcfd), followed by the Russian Federation (57 bcfd), Canada (15.5 bcfd), Iran (13 bcfd), and Qatar (11 bcfd).[vii]

The United States is also the world's largest consumer of natural gas, using 66 bcfd in 2010. This is the energy equivalent of 11.4 million barrels of oil per day.[8] Other major consumers are the Russian Federation at 40 bcfd, Iran at 13 bcfd, China at 10.5 bcfd, and Japan at 9 bcfd.[viii]

In 2010, natural gas accounted for 24% of the world's energy consumption, third behind petroleum's 34% share and coal's 30% share. Natural gas is used globally for electricity generation, for heating and cooking, as transportation fuel, as the primary feedstock for hydrogen production, and in the production of fertilizers.

Natural gas is also used to produce synthetic fuel via the Fischer-Tropsch process invented in Germany in the 1920s. This gas-to-liquids (GTL) process is used commercially by Shell in Bintulu, Malaysia, and in Ras Laffan, Qatar, and by SASOL in South Africa.

Nuclear Power

Nuclear power is the production of electricity using a controlled nuclear fission reaction as the energy source. Nuclear power was commercialized only in the past half-century. One of the early drivers of nuclear power development was for use in powering submarines and aircraft carriers operated by the U.S. and USSR navies, but commercial development for peacetime purposes was taking place concurrently.

In the USSR in 1954, the 5-megawatt (MW) Obninsk Nuclear Power Station was commissioned and was the first nuclear plant to produce electricity for the grid. Two years later, the 50-MW Calder Hall nuclear plant was opened in the United Kingdom, and is generally considered the first commercial nuclear power plant. The first nuclear power plant to be commissioned in the United States was the 60-MW Shippingport Atomic Power Station in Pennsylvania in 1957.

Did you know? While France receives the largest percentage of its electricity from nuclear power (over 75%), the United States has by far the most nuclear power capacity of any country.

---

[8] 5,800 cubic feet of natural gas has the energy content of one barrel of oil. This is commonly referred to as a barrel of oil equivalent, or BOE, and is a measure used to compare different forms of energy relative to oil.

Today there are approximately 440 nuclear reactors operating in 30 countries. Nuclear power produced 14% of the world's electricity in 2010.

While France produces approximately 80% of its electricity with nuclear power, the United States has by far the largest overall nuclear power capacity. In 2010, the U.S. produced 807 billion kilowatt hours (kWh) of electricity from nuclear power, followed by France at 410 billion kWh, Japan at 280 billion kWh, Russia at 159 billion kWh, and South Korea at 142 billion kWh.[ix]

Nuclear power is one of the most controversial sources of energy. Proponents of nuclear power argue that a normally functioning nuclear power plant is one of the most environmentally friendly sources of power available. Opponents argue that the risks from nuclear power are too great. This controversy will be explored in depth in a later chapter.

Summary

The nonrenewable forms of energy discussed in this chapter account for over 80% of the world's current energy consumption for reasons that boil down to cost, convenience, reliability, and scalability. For centuries, these energy sources have driven economic growth and improved standards of living for many people. But increasing consumption of nonrenewable energy is unsustainable, and there are many open questions about how the world will transition to more sustainable energy sources. Renewable energy, which will play an increasingly important role during this transition, will be explored in the next chapter.

References

[i] U.S. Energy Information Administration (EIA), DOE/EIA-0484(2011), *International Energy Outlook 2011*, September 2011, 87, http://www.eia.gov /forecasts/ieo/pdf/0484(2011).pdf.

[ii] EIA, *Long Term World Oil Supply*, July 28, 2000, http://www.eia.doe.gov/pub /oil_gas/petroleum/presentations/2000/long_term_supply/index.htm.

[iii] BP, *BP Statistical Review of World Energy 2011*, http://www.bp.com /sectionbodycopy.do?categoryId=7500&contentId=7068481.

iv EIA, *Annual Energy Review 2009*, DOE/EIA-0384(2009), August 2010, xxiii, http://www.eia.gov/FTPROOT/multifuel/038409.pdf.

v Ben Lefebvre, "US Could Become Net Fuel Exporter," *Downstream Today.com*, November 10, 2010, http://www.downstreamtoday.com /news/article.aspx?a_id=24640.

vi U.S. Environmental Protection Agency (EPA), *How Does Electricity Affect the Environment?* last updated August 10, 2009, http://www.epa.gov /cleanenergy/energy-and-you/affect/index.html.

vii BP, *BP Statistical Review of World Energy 2011*, http://www.bp.com /sectionbodycopy.do?categoryId=7500&contentId=7068481.

viii Ibid.

ix World Nuclear Association (WNA), "World Nuclear Power Reactors & Uranium Requirements," January 1, 2012, http://www.world-nuclear.org /info/reactors.html.

Renewable Energy

Energy of the Past and the Future

The fuel of the future is going to come from fruit like that sumac out by the road or from apples, weeds, sawdust—almost anything. There is fuel in every bit of vegetable matter that can be fermented. There's enough alcohol in one year's yield of an acre of potatoes to drive the machinery necessary to cultivate the fields for a hundred years.

—Henry Ford, 1925

Henry Ford may have been a bit ahead of his time, but he was right about one thing: the energy of the future will have to come increasingly from renewable energy. Over the past 250 years, humans have consumed an ever-increasing amount of fossil resources like coal, oil, and natural gas. But as these resources are depleted, the world must transition to renewable sources of energy.

Transition to Sustainability

The word "sustainability" means different things to different people. My interpretation of sustainable energy is energy that can be produced: (1) without degrading the environment; (2) within the carrying capacity of the ecosystem; and (3) without putting future generations at a significant disadvantage. In a nutshell, it is energy that doesn't increase pollution, that is produced within the annual solar budget of the planet, and that doesn't deplete natural resources.

This is an idealized definition, and in fact probably none of our existing energy sources could strictly meet this definition. My own personal metric is to assume that a particular process would be run for hundreds of years and evaluate how it would impact the environment. The lower the overall environmental impact, the higher the level of sustainability.

Some renewable sources are less sustainable than others, and may even be less desirable than the fossil fuels they seek to replace. To illustrate, consider one renewable fuel that petroleum ultimately replaced: whale oil. Whale oil is certainly a renewable fuel, but for many people this would not be an ethical source of fuel. Further, it isn't sustainable if whale populations are endangered due to demand for whale oil.

Given a choice, most people would likely choose petroleum over whale oil for a variety of reasons. The idea of killing whales so we could have fuel would probably trouble most people more so than the implications of petroleum usage.

This is, of course, an extreme example, as most of the world's biofuels are plant-based. But for just about every type of renewable energy, there are similar issues of ethics, sustainability, and economics that must be navigated during the transition from fossil fuels. As with all energy sources, we will be forced to make trade-offs.

Did you know?   Nearly 85% of the world's use of renewable energy is either hydroelectricity or biomass used for heating and cooking.

In theory, a truly renewable energy source should be a sustainable energy source, but in fact renewable energy is sustainable to varying degrees. A renewable fuel that depletes resources is not sustainable, and would ultimately pose the same sorts of issues as those related to the dependence on fossil fuels.

For example, to gather and convert energy of any sort, certain inputs are required. Consider the production of oil. Energy inputs are required to operate the drill and the pumps, and then to transport the oil. Water may need to be injected into the well. Energy and water are both required for refining the oil into finished products. In addition, inputs of energy and raw materials are required to build the pipelines, trucks, and ships to move the oil, as well as the refinery equipment needed to process the oil.

It is obvious that in the long run, oil production is unsustainable because it isn't renewable.[1] What may be less obvious is that other factors may render oil production unsustainable long before the resource depletes. For instance, if water from a depleting aquifer is used in the process of producing the oil, depletion of that aquifer could render the field unproductive even though there is plenty of oil left in the ground. In short, there are other sustainability factors to consider when producing energy.

The same is true when considering renewable energy. There are certain types of "renewable" energy that are dependent on fossil fuels for their production. In some cases, it is not clear that they would be viable sources of energy without the fossil fuel inputs into the production process. In such cases, these fuels are not truly renewable, due to their fossil fuel dependence, even though many of them are treated as renewable.

Energy whose production depletes aquifers faster than they can be recharged, degrades the topsoil, consumes nonrenewable resources, or causes pollution to build up in the environment might be called renewable, but it isn't sustainable. It might even appear to be sustainable for decades. For someone who lived out their life during the 20th century, oil production was, for all practical purposes, sustainable. They saw global oil production climb during their lives, and oil was almost always available to them—so it was sustainable over that time frame.

Under a strict interpretation, virtually none of the energy sources we consider to be renewable are truly renewable. Wind turbines are made of steel, the production of which is heavily dependent on coal. Growing crops for use in the production of ethanol is typically done with fertilizer made from natural gas, and pesticides and herbicides derived from petroleum. Biodiesel production uses methanol, which is normally made from natural gas.

However, in many cases the use of nonrenewable energy in the production of renewable energy is simply an economic choice. Methanol made from natural

---

[1] Technically speaking, since fossil fuels are derived from biomass, they are renewable, but only over extremely long time spans. The key issue is that we use these resources at such a fast rate relative to the time frame over which they form that they are essentially nonrenewable and we treat them as such.

gas is much cheaper than methanol made from wood, but methanol can be produced from wood. So what we are really interested in determining is whether a renewable energy source whose production uses fossil fuel can transition away from the use of fossil fuel inputs. If so, even though the process is unsustainable in its current form, it eventually could be sustainable.

Beyond the question of sustainability, there are important ethical questions about the use of some renewable energy sources. One argument in recent years is that widespread use of renewable fuels leads to certain undesirable land use changes (e.g., conversion of forested land to farmland). Another is that use of food crops for renewable fuel drives food prices up and causes additional hardships on poor people who are already struggling to survive. These arguments can be more complicated than they might first seem, and will be explored in more detail in later chapters. For now, let's take a closer look at the major sources of renewable energy.

Renewable Primary Energy Sources

There are many renewable options available for displacement of fossil-based heat and power. Solar and wind power receive the bulk of the media coverage, but in fact, the vast majority of renewable energy in the world falls into two categories: traditional biomass and hydroelectricity.

Traditional Biomass

Approximately two-thirds of the renewable energy in the world is in the form of traditional biomass.[i] Biomass energy simply refers to energy from recently living plants or animals.[2] In developing countries, the overwhelming majority of the energy consumed is provided by fuel wood, which is generally the cheapest fuel option available. Fuel wood is the main energy source for cooking for most of the developing world, and is the primary source of energy for over 2 billion people.[ii]

Wood has been used to heat homes for thousands of years. Until the 20th century, 90% of U.S. homes were heated with wood.[iii] That percentage fell during the 20th century as homeowners turned increasingly to fossil fuels for their home heating needs. But interest in wood for home heating surged during the energy crisis in the 1970s.

---

[2] Energy from biomass is derived almost exclusively from plant matter.

As with other energy sources, using wood for fuel has trade-offs. The majority of the wood used for cooking is burned in open cook stoves. This process is inefficient and leads to excessive consumption of wood. In some developing countries, excessive consumption has led to deforestation and desertification (see Figure 3-1).

Another trade-off is that use of wood in open cook stoves results in particulate emissions. The emissions from cooking with wood have been identified as a risk factor in acute lower respiratory infection, which is the chief cause of death in children in developing countries.[iv]

High-efficiency biomass stoves have been developed to mitigate some of the problems associated with cooking over an open fire. By operating more efficiently, less fuel is required, and the air pollution associated with open fires is diminished. Because of the advantages of high-efficiency biomass stoves, a number of programs by governments and charitable organizations have emerged to disseminate these stoves to developing countries.[v]

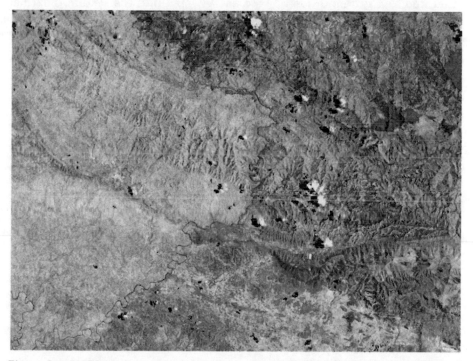

Figure 3-1. NASA aerial satellite photo showing the border between the heavily deforested Haiti to the left and the Dominican Republic to the right (Source: NASA/Goddard Space Flight Center Scientific Visualization Studio)

Using wood to heat homes and businesses can also result in a high level of particulate emissions. In addition, open fireplaces suffer efficiency losses from heat exiting the chimney. Advanced wood combustion (AWC) systems have been developed to address these two issues.

AWC systems are operated at higher temperatures than a normal fireplace. In these systems, the wood is first gasified (converted to a gas) and the resulting gases are combusted. Conditions are carefully controlled to ensure an efficient combustion. AWC has grown in importance in Europe over the past 20 years, with more than 1,000 systems now installed in Austria alone.

In addition to being used for heating, wood can be used to produce electricity from combustion or co-combustion (e.g., co-fed with coal in a coal-fired steam plant). However, the most efficient usage of wood is in a combined heat and power (CHP) application to produce electricity and hot water.

The thermal efficiency of a system is defined as the usable heat or work generated by a system divided by the energy input into the system. Thermal efficiencies of CHP systems can approach 90%, whereas a wood-based electricity-only application generally has a thermal efficiency below 30%.

For example, if 1,000 British thermal units (BTUs)[3] of wood produce 0.09 kilowatt hour (kWh) of electricity (equivalent to 300 BTUs), the thermal efficiency is 30%. If 600 BTUs of hot water are also utilized, the thermal efficiency increases to 90%.

ENERGY, POWER, AND UNITS OF MEASUREMENT

There are a number of potentially confusing units of measurement for energy and power. The first thing to understand, however, is the difference between energy and power. Technically speaking, energy refers to the capacity of a system to do work. In this definition, "a system" could be a gallon of gasoline that contains 115,000 British Thermal Units (BTUs)—a unit of energy. In addition to the BTU, some other units of energy are the joule (J), the calorie (cal), and the watt hour (Wh). Multiples of these units have abbreviations like kilo (one thousand) or mega (one million), so one kilowatt hour (kWh) is one thousand watt hours. Each of these units can be converted into the other. One BTU is equal to 1,055 joules, 252 calories, or 0.29 watt hours.

---

[3] BTU is the common unit in the U.S., but in Europe and much of the rest of the world it is joules; 1 BTU is equal to approximately 1,055 joules.

Power is the rate at which energy is consumed or generated. One BTU of gasoline refers to the energy content, but gasoline consumption over time could be measured in BTUs/hour, a unit of power. Other units of power are joules/second, calories/day, watts, and horsepower.

A 100 megawatt (MW) power plant is capable of generating energy at the rate of 100 megawatt hours (MWh) per hour. People frequently confuse the energy unit of watt hours with the power unit of watts. This is probably because other measures of power are defined per unit of time (e.g., calories/hour), and therefore it would seem logical that a kilowatt hour would be a unit of power. Alas, it is not. However, it should be clear that a joule/second is a unit of power, because it is energy consumed over time. In fact, that's what a watt actually is: 1 watt = 1 joule/second. So a watt is a rate of energy consumption, but the time element has been incorporated into the definition. Someone thought it would be a good idea to call it a watt instead of a joule/s, and many people have been confused ever since.

The city of Saint Paul, Minnesota, started up a wood-based CHP plant in 2003. The plant generates 25 megawatts (MW) of electricity and up to 65 MW of thermal energy from wood waste generated in the Twin Cities (Saint Paul/Minneapolis) metro area. The renewable electricity is supplied to the local electric utility and the thermal energy is used to heat buildings throughout downtown Saint Paul, including the Minnesota State Capitol Complex.

Globally, the usage of biomass for power production, heating, and combined heat and power has increased substantially in the past decade. The biomass heating market has seen strong growth rates in Northern Europe, driven in large part by imported fuel pellets.

In Sweden, biomass recently surpassed oil in the production of power for the first time. Denmark currently obtains an estimated 10% of its power from biomass. Germany, Austria, Finland, Belgium, and the Netherlands have all seen strong growth in the use of biomass for energy, largely in response to concerns over their energy supplies and a desire to lower their net carbon dioxide emissions.

Because of the ability to produce firm power,[4] the global use of biomass for energy production is likely to continue growing strongly. Countries that

---

[4] Firm power is power that is intended to be available on demand at all times even during adverse conditions. Intermittent power on the other hand varies according to outside factors. Coal-fired power is considered to be firm power, and wind power is considered to be intermittent power.

have made commitments to reduce greenhouse gases, those with hot water demands for a majority of the year (e.g., Sweden), and those without access to cheap coal or natural gas will likely see the strongest growth rates.

One of the strongest growth areas for biomass over the past decade has been its use to produce liquid fuels. Liquid fuels from biomass—biofuels—will be covered in more depth in Chapter 11.

Hydroelectricity

Hydroelectricity is electricity produced by utilizing the flow of water as the power source for a generator. Hydroelectricity is the second most common form of renewable energy, behind traditional biomass. Four of the five largest electric power stations in the world are hydroelectric plants.

Hydroelectricity was originally developed in the second half of the 19th century, and several hundred hydroelectric plants were built worldwide by 1900. During the 20th century, hydroelectric power continued to gain in popularity, and projects became larger in scale.

In 1936, the 1.3-gigawatt (GW) power plant at the Hoover Dam on the Nevada/Arizona border in the U.S. was the world's largest hydroelectric plant. By 1942, it had been surpassed as the world's largest by the 6.8-GW power plant at Grand Coulee Dam in Washington State, which remains the largest electricity-generating plant of any type in the U.S. today.

Did you know? Four of the five largest power plants (by capacity) in the world are hydroelectric plants.

The 1980s saw the construction of three major facilities in South America. In 1984, Brazil's Tucuruí Dam was briefly home to the world's largest hydroelectric plant, at 8.4 GW, but two years later, Venezuela completed the second stage of its power station at the Guri Dam, reaching a capacity of 10.2 GW. Brazil's Itaipu Dam first started producing power in 1984, and by 2007 the capacity had been increased to 14 GW.

The Three Gorges Dam in China is presently the world's largest electrical power plant of any type at 18.3 GW of installed capacity, but it is undergoing an expansion that will bring the total installed capacity to 22.5 GW. That will make the capacity almost four times greater than the world's largest coal-fired power plant.

Electricity produced from hydropower has a lower environmental impact than many other sources of electricity. There are no emissions from the ongoing operations of a hydropower plant.

However, large hydroelectric plants do impact the environment. When dams are constructed, land areas must be flooded, displacing people and drastically changing the wildlife habitat.

The massive Three Gorges Dam in China displaced an estimated 1.4 million people, and may displace a total of 4 million people over the next decade.[vi] Hydroelectric projects in the U.S. Pacific Northwest disrupted the migration patterns of a number of species of salmon, drastically reducing the number of salmon in the region and pushing some species onto the endangered species list.

Over the past decade, most of the world has seen modest growth in hydro-electricity consumption. This is largely because many of the best sites for hydroelectric dams have already been developed. The exception to this is in the Asia Pacific region, where hydroelectric consumption more than doubled over the past decade. The region currently accounts for 32% of global hydroelectric consumption, and that percentage is likely to increase as countries continue to develop hydroelectric power plants.

Wind Power

The power of the wind has been used for thousands of years to propel ships with sails, to pump water, and to grind grain. The wind was first used to make electricity near the end of the 19th century, but it was only in the past two decades that global wind power capacity began to expand rapidly.

From 6.1 GW in 1996, global wind power capacity grew by more than a factor of 30, to nearly 200 GW, by 2010. Over the five-year period from the end of 2005 to the end of 2010, global wind power capacity increased by an average of 27% per year.

In 2010, China surpassed the U.S. for the world's largest installed capacity of wind power, at 44.7 GW. Capacity in the U.S. wasn't far behind at 40.2

GW. Rounding out the top five were Germany at 27.2 GW, Spain at 20.7 GW, and India at 13.2 GW.[5]

Did you know? In 2010, 19.4% of global electricity production came from renewable sources. Approximately 83% of the renewable electricity came from hydropower, with most of the remainder contributed by wind, solar, and geothermal power.

Despite the impressive growth rate of installed wind power capacity, wind remains a very small component of overall renewable energy production. In 2010, wind provided 2.3% of the electricity in the U.S. and 1.2% of the electricity in China.[vii] However, specific regions can produce much higher percentages of wind-derived electricity. In 2010, wind-generated electricity reached 21.9% of total demand in Denmark, 17% in Portugal, 16.4% in Spain, and 10.5% in Ireland. In the U.S., Iowa and Texas, respectively, obtained 15.4% and 7.8% of each state's electricity from wind power in 2010.

The biggest attraction of wind power is that when the wind blows, the electricity produced can directly back out fossil fuel–derived electricity from the grid while producing no direct emissions.[6] The biggest disadvantage is that the wind doesn't always blow, meaning that installed wind power capacity has to be backed up by firm power sources.

The extent to which wind power must be backed up depends on the capacity factor, which varies by location. In consistently windy locations, wind generation might be counted on to contribute electricity to the grid up to 45% of the time on an annual basis. However, if there are times of the year—even if annual capacity factors are high—during which wind generation falls to lower levels, then utilities must plan to back up wind based on its lower output.

---

[5] Production and consumption figures for many of the renewable energy sources discussed here were obtained from REN21's *Renewables 2011 Global Status Report* (reference i).

[6] Wind power, like all other sources of electricity production, does have indirect emissions. For example, the turbines are made from steel, the production of which is heavily dependent on coal.

For example, consider a community that requires 100 MW of electricity capacity. If a 100-MW wind farm is built to serve that community, a 30% capacity factor for the plant would mean that during the course of the year the plant has to be backed up by an average of 70 MW of a firm power source. However, if there are times of the year during which the wind power capacity factor is lower, there must be a higher level of backup available. In the worst case—if there are times of the year during which the wind plant produces no electricity—the plant may need to be backed up by 100 MW of firm power (unless, of course, suitable energy storage solutions are available—in which case the stored energy could be drawn upon for some of the backup power).

Two other oft-cited disadvantages of wind power are the noise from the turbines, and the fact that birds and bats are sometimes killed by the turbines. The noise issue often results in opposition to wind farms from local residents—a standard and understandable NIMBYist[7] response.

The issue of bird and bat kills brings a broader level of opposition from many animal conservation and environmental groups. A frequently cited example is a 2008 study of a wind farm in Altamont Pass, California, that estimated the turbines there kill an average of 80 golden eagles and a total of about 10,000 birds annually.[viii]

Estimates of bird kills from wind turbines in the United States range from 150,000 up to about 500,000, according to the American Wind Energy Association (the U.S. lobby for the wind industry). In context, the U.S. Forest Service has estimated that each year 550 million birds are killed in collisions with buildings, 130 million are killed by power lines, 100 million are killed by cats, and 80 million in collisions with automobiles.[ix]

Thus, wind power is not immune to the trade-offs we must make with any of our energy sources. On the plus side, wind power has the potential to back out fossil fuels from power plants, and that has distinct environmental benefits. On the negative side, wind power often requires a high level of firm power backing it up—which is generally unaccounted for in the reported costs for producing wind power. Further, the number of birds and bats killed by wind power is expected to rise as additional wind power capacity is installed.

---

[7] NIMBY = Not In My Backyard.

Solar Power

Most of our energy sources can be traced to the power of the sun. The ancient biomass that produced coal, oil, and natural gas can be thought of as fossilized sunshine. The energy of the sun enables hydropower through the cycles of evaporation and rain. Wind is produced as the sun unevenly heats the earth and causes air to move between warmer and cooler locations.

However, the indirect capture of the sun's energy is relatively inefficient. Plants are able to capture and store the sun's energy via photosynthesis, but the efficiency of solar capture can be as low as 0.1%. Intensely cultivated crops can reach 2% to 4% photosynthetic efficiency, but this is a small fraction of what can be achieved by direct capture of solar power.

There are three primary methods of producing energy via solar power: solar photovoltaics, concentrating solar power, and solar heating.

Solar Photovoltaics

The first major method of producing energy via solar power uses solar photovoltaic (PV) cells. Certain materials, such as various types of silicon or cadmium telluride, are capable of producing electricity when struck by solar radiation. Solar PV cells are produced using materials that are susceptible to this photoelectric effect.

Solar PV cells are capable of converting solar radiation into energy at a much higher efficiency than plants. While most commercial solar PV cells convert solar radiation at efficiencies ranging from 10% to 15%, experimental cells have managed to increase the efficiency to above 40%.

Like wind power, the solar PV market is small relative to the total electricity market, but it is growing rapidly. During 2010, solar PV capacity was added in more than 100 countries, and the estimated global capacity at the end of 2010 was 40 GW—a sevenfold increase over the previous five years. Much of the growth was due to the construction of a number of utility scale systems (generally multi-megawatt facilities designed to service hundreds or thousands of customers). There are presently over 5,000 utility scale systems, accounting for nearly 25% of global solar PV capacity.

Because of policies that are favorable toward solar PV, EU countries dominate global capacity. At the end of 2010, Germany had by far the largest solar PV capacity at 17.3 GW, which was more than the combined capacity of the rest of the top five countries, and 44% of global capacity. Spain's 3.8 GW of solar PV capacity was enough for second place globally, followed by Japan at 3.6 GW, Italy at 3.5 GW, and the U.S. at 2.5 GW.

Concentrating Solar Power

The second major method of producing energy from solar radiation is called concentrating solar power (CSP). CSP systems use lenses or mirrors to concentrate the sun's rays, much like a magnifying glass. The concentrated rays are then used to produce heat. The heat may be used to generate steam directly, which is then passed through a turbine to produce electricity. Alternatively, the heat may be used to produce molten salt, which retains heat when the sun doesn't shine and can potentially enable these plants to run for 24 hours a day.[x]

Total installed capacity of CSP at the end of 2010 was 1.1 GW, and was located primarily in two countries. Spain leads the world in global CSP capacity with 632 MW of capacity, followed by the U.S. at 509 MW. However, a number of countries are either building or planning CSP systems, including several countries across North Africa and the Middle East, as well as Australia, South Africa, Mexico, and Italy.

CSP capacity grew by 77% in 2010 and has increased by an average annual rate of 25% over the past five years. Additional capacity currently under construction is 2.6 GW, and growth rates are expected to remain high. The International Energy Agency estimates that in sunny countries, CSP can become competitive for peak and intermediate power by 2020, and for base load power by 2025 to 2030.[xi] The IEA also estimates that CSP could provide over 11% of global electricity by 2050.

Solar Heating

The final category of energy production from solar radiation is solar heating. This takes the form of solar hot water and space heating for homes, as well as industrial process heat. The process can be as simple as water moving through black tubing outdoors to absorb heat from the sun.

Global capacity of solar heating applications is far larger than that of either solar PV or CSP. At the end of 2010, total global capacity of solar hot water and space heating was 185 GWth.[8]

There are more than 70 million solar hot water systems globally, with most of them located in China. As a result, China has the majority of the global capacity of solar heating systems, with 118 GWth of capacity at the end of 2010. In addition to China, the top five countries in solar heating capacity include Turkey and Germany, each with 8.4 GWth, Japan with 4.0 GWth, and Greece with 2.9 GWth.[9]

Solar heating installations are expected to continue to grow rapidly. Many countries—including Israel, Spain, India, South Korea, and Uruguay—have mandates for solar hot water. Within the U.S., Hawaii is presently the only state that mandates solar hot water systems in new single-family dwellings (see Figure 3-2).[10]

Figure 3-2. Solar water heater on the author's home in Hawaii (Photo by Courtney Rapier)

---

[8] GWth refers to gigawatts of thermal energy, as opposed to gigawatts of electrical energy (GWe, or simply GW).

[9] These numbers exclude swimming pool collectors. If those are included, the U.S. jumps to second place with 15.0 GWth of solar heating capacity.

[10] Although there is a mandate in place in Hawaii, some new homes request and receive exemptions from the mandate.

Solar Trade-offs

The trade-offs for solar power are primarily of cost and convenience. The cost of solar power—especially solar PV—has been falling, but it is expected to remain well above the cost of producing electricity from more conventional sources such as coal, natural gas, or hydropower (see Figure 3-3). The higher cost has limited the growth of solar power to locations in which traditional power production is very expensive, or locations that provide generous incentives for the production of solar power. But solar panels have been plummeting in price, declining by two-thirds over the past three years and 50% just in 2011. If that trend continues, solar PV may become cost competitive with coal-fired power before the end of the decade.

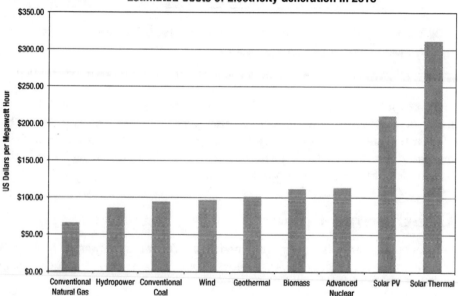

Figure 3-3. Estimated levelized cost[11] of producing electricity in 2016 (Data source: EIA, *Annual Energy Outlook 2011*[xii])

Solar power also suffers from the same intermittency problem as wind power. The U.S. Energy Information Administration (EIA) estimates that the

---

[11] The levelized cost is the break-even cost for producing electricity from various sources.

capacity factors for gas, coal, and nuclear electricity are in the range of 85% to 90%, for geothermal 92%, for hydropower 52%, for wind 34%, and for solar PV and solar thermal 25% and 18% respectively.

This means that, like wind power, solar power must be backed up by firm power. However, there are some important considerations to keep in mind. First is that most of the time that solar power isn't producing electricity—during the night—corresponds to the lowest demand period. Thus, the level of backup power required, particularly in sunny locations, is fairly predictable and can be planned. If the need for backup power can be planned, the backup power system can be operated more efficiently than if the system has to be cycled up and down frequently as demand rises and falls unpredictably.

Did you know?   The price of solar panels dropped by around 50% in 2010, which was primarily driven by huge increases in polysilicon supplies.

Peak output from solar panels also roughly corresponds to peak demand from power consumers—which is also when power costs tend to be highest.[12] Thus, some advocates have argued that solar power should be evaluated on the basis of peak power demand, which would make the economics of solar power more favorable.

Geothermal Power

Geothermal energy is energy obtained from the earth's internal heat. It is one of the most environmentally benign sources of energy, producing little to no emissions during normal operation.

Geothermal electricity is produced when the heat from the earth is used to produce steam, which is then passed through a turbine. Electricity produced in this way generally requires fairly shallow geothermal reservoirs (less than

---

[12] Daily peak power demand actually occurs a bit after the daily peak output for the solar panels, but at a time when the solar panel output is generally not far from peak power.

2 miles deep). Geothermal electricity has a high capacity factor, and the cost of generation is comparable to that of coal-fired generation.

Geothermal energy can be also be used for heating or cooling. Hot springs or water circulating in hot zones can be used to heat buildings. Geothermal heat pumps take advantage of the earth's temperature a few feet below the ground—consistently 50° to 60°F—to heat buildings in the winter and cool them in the summer.

In 2010, 24 countries operated geothermal plants and 78 countries used geothermal directly for energy. About 70% of the geothermal energy for direct use was through geothermal heat pumps.

Total geothermal electricity capacity was 11 GW at the end of 2010. Capacity was led by the U.S. with 3.1 GW of capacity, followed by the Philippines at 1.9 GW, Indonesia at 1.2 GW, Mexico at almost 1 GW, and Italy at 0.9 GW. On a per capita basis, Iceland leads the world with 0.6 GW of capacity, which accounted for 26% of the country's electricity in 2010.

Did you know?   The U.S. oil company Chevron is the world's largest commercial producer of geothermal energy.

The global capacity of geothermal for direct usage was 51 GWth in 2010, with the U.S. again leading with 12.6 GWth of capacity, followed by China at 9 GWth, Sweden at 4.5 GWth, Germany at 2.5 GWth, and Japan at 2.1 GWth.

A small portion of global geothermal capacity is in the form of deep geothermal energy. This involves drilling much deeper into the earth, which opens up the potential of geothermal energy to countries that do not have shallow geothermal resources. The global potential for deep geothermal is immense. A recent assessment by MIT[xiii] estimated that the potential for deep geothermal in the U.S. was greater than 2,000 times the current energy consumption of the U.S.

Despite the potential for deep geothermal, hurdles remain. Probably the most serious issue is that drilling has been implicated in the generation of earthquakes. There have also been reported issues of difficulty drilling through some of the formations in order to reach the required depths.

Therefore, deep geothermal is presently an experimental technology with a seemingly great deal of potential.

Relative to many other energy options, the trade-offs for geothermal power are minimal. The primary issues are that a well can suddenly stop producing steam, and sometimes gases can escape from the holes drilled in the ground. The biggest disadvantage is that shallow geothermal is only available in limited locations around the earth. So until deep geothermal is fully commercialized, geothermal will be geographically limited.

Ocean Energy

There are several sources of renewable energy from the ocean that are either still in an experimental stage or presently have limited commercialization. There are over 100 ocean energy projects currently in development with a cumulative capacity of over 1 GW.

Tidal power is a form of hydropower. As tides rise and fall, the water moving inland and back out can be passed through a turbine, utilizing the same principles as hydroelectric power plants at dams. A 240-MW tidal power system has been operated in France since 1966. At present this is the bulk of the world's 262 MW of tidal power capacity. However, high energy prices in recent years have sparked increasing interest in tidal power. New plants are being planned or are under construction in South Korea, Scotland, and India.

Wave energy utilizes the power of ocean waves to produce electricity. Some devices utilize floating buoys that produce electricity as the waves rise and fall. Other devices face perpendicular to the waves and capture the force of the wave as it strikes the surface. The world's first commercial wave power plant was commissioned in Scotland in 2000 and has been operating continuously since. Plant capacity is 500 kW and plant availability is reported to be over 90%.

Ocean thermal energy conversion (OTEC) utilizes the temperature differences between the deep ocean and the water's surface to drive a heat engine. Because of the relatively small temperature differences (~35°F), the maximum theoretical efficiency of these systems is below 10%. Japan, India, and the U.S. are among the leading countries working to advance the development of OTEC.

Summary

Renewable energy has played an important role in human civilization for thousands of years. As the world discovered coal, oil, and natural gas, it relied increasingly on those sources, and continued development of many renewable technologies stagnated. However, as the world approaches the end of the fossil age, renewable energy is experiencing a renaissance as the world grapples with the problem of transitioning to a post–fossil fuel economy. Due to the magnitude and breadth of the world's fossil fuel usage, a wide variety of renewable energy technologies will be required to supply the world's energy in the coming decades.

References

[i] Renewable Energy Policy Network for the 21st Century (REN21), *Renewables 2011 Global Status Report (GSR)*, July 12, 2011, http://www.ren21.net/Portals/97/documents/GSR/REN21_GSR2011.pdf.

[ii] Food and Agriculture Organization (FAO) of the United Nations, "Wood Energy," last updated January 25, 2012, http://www.fao.org/forestry/energy/en/.

[iii] U.S. Department of Energy (DOE) Office of Energy Efficiency and Renewable Energy (EERE), "Wood and Pellet Heating," last updated February 9, 2011, http://www.energysavers.gov/your_home/space_heating_cooling/index.cfm/mytopic=12570.

[iv] Kirk R. Smith et al., "Indoor Air Pollution in Developing Countries and Acute Lower Respiratory Infections in Children," *Thorax* 55, no. 6 (June 2000): 518–532.

[v] Daniel deB. Richter Jr. et al., "Wood Energy in America," *Science* 323 (March 2009): 1432–1433.

[vi] Christopher Bodeen, "China Plans to Relocate Millions near Gorges Dam," *Associated Press*, October 13, 2007, http://articles.boston.com/2007-10-13/news/29225490_1_china-plans-three-gorges-dam-landslides.

vii International Energy Agency (IEA) Wind, *IEA Wind 2010 Annual Report*, July 2011, http://www.ieawind.org/IndexPagePOSTINGS/IEA Wind 2010 AR _cover.pdf.

viii Robert Bryce, "Windmills Are Killing Our Birds," Wall Street Journal, Opinion page, September 7, 2009, http://online.wsj.com/article /SB10001424052970203706604574376543308399048.html#articleTabs%3D article.

ix Wallace P. Erickson, Gregory D. Johnson, and David P. Young Jr., "A Summary and Comparison of Bird Mortality from Anthropogenic Causes with an Emphasis on Collisions," USDA Forest Service, 2005, http://www.fs.fed.us/psw/publications/documents/psw_gtr191/Asilomar /pdfs/1029-1042.pdf.

x Zachary Shahan, "World's First Molten Salt Concentrating Solar Power Plant Opens," *CleanTechnica*, July 26, 2010, http://cleantechnica.com/2010 /07/26/worlds-first-molten-salt-concentrating-solar-power-plant-opens/.

xi International Energy Agency, "Technology Roadmap: Concentrating Solar Power," 2010, http://www.iea.org/papers/2010/csp_roadmap.pdf.

xii U.S. Energy Information Administration, DOE/EIA-0383(2011), *Annual Energy Outlook 2011*, April 2011, http://www.eia.gov/forecasts/aeo /pdf/0383(2011).pdf.

xiii Massachusetts Institute of Technology (MIT), *The Future of Geothermal Energy*, 2006, http://geothermal.inel.gov/publications/future_of_geothermal _energy.pdf.

Energy Production

From the Source to the Consumer

Formula for success: rise early, work hard, strike oil.

—J. Paul Getty

When humans first tamed fire, they needed energy sources to feed that fire. Thus the history of energy production greatly predates human civilization. But as civilizations grew, they demanded greater and more concentrated sources of energy in the form of fossil fuels. This chapter details how we produce the fossil fuels we use today, as well as some of the environmental and social costs of producing those energy sources.

Coal Production

Coal was the first energy source produced on a large commercial scale. While coal had been used for centuries, usage began to accelerate during the 1600s due to widespread deforestation in England. By the end of the 1600s, England was the world's leading coal producer, accounting for 80% of global coal production.[i]

Coal quickly became the fuel of choice across England, and then usage began to skyrocket during the Industrial Revolution in the 18th century. During the second half of the 19th century, coal overtook wood as the world's predominant source of energy. Global use of coal continued to grow during the 20th century, and was the world's most widely used energy source until it was overtaken by oil in the second half of the 20th century.

Forms of Coal

Coal comes in many different forms. Peat is a coal precursor, i.e., it would eventually become coal if subjected to the right conditions over time. Lignite, or brown coal, has properties intermediate between those of peat and other forms of coal. The energy density of lignite is similar to that of many types of wood. Lignite is the lowest grade of coal, and it is used primarily for the production of electricity in power plants.

Subbituminous and bituminous coal are of a higher quality than lignite. Both have lower moisture content and higher energy content than lignite, with bituminous coal having the highest quality of the three. Like lignite, sub-bituminous coal is used primarily for electricity production. In addition to being used for electricity production, bituminous coal is used to produce coke, which is in turn used in the production of steel.

Anthracite is an even better fuel than the other types of coal. It contains fewer impurities and has the highest heating content of the major types of coal. The heating content of anthracite can be more than double that of lignite, and as a result of the high heating content and low impurity levels, anthracite is primarily used for heating purposes.

Coal Mining

Coal is predominantly produced by either mining it from underground or excavating it from the surface in open pits. After coal is extracted from a mine, it is moved by truck, rail, and/or barge to its final destination.

Underground mining is responsible for about 60% of global coal production, and it is conducted primarily by using either one of two techniques. *Room-and-pillar mining* involves carving out underground rooms from the coal, and leaving coal pillars behind to support the roof of the room. The advantage of this method is that it can be done at a lower capital cost than other techniques, but the recovery of coal is lower than with some techniques because the pillars can take up to 40% of the area of the room.

Longwall mining is a more productive mining technique, often extracting up to 80% of the coal in a coal seam and at much higher production rates than is possible with room-and-pillar mining. Longwall mining is carried out underneath a self-advancing hydraulic roof support. Underneath the support a shearer with cutting drums is moved across the coal seam. As coal is removed from the seam, it falls into a conveyor system that eventually moves the coal out of the mine.

In areas where a coal seam is near the surface, surface mining can extract more than 90% of the coal from the seam. With surface mining, the dirt and rocks covering the seam are first removed, and then the coal is extracted with excavation equipment. There are several variations of surface mining, including strip mining, open-pit mining, and mountaintop removal mining.

Coal Consumption

Today, the world produces approximately 7 billion metric tons of coal per year.[ii] This is about 30% of the world's total primary energy production. Over the past three decades, global production of coal has increased by 90%. Globally the coal industry employs an estimated 7 million people.[iii] The majority, about 5 million, are employed in China.

As was the case in England during the 18th century, industrializing countries often rapidly increase their rate of coal consumption. Over the past decade, coal consumption in China, India, and Vietnam—three rapidly developing countries—increased by 133%, 92%, and 192% respectively. In comparison, coal consumption over this same time period declined by 8% in the United States and by 14% in the European Union. But even in the developed world—as Jeff Goodell aptly noted in *Big Coal*[iv]—"our shiny white iPod economy is propped up by dirty black rocks."

Safety and Environmental Considerations

As coal became widely adopted in England in the 18th century, the air quality in England's cities diminished. Rickets—a disease caused by vitamin D deficiency that can be brought on by inadequate exposure to sunlight—was a common ailment. Even in the modern era, coal pollution continued to cause premature deaths in major cities in the UK and the U.S.

One famous incident took place in London in 1952, when a period of unusual weather in December caused a layer of smog—primarily from coal combustion—to settle over the city. Estimates are that 4,000 to over 12,000 people died prematurely as a result of exposure to this smog, and an estimated 100,000 people were sickened. In the U.S., serious coal-related air pollution events have occurred in New York City, Saint Louis, and Donora, Pennsylvania. While stricter air pollution laws have greatly reduced coal-related air pollution in much of the developed world, many cities in China are still plagued by air pollution from coal-fired power plants.

Coal mining has historically been a dangerous occupation, and it continues to be highly dangerous in certain countries. In the U.S., more than 100,000 coal miners were killed in accidents during the 20th century.[v] Numerous others suffered from long-term illnesses as a result of breathing coal dust.

The fatality rate in the U.S. has fallen dramatically in recent years as a result of improvements in technology and stricter safety standards, but globally the number of annual fatalities remains high. In China, for example, thousands are killed each year in the coal-mining industry, and the death rate per million tons of coal extracted is 30 to 50 times the rate in the developed world.[vi]

Coal mining also impacts the environment. As surface-mining techniques became more prevalent in the U.S., the Surface Mining Control and Reclamation Act of 1977 was passed in part to ensure that land that had been altered by mining was ultimately reclaimed.

In more recent years, the practice of mountaintop removal has come under criticism. This practice sometimes involves dumping the mountaintop overburden into neighboring valleys, which can bury streams and change the hydrology[1] of the area. Studies have documented that this practice can lead to increased flooding of downstream areas and a degradation of downstream water quality.[vii]

Oil Production and Refining

Humans have a long history of using oil in small volumes for lighting and heating, for medicinal purposes, and even in warfare. But the modern oil industry began when several oil wells were drilled in Europe, Russia, and

---

[1] Hydrology refers to the movement of water on and under the surface of the land.

North America around the middle of the 19th century. As more oil was discovered, the industry spread and began to build refineries, initially to remove kerosene—which was valued as an energy source for lighting and heating—and later to provide transportation fuel.

Today, the methods of oil production encompass many categories, including several different types of unconventional oil production.

Discovery and Extraction

The first step in the production of oil is to discover an oil reservoir. This often involves the propagation of seismic waves into the earth and interpreting the reflected shock waves to determine whether a geological formation might contain oil.

Once a suitable prospect has been found, an exploratory well[2] is drilled to assess the quality and quantity of recoverable oil in the reservoir. If the prospect is deemed to be economical, then the development phase begins.

During the development phase, a hole is drilled into the zone where the petroleum deposit is located. The hole is lined with sections of pipe—the casing—that are then cemented into place. The casing serves to prevent sections of the drill hole from collapsing and to prevent contamination of fresh water by the oil that is produced.

Once the casing has been cemented into place, it must be perforated to allow oil to flow into the pipe so it can be extracted. This is done by lowering explosive charges into the oil production zone and setting them off, creating holes through the casing and cement. The explosions also create cracks in the reservoir rock surrounding the casing, which helps to facilitate the flow of oil into the pipe.

The cracks may be further opened by fracturing, or "fracking," the formation. This involves pumping water, chemicals, and a proppant down the well under high pressure to break open channels in the reservoir rock. The proppant can be a material such as sand that is designed to hold the cracks open once they are formed. In some formations, acids are used to perform a similar function of opening up channels for facilitating the flow of oil through the rock.

---

[2] An exploratory well is commonly called a "wildcat well."

Conventional Oil Production

The first stage of commercial production is called primary recovery. During this phase, the pressure of the oil and gas in the formation drives the oil into the wellbore. Typically about 10% of a reservoir's oil can be produced during this phase.

Secondary recovery involves the use of artificial pressure by injecting water or natural gas, for example, into the reservoir. The injected fluid then pushes the oil into the wellbore. Use of secondary recovery methods pushes the recovery rate up to 20% to 40% of the reservoir's oil.

Recovery rates can be increased to 60% or even more through the use of tertiary, or enhanced oil recovery (EOR), techniques. There are three primary methods of EOR: gas injection, thermal recovery, and chemical injection. Each of these methods works by changing the flow properties of the oil so it can more easily move through the reservoir.

With gas injection, a gas that is miscible[3] with the oil—such as carbon dioxide—is injected into the well. The gas lowers the viscosity[4] of the oil and sweeps it toward the production well. Approximately 60% of the EOR production in the United States occurs by gas injection.

Thermal recovery involves heating the oil in the reservoir. This is usually done by injecting steam into the well. Thermal recovery accounts for nearly 40% of the EOR in the U.S.

The final primary EOR technique is chemical injection. During this process, chemicals such as detergents are injected into the well. They reduce the surface tension of the oil, which allows it to flow more easily through the reservoir. Around 1% of the EOR in the U.S. is from chemical injection.

Techniques for conventional oil recovery and EOR can be classified as on-shore, shallow water (water depth of less than 1,000 feet), deepwater (water depth between 1,000 and 2,500 feet), or ultra-deepwater (water depth greater than 2,500 feet).[viii]

---

[3] *Miscible* means the formation of a single phase when two different substances are mixed together. *Immiscible* means that two or more phases are formed upon mixing, such as when oil is mixed with water.

[4] Viscosity refers to the ability of a fluid to flow.

Unconventional Oil Production

Unconventional oil production typically involves very heavy oil resources that require special processing before they can be refined. The resource can be oil sands, bitumen,[5] or oil shale. However, conventional oil production in difficult-to-reach locations—such as deepwater or in the Arctic—is sometimes also classified as unconventional oil production.

Did you know? The world has consumed approximately 1 trillion barrels of oil since the oil age began in the mid-19th century. That is enough oil to cover the state of New York to a depth of 3.7 feet.

Most unconventional heavy oil production today occurs in the Athabasca oil sands In Alberta, Canada, and in the Orinoco oil sands in Venezuela. The deposits in the Orinoco Belt are estimated to contain up to 1.2 trillion barrels, with over 200 billion barrels technically recoverable.[6] The oil sands in Alberta contain an estimated 1.7 trillion barrels, with about 10% (170 billion barrels) of that being technically recoverable. For reference, Saudi Arabia's proven reserves of conventional crude oil are estimated to be 267 billion barrels.

Unconventional heavy oil is commercially produced by adding heat to the oil. This may be done by mining the deposit and then extracting the oil in a processing plant, or it may be done in place by injecting steam into the ground to reduce the oil's viscosity so it may be extracted by conventional methods.

As the ratio of oil prices to natural gas prices increases, the economics for techniques such as steam-assisted gravity drainage (SAGD) become more attractive for producing heavy oil. SAGD involves drilling two horizontal wells, one approximately 15 feet above the other. Steam—usually produced from natural gas—is injected into the upper well, which heats the oil and allows it to flow to the lower well, where it is then pumped out of the ground. This technique is particularly attractive in the Athabasca oil sands

---

[5] Bitumen is naturally occurring asphalt.

[6] Technically recoverable oil is defined as oil that is recoverable using known exploration and production technology, but without regard to cost.

because it provides a use for stranded natural gas reserves.[7] In areas where natural gas can reach the marketplace, SAGD can still be competitive at a high enough oil to natural gas price ratio.

In contrast to the other heavy oils, oil shale[8] consists of sedimentary rock that contains heavy organic compounds called kerogen. Oil shale lacks the tarry or sticky qualities of heavy oil deposits, and more processing is required to produce oil from oil shale.

Global estimates of technically recoverable oil shale reserves are around 3 trillion barrels. Commercial grades of shale may yield 0.5 to 1 barrel of oil per metric ton of shale, but there is little commercial production of oil from shale globally because of poor economics.

OIL SHALE DEVELOPMENT: IMMINENT FOR OVER A CENTURY

During the 2012 U.S. presidential campaign, then-candidate Michele Bachmann made the claim, "We have more oil in three Western states in the form of shale oil than all the oil in Saudi Arabia." What Bachmann was referring to is the Green River Formation, a geologic formation that encompasses parts of Utah, Colorado, and Wyoming and contains an oil shale resource estimated at more than 2 trillion barrels.

But a *resource* is not the same as a *reserve*. An analogy to help understand the difference is to consider the amount of dissolved gold in the oceans. All of the gold in the ocean would be the resource—and it is enormous. The value of this resource would amount to trillions of dollars if the gold could be economically recovered. But the gold is at such a dilute concentration that even though it could technically be recovered, it can't be economically recovered. Thus even though the resource is huge, the reserve—the amount that can be economically recovered with existing technology—is zero.

This is similar to the situation with the oil shale in the Western U.S. Over 100 years ago, the headline of a Colorado newspaper declared "Oil Shale Development Imminent." But despite developmental work, the oil shale has never been developed, because processing the shale into oil has always been costly relative to

[7] Stranded natural gas reserves are natural gas reserves that can't economically reach the marketplace.

[8] The oil produced from processing oil shale is shale oil. Another category of oil unrelated to this is deposits of oil found within shale deposits. This type of oil can be produced with horizontal drilling combined with fracking, and has led to increased oil production in the U.S. in recent years.

the oil that is produced. One of the costs is the energy inputs, and those—along with other processing costs—tend to increase as the price of oil increases. This has always put the economics of oil shale out of reach even as oil prices climbed.

Oil Refining

Once oil is extracted, it is transported to an oil refinery for conversion into final products such as gasoline, diesel, jet fuel, fuel oil, and asphalt.

The level of refining required depends on the quality of the crude oil. There are numerous different types of crude oil, and the quality of the crude oil is indicated by the crude oil assay. Figure 4-1 shows a comparison of two different generic types of crude oil. Crude oils that have very high density—designated in the assay by a low API gravity[9]—are called heavy crudes. If a crude oil has high sulfur content, it is called a sour crude. Crudes may also have varying contents of heavy metals that complicate processing.

Volume %	Generic Light Sweet	Generic Heavy Sour
Gas (Initial Boiling Point to 99°F)	4.4	3.4
Straight Run (99 to 210°F)	6.5	4.1
Naphtha (210 to 380°F)	18.6	9.1
Kerosene (380 to 510°F)	13.8	9.2
Distillate (510 to 725°F)	32.4	19.3
Gas Oil (725 to 1050°F)	19.6	26.5
Residuals (Boiling Point > 1050°F)	4.7	28.4
Total	100.0	100.0
Sulfur %	0.3	4.9
Gravity, °API	34.8	22
Nickel, ppm	26	44
Vanadium, ppm	2.9	139
Iron, ppm	8	17

Figure 4-1. Comparison of two simplified crude oil assays

The crude oil assay indicates expected products from processing the crude, as well as what type of processing is needed to meet market specifications. In this example, the amount of product that boils off as the temperature is

---

[9] The API gravity is a measure of how heavy or light oil is relative to water. If the API gravity is above 10, the oil is lighter than water and would float. If it is less than 10, it is heavier than water and would sink.

raised to 99°F is called "gas." As Figure 4-1 shows, this is 4.4% for the light crude and 3.4% for the heavy crude.

Crudes that are heavy and/or sour trade at a discount to light, sweet crudes, because they require more processing. Refineries must be specifically configured to process crudes that are heavy and/or sour, but depletion of light, sweet crude supplies has caused many refineries to make the capital investments required to process the lower grades.

The first step in the refining of crude oil is removal of salt and water. The oil then undergoes distillation, where different fractions are separated according to boiling point ranges (as shown in the assay).

The lightest fraction, or cut, in crude oil consists of a mixture of light gases. This gas mixture includes dissolved methane, ethane, propane, some butane, and some trace higher gases. This fraction can be purified for sales or conversion to various petrochemicals such as ethylene or propylene, or it can end up as fuel gas to help satisfy a refinery's need for steam.

The next fraction is straight-run, or natural, gasoline. Gasoline is a mixture of hydrocarbons that is partially characterized by a specific boiling-point range, and the gasoline you purchase at the gas station contains many different blended components. One of these components is usually light, straight-run gasoline. This fraction contains compounds like butane, octane, and many branched and cyclic hydrocarbons that boil in a specific range. However, most finished gasoline has been subjected to additional processing. The straight-run gasoline is what is distilled from the crude oil with no additional processing.

The next fraction is naphtha. Small amounts of naphtha can be blended into gasoline, but the octane rating[10] for naphtha is very low. More commonly, naphtha is fed to a catalytic reformer, which processes the naphtha and boosts the octane rating from less than 40 to greater than 90.

The fraction just heavier than naphtha is kerosene (also called "jet"), which starts to get into the range of the distillate fractions. This fraction has greater energy content per gallon than the lighter fractions, but is too heavy (i.e., the boiling point is too high) to be blended into gasoline.

---

[10] The octane rating refers to the tendency of a fuel to pre-ignite. Fuels with low octane ratings will ignite early in an engine, which will cause the engine to knock.

The sulfur components start to become more concentrated in the heavier fractions, so kerosene is typically subjected to hydrotreating. In this step, hydrogen is added to the kerosene in a reactor to convert sulfur compounds into hydrogen sulfide, which is then removed. Kerosene is used as fuel for jet engines and for some portable heating and lighting applications, and it may also be blended into diesel.

The next fraction is distillate (specifically, No. 2 Distillate; kerosene is sometimes called No. 1 Distillate). Like kerosene, this fraction contains sulfur (as do all the heavier fractions) and must be subjected to additional treatment. Distillate has two major end uses: as diesel fuel and as home heating oil. In fact, as indicated in the assays shown in Figure 4-1, a substantial portion of a barrel of oil ends up as heavy distillate. For the light, sweet crude assay, an estimated 32.4% ends up as distillate (i.e., the 32.4% of the components will boil off in the boiling range characterized as "distillate"), and for the heavy, sour crude assay, 19.3% ends up as distillate.

The fraction following distillate is gas oil, which is also known as fuel oil or heavy gas oil (distillate also being known as light gas oil). This fraction is typically processed in a catalytic "cracker" to make cracked gasoline. Cracking involves breaking heavy, long-chain hydrocarbons down into shorter hydrocarbons that boil in the gasoline range. The cracked gas is then blended into the gasoline pool.

The final cut, residuals, or just plain "resid," is of great interest when the economics of heavy crudes versus light crudes are compared. Note in the assays in Figure 4-1 that less than 5% of the barrel of light crude ends up as resid, whereas the heavy crude yields over 28% resid. Resid is sold as asphalt and roofing tar, and it is not as valuable as gasoline or distillate. Therefore, more and more refiners are installing a piece of equipment called a *coker* to further process the resid.

A coker thermally cracks the resid by subjecting it to extremely high temperatures and converts it into additional gasoline, diesel, and gas oils. The economics of doing this are often very attractive, given the historical price spread between light crude oil and heavy crude oil. A coker can convert over 80% of the resid into valuable liquid fuels.

Safety and Environmental Considerations

The production, transportation, and refining of crude oil pose a number of safety and environmental considerations. Certain types of oil production—such as offshore or unconventional oil—have higher potential to impact the environment.

Millions of gallons of oil and fuel are spilled each year throughout the petroleum supply chain. We are all familiar with images from the *Exxon Valdez*, which spilled 11 million gallons of crude oil in Prince William Sound in 1989.[11] While such tanker spills are rare, they can do tremendous damage to ecosystems when they occur.

Less rare are any number of pipeline leaks that occur as oil is transferred from beneath the earth to refineries and then to consumers around the world. The recent Deepwater Horizon oil spill leaked nearly 200 million gallons of oil into the Gulf of Mexico following a blowout deep below the ocean that took months to cap.

Did you know?   A 1979 underwater oil well blowout in Mexico's Bahia de Campeche flowed uncontrollably for nine months before being capped.

In addition to accidents, there have been a number of cases where waste from petroleum production operations has been dumped into the environment. One example of this took place in Ecuador, where oil byproducts were dumped into unlined pits and contaminated the soil and waterways. The Niger Delta has become extremely polluted with oil due to accidental spills as well as vandalism, sabotage, and theft from pipelines.

Development of oil sands poses additional environmental considerations. The process requires the removal of the land above the deposit, uses a lot of water, and generates a lot of wastewater. The wastewater often ends up in tailings ponds containing toxic byproducts of the extraction process. These tailings ponds have been responsible for a number of documented bird fatalities.

---

[11] Globally, drivers and boaters spill nearly twice this much fuel every year. This often contributes to smog, but does not have the same impact on the ecosystem as a large spill in a single location.

The burning of petroleum products—as with the combustion of all fossil fuels—emits greenhouse gases believed to be contributing to global warming. Smog is also a major issue that can be caused by vehicle emissions, particularly in large cities.

As with the coal-mining industry, millions of people are employed globally in the oil industry, and thousands are killed each year in accidents. Historically, there have been many major accidents that killed large numbers of employees as well as private citizens, and damaged personal property. For example, in 2005, an explosion at a BP refinery in Texas killed 15 people, injured over 170, and caused tens of millions of dollars in property damage.

Natural Gas Production

Natural gas and petroleum are both products of the decay of organic matter within the earth. Petroleum is a mixture of hydrocarbons, and natural gas primarily consists of the simplest hydrocarbon—methane. Therefore, natural gas and petroleum are generally found together. (Natural gas is also found in coal deposits.)

Oil fields will contain some natural gas, and natural gas fields will contain heavier hydrocarbons (i.e., light petroleum fractions). Whether oil or natural gas is the predominant deposit is a function of the conditions the buried matter experienced over time. The deeper the organic material was buried, the more pressure and temperature it experienced. Higher temperatures and pressures favor the formation of natural gas.

METHANE HYDRATES: THE ICE THAT BURNS

Because of advances in hydraulic fracturing, U.S. oil and gas production has started to grow in recent years. Resources that were formerly uneconomical are now being developed in places like North Dakota, Texas, and Pennsylvania. While it is too early to tell how long these production increases can continue, this does show the importance of technology improvements when it comes to increasing energy supplies.

Another potential energy supply for the future is called methane hydrates, also known as methane clathrates. Methane hydrates are compounds in which methane forms an ice-like crystalline compound with water. Methane hydrates are flammable in the crystalline form, and methane can be extracted from them and burned.

The methane hydrate resource is immense—much larger than the conventional resource base for natural gas. But the deposits occur primarily on and under the ocean floor, and there is presently no way to economically extract them.

Beyond the economic issue is the fact that methane is a powerful greenhouse gas, and development of the hydrates would both increase the amount of methane in the atmosphere, as some would be lost to the air during processing, and increase the atmospheric carbon dioxide concentration as the methane is burned for power.

Nevertheless, countries are working to commercialize the extraction of methane hydrates. Japan and China are both engaged in long-term commercialization efforts, and the United States is conducting research into the potential of methane hydrates.

The exploration and production of natural gas is similar—and in many aspects identical—to the process for finding and producing petroleum. Refining of natural gas is much simpler than petroleum refining. It generally consists of removing heavy hydrocarbons for processing in an oil refinery, and removing impurities such as water and hydrogen sulfide.

The Shale Gas Revolution

As with petroleum, hydraulic fracturing, or "fracking," is used on many gas wells to break open channels in the reservoir rock that facilitate gas flow to the well bore. Fracking was first commercially introduced in the oil and gas industry in 1949, and application of the technique grew rapidly in the oil and gas fields of Oklahoma and Texas. Fracking increases the amount of oil and gas that can be recovered from a field, and it is credited with boosting recoverable U.S. oil reserves by 30% and natural gas reserves by 90%.[ix]

In recent years, fracking has been used in conjunction with horizontal drilling to extract natural gas from shale deposits. Shale gas typically can't be economically produced via conventional methods.

Shale gas reserves exist in many countries around the world (see Figure 4-2), with the U.S. Energy Information Administration (EIA) projecting that "adding the identified shale gas resources to other gas resources increases total world technically recoverable gas resources by over 40 percent to 22,600 trillion cubic feet." (Global consumption of natural gas was 112 trillion cubic feet in 2010.)[x]

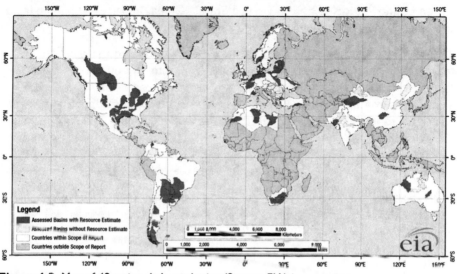

Map of Shale Gas Basins in the U.S. and 14 World Regions

Figure 4-2. Map of 48 major shale gas basins (Source: EIA)[xi]

China is estimated to have the most technically recoverable shale gas, with 1,275 trillion cubic feet (tcf). This is 12 times greater than China's conventional gas reserves and could ease pressure in the global marketplace from China's growing energy needs.

Shale gas that contributes to China's energy supplies could ease pressure on China's energy demands in the global marketplace. This is likely why in 2009 U.S. President Obama signed an agreement with Chinese President Hu Jintao to share U.S. knowledge on shale gas development and help China develop its shale gas reserves.

Many other countries have large shale gas resources. Behind China, the top five technically recoverable shale gas resources[12] are located in the United States with 862 tcf, Argentina (774 tcf), Mexico (681 tcf), and South Africa (485 tcf).

---

[12] This according to the EIA assessment, which did not examine Russia or the Middle East because their large conventional gas reserves are expected to remain the dominant source of gas production for the foreseeable future.

Exploration and/or development of shale gas is underway in more than a dozen countries, including the United States, China, India, Canada, Australia, the United Kingdom, Poland, and Germany.

The Barnett Shale geological formation in Texas became one of the early major economic successes in shale gas development, ultimately becoming the largest source of natural gas in the U.S. Spurred on by the success in Texas, fracking has expanded out of traditional oil-and-gas producing areas and into more densely populated areas of the country such as the East Coast of the U.S.

■ **Did you know?** Not only has hydraulic fracturing dramatically increased natural gas production, but it is also the primary driver behind the increases in U.S. oil production that began in 2009.

The Marcellus Shale is a geological formation underlying most of West Virginia, northern and western Pennsylvania, western New York, and eastern Ohio. Conventional fracking has been carried out on gas wells in the region for decades, but over the past five years unconventional fracking[13] has been increasingly used to extract gas from the Marcellus Shale.

Environmental Implications of Fracking

As unconventional fracking has been increasingly used in more populated areas, concerns have been raised about the potential for the technique to harm the environment. The primary issue is the potential for fracking fluids—water mixed with a cocktail of chemicals, some of which are carcinogens—to migrate into the groundwater as a result of the fracking process.

In fact, a number of people have reported that their water was contaminated in areas where fracking was taking place. In 2010, gas driller Cabot Oil was cited by the Pennsylvania Department of Environmental Protection for contaminating 14 water wells during Cabot's Marcellus Shale drilling operations.

---

[13] Unconventional fracking utilizes horizontal drilling and requires much greater volumes of water than does conventional fracking.

The Cabot case provides a perfect example of why fracking has become controversial in the area. The reason the water wells were contaminated was determined to be not a result of fracking fluids migrating from the fracking zone, but rather because the gas wells were improperly cemented.

These gas wells do pass through the water table, but the fracking takes places thousands of feet below the water table. Between the fracking location and the water table, the rock presents a formidable barrier against migration of the chemicals. Thus, fracking proponents argue that there is zero chance of contaminating a water table because of the fracking process, and that there has never been a documented case of water being contaminated via fracking.

However, the fracking fluids must be transported to the site, pumped down the well, and ultimately recycled or disposed. If fracking fluid leaks out into the environment during any stage of a fracking operation, it is irrelevant to impacted people whether it was the physical act of fracking, or simply operations supporting the fracking, that resulted in the contamination. In any case, the negative impact will be associated with the fracking.

Ultimately, even if there is zero risk of chemical migration from the fracking zone into the groundwater, accidents are going to happen such as the one that resulted in Cabot's citation. The production of energy—coal, oil, natural gas, even biofuels—has always been accompanied by accidents that injure people and harm the environment. As the number of operations and individual operators increases, so will the risks.

Fracking Trade-Offs

Fracking provides a classic example of energy trade-offs. Development of the Marcellus Shale can indeed increase the level of energy security for the U.S., but some people are going to be impacted by developments in the area. For some, it will mean jobs and a higher standard of living. For others, the impact will be inconvenience, such as more noise and traffic. And for some, the impact has already been contaminated groundwater.

Because of the stakes involved, it is likely that development in shale deposits across the U.S.—and indeed the world—will continue to grow. A U.S. Department of Energy (DOE) panel that was created by President Obama to study the issue concluded that fracking can be done in an environmentally responsible way, but major steps must be undertaken to protect the environment.

The issue of fracking in areas like New York and Pennsylvania will continue to pit development versus those who would rather preserve their existing way of life. This is not an issue specific to fracking; opposition to development will take place any time an extractive industry moves into a populated area for the first time, be it natural gas production, logging, or coal mining.

Did you know? Geologists have linked fracking to earthquakes in Oklahoma and Ohio.

Such opposition is understandable by those who are impacted by the development, and if development is to proceed, then governments and companies must work to minimize the impact on the local population.

However, this is a two-way street. History tells us again and again that such lucrative revenue streams are irresistible to private companies and governments alike. Therefore, people are likely to continue to be impacted by fracking operations. Even if their primary goal is to prevent fracking in their area, protesters should spend considerable energy providing input into the regulatory process because of the likelihood that fracking will continue to expand.

Summary

The fossil fuels discussed in this chapter will continue to provide the majority of the world's energy for many years. As conventional supplies deplete, the world will turn increasingly to unconventional methods of production. However, unconventional methods often have higher costs and a higher environmental footprint than conventional methods, and therefore strict regulations must be applied to protect the environment.

Some would argue that the environmental footprint of burning fossil fuels is too high and that the threat from climate change is so great that fossil fuels must not continue to be used to provide the majority of the world's energy. That brings us to the issue of climate change, the topic of Chapter 5.

References

[i] Donald G. Kaufman and Cecilia M. Franz, *Biosphere 2000: Protecting Our Global Environment* (New York: HarperCollins College Publishers, 1993).

[ii] BP, *BP Statistical Review of World Energy 2011*, "Coal Consumption," http://www.bp.com/sectiongenericarticle800.do?categoryId =9037185&contentId=7068613.

[iii] World Coal Institute (WCI), *Coal: Meeting Global Challenges*, May 2006, www.worldcoal.org/bin/pdf/original_pdf_file/coal_meeting_global_challenges _report(03_06_2009).pdf.

[iv] Jeff Goodell, *Big Coal: The Dirty Secret Behind America's Energy Future* (Boston: Houghton Mifflin Harcourt, 2006).

[v] Ian Urbina, "Toll Mounts in West Virginia Coal Mine Explosion," *New York Times*, April 5, 2010, http://www.nytimes.com/2010/04/06/us /06westvirginia.html.

[vi] Wang Huazhong, "China Coal Mine Deaths Fall 'but Still Remain High,'" *China Daily*, February 26, 2011, http://www.chinadaily.com.cn/china /2011-02/26/content_12081456.htm.

[vii] Margaret A. Palmer et al., "Mountaintop Mining Consequences," *Science* 327, no. 5962 (January 8, 2010): 148.

[viii] Morgan Downey, *Oil 101* (New York: Wooden Table Press, 2009).

[ix] Carl T. Montgomery and Michael B. Smith, "Hydraulic Fracturing: History of an Enduring Technology," *Journal of Petroleum Technology*, December 2010, http://www.spe.org/jpt/print/archives/2010/12/10Hydraulic.pdf.

[x] U.S. Energy Information Administration (EIA), "World Shale Gas Resources: An Initial Assessment of 14 Regions Outside the United States," April 5, 2011, http://www.eia.gov/analysis/studies/worldshalegas/.

[xi] Ibid.

Global Warming

How Do You Stop a Hurricane?

> *The warnings about global warming have been extremely clear for a long time. We are facing a global climate crisis. It is deepening We are entering a period of consequences.*

—Al Gore

> *With all of the hysteria, all of the fear, all of the phony science, could it be that man-made global warming is the greatest hoax ever perpetrated on the American people?*

—James Inhofe, U.S. Senator

There are few issues that are as polarizing as the topic of global warming. On one side are proponents of the theory that human activity is contributing to climate extremes, and that rising greenhouse gas emissions pose a serious threat to life on earth. On the other side are people who believe that global warming is at a minimum grossly exaggerated, at worst a scam, and that enacting drastic measures to address the issue will result in economic calamity. On each side are people who feel strongly about their position, and who believe that if the other side prevails the results will be disastrous.

This chapter explains the science behind global warming, examines some of the reasons that it is a controversial topic, and considers the political and economic issues involved in attempting to bring greenhouse gas emissions under control. But to be clear, I am not attempting to present the scientific case either for or against global warming, but rather to better familiarize readers with the issue.

What Is Global Warming?

The earth's climate can be influenced by a number of different factors. Small wobbles in the earth's orbit, changes in the level of solar activity, changes in ocean currents, and even major volcanic eruptions can all contribute toward the warming and cooling of the earth.

One of the factors that influences the earth's climate is the greenhouse effect. The surface of the earth is warmed by short-wavelength (visible) solar radiation that passes through the earth's atmosphere. As solar radiation causes surfaces to warm, energy is reemitted from those surfaces in the form of infrared radiation.

Infrared radiation has longer wavelengths than the visible radiation from the sun, and it interacts with the atmosphere in a different way. The atmosphere contains certain gases—water vapor, methane, and carbon dioxide, to name a few—that absorb the infrared radiation from the surface of the earth and radiate some of that energy back toward the earth. This is analogous to a greenhouse, where glass blocks some of the infrared radiation and reflects it back into the greenhouse.

■ **Did you know?**   The term "greenhouse effect" is actually a misnomer. While a greenhouse glass will in fact reflect some infrared radiation back into the greenhouse in a way that is similar to the atmosphere reflecting infrared radiation back to earth, the primary heating mechanism in a greenhouse is the prevention of airflow that would otherwise cool the interior.

The result of the heat being radiated back to the earth is that the earth is about 60°F warmer than it would be without a greenhouse effect. Because greenhouse gases in the atmosphere are responsible for the greenhouse effect, it stands to reason that if the atmospheric concentration of those greenhouse gases increases, then so should the surface temperature of the earth.

Climate change that is induced by increasing greenhouse gas concentrations is commonly called global warming. However, in recent years, this has been increasingly referred to as "climate change," since the overall impact to climate is more complex than a mere rise in the earth's temperature. I tend to use the two terms interchangeably, but will more often use "global warming" simply because that is the phrase that is most familiar to the layperson.

The Controversy

There is no dispute that there is a greenhouse effect on earth. The reason for the greenhouse effect is well understood. In fact, it is only because of the greenhouse effect that life as we know it on the earth is possible. Without the greenhouse effect, the average surface temperature of the earth would hover around 0°F.

There is also no dispute that greenhouse gases, like carbon dioxide (CO_2), are accumulating in the atmosphere as humans burn through ancient carbon sources like coal, oil, and natural gas. The atmospheric CO_2 concentration has increased from about 285 parts per million (ppm) in preindustrial times to 320 ppm in the 1960s to the present value of 390 ppm (see Figure 5-1).

It is clear from our scientific understanding of the greenhouse effect that increases in the atmospheric CO_2 concentration *should* cause the surface temperature of the earth to warm, and if the concentration continues to increase, this *should* lead to further warming. Despite this, a large number of people are skeptical of the idea that human activity is causing the earth's climate to change.

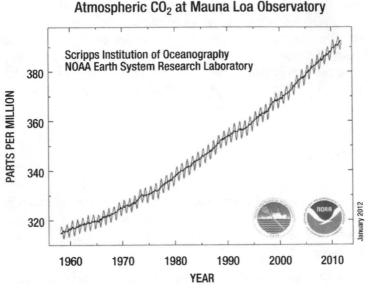

Figure 5-1. Historical atmospheric CO₂ concentrations at Hawaii's Mauna Loa Observatory (Graphic source: National Oceanic and Atmospheric Administration)

A poll conducted in the U.S. in 2011 showed that a strong majority—83%—believes that the earth is warming, but only a minority of those polled attributed it primarily to human activity. Respondents were split along political lines: 37% of Democrats attributed the warming primarily to human activity, but only 14% of Republicans agreed.[i]

Skepticism is not limited to the U.S. A 2010 poll by Cardiff University in the UK showed that 40% of those surveyed thought that climate change concerns were exaggerated, and less than one-third believed that climate change was primarily a result of human activity.

So if the science behind the greenhouse effect is understood, why are so many people skeptical of the idea that human activity is primarily responsible for global warming?

Understanding the Skepticism

People may be skeptical of the science behind climate change for various reasons. The science of why there is a greenhouse effect is clear, but the specific impacts on climate come from projections based on climate models.

Some skeptics feel that because complex feedback mechanisms are involved in modeling the climate, the certainty of the results have been overstated. In fact, the reason that "global warming" eventually morphed into "climate change" is that the climate impact was much more complex than simply a warming earth.

To put this in the context of why some people have doubts, consider the accuracy of your local weather forecast. Some skeptics argue that if science can't model the weather a week in advance, it can hardly predict years in advance the climate impacts due to the greenhouse effect.

Another common reason for skepticism is that some people have a hard time believing that the relative contribution of CO_2 can have a major impact on the climate. There are a number of greenhouse gases in the atmosphere, but water vapor is the greenhouse gas in the greatest abundance and with the dominant contribution to the greenhouse effect.

The concentration of water vapor in the atmosphere is 3% to 4%.[ii] The concentration of CO_2 in the atmosphere is 390 ppm, which is 0.039%. So, there is about 100 times more water vapor than CO_2 in the atmosphere, and water vapor contributes an estimated 75% of the earth's greenhouse effect.[iii] (A report from the U.S. Department of Energy (DOE) attributed as much as 95% of the greenhouse effect in the lower atmosphere to water vapor).[iv]

Thus, even if the atmospheric concentration of CO_2 doubles from current values due to continued burning of fossil fuels, there will still be around 50 times more water vapor in the atmosphere. Some skeptics argue that this relatively small contribution could not have a major impact on the climate.

However, once again there are complex feedback mechanisms in play. For example, as the earth warms, methane that is locked up in permafrost can leak into the atmosphere. Methane is a more powerful greenhouse gas than CO_2, so this has the potential to set up a positive feedback loop: as the earth warms, methane is released, and this causes more warming.

The world's oceans—the largest global sink of CO_2—also play an important but complex role. As the oceans warm, they can absorb less CO_2, setting up the potential for a greater portion of future global CO_2 emissions to remain in the atmosphere. These are the sorts of feedback mechanisms that the climate models must attempt to incorporate.

There are other people who accept the science behind global warming and accept that there will be some warming, but believe temperature increases will be small and are not cause for undue concern.

■ **Did you know?** Some of the CO_2 that is absorbed by the oceans dissolves and forms carbonic acid. This has slightly decreased the pH of the world's oceans as atmospheric CO_2 concentrations have increased, a process referred to as "ocean acidification."[1]

However, it is important to bear in mind that projected temperature increases are global averages, and some areas are apt to see more extreme temperature changes than others. In addition, temperature variations can change the intensity of the weather and shift global climatic zones. Some areas that currently experience cold climates might become more temperate, but then some temperature zones may become drier and unable to sustain agriculture.

Some arguments against global warming are simply based on misinformation. An example of this is the oft-repeated claim that volcanoes contribute more CO_2 to the atmosphere than do humans. This claim is false. According to the U.S. Geological Survey, volcanoes emit approximately 130 million metric tons of CO_2 into the atmosphere each year.[v] In contrast, the burning of fossil fuels contributed 33.2 *billion* metric tons CO_2 to the atmosphere in 2010—255 times the estimated level contributed by volcanoes.

Obstacles to Action

The reality is that global warming is a complex issue, but it is one that is viewed by many as the most pressing environmental issue facing humankind. Still, developing an internationally agreeable mitigation plan has proven to be difficult, for both political and economic reasons.

One reason for this difficulty is that humans tend to discount the future, which means that we usually are unwilling to pay $1 today to avert $1 of future costs. The greater the uncertainty about those future costs, the heavier the future is likely to be discounted (i.e., the less we are willing to pay). Because there is some uncertainty about specific impacts of global

---

[1] Some people have suggested that the term "ocean acidification" is misleading, because even though the pH of the oceans is declining, the pH is actually alkaline, or basic (the opposite of acidic). Thus, they have argued for characterizing the change as "becoming less basic," or "neutralizing."

warming—and because a large portion of the general public remains skeptical that global warming is a result of human activity—some countries have been unwilling to commit major public funding to reducing greenhouse gas emissions.

A second reason for the difficulty in developing an internationally agreeable mitigation plan is that people often act in their own self-interest, even when these interests conflict with those of the global population. This is a dilemma known as the *tragedy of the commons*, first used to describe a situation in which individuals are allowed to graze their herds on public lands. Individuals will seek to maximize their personal gain when accessing a common resource, and this leads to overuse of the resource by individuals acting in their self-interest. Hence the asset may ultimately be destroyed by those self-interests.

Many countries display this sort of behavior on the issue of CO_2 emissions. While a majority of countries may agree that global warming is taking place and that carbon emissions must be regulated, some countries have refused to participate in global agreements because of concerns about how their economies would be impacted.

There have been international treaties aimed at reducing CO_2 emissions. The most famous is the Kyoto Protocol, a treaty that was ratified by nearly every country in the world. The treaty became effective in 2005 and commits certain developed countries to reduce their collective greenhouse gas emissions. However, it contains no quantitative requirement of reductions for developing countries, and the United States cited this as a reason when it refused to ratify the treaty. Thus, global CO_2 emissions have continued to rise despite the treaty.

Case Study: United States

For most of the 20th century, the United States was by far the world's largest emitter of CO_2. The U.S. is also a high per capita emitter of CO_2. As Figure 5-2 shows, in 2010 there were nearly 20 metric tons of CO_2 emitted for every person living in the U.S.[2] Thus, as global concern over global

---

[2] The U.S. Census Bureau indicates that the 2010 U.S. population was 309 million people, and the *BP Statistical Review of World Energy 2011* put 2010 U.S. emissions at 6.1 billion metric tons.

warming escalated, the U.S. came under increasing international pressure to reduce CO_2 emissions.

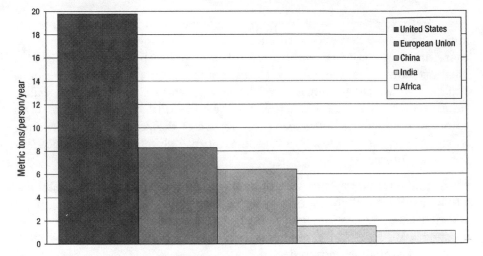

Per Capita CO_2 Emissions 2010

Figure 5-2. Per capita CO_2 emissions for various regions of the world (Data source: Emissions data is from BP *Statistical Review of World Energy 2011* and population data is from the *CIA World Factbook*)

There has also been pressure within the U.S.—especially among Democrats[3]—to reduce greenhouse gas emissions in the U.S. But as reported in the Reuters/Stanford/Ipsos poll mentioned earlier in the chapter, Republicans are less likely than Democrats to attribute climate change to human activity—and the U.S. has a substantial conservative population. Thus, attempts to regulate carbon emissions in the U.S. at the federal level have been mostly unsuccessful, and the U.S. has resisted pressure to sign on to international agreements such as the Kyoto Protocol.

However, in 2009 the U.S. Environmental Protection Agency (EPA) made a determination that greenhouse gases fall under the Clean Air Act definition of air pollutants and threaten the public health. This ruling would have given the EPA the authority to regulate greenhouse gas emissions, but, unsurprisingly, Republican lawmakers introduced legislation to block the EPA from enforcing the ruling.

---

[3] Al Gore is one of the prominent Democrats urging action on greenhouse gas emissions.

There has been some successful legislation at the state level. California, one of the most liberal states in the U.S., passed legislation to cap emissions at 1990 levels by 2020, which would be approximately 25% lower than present day emissions. A number of traditionally Democratic states followed California's lead, but prospects for meaningful legislation at the U.S. federal level appear to be slim.

Despite the political stalemate in the U.S. over enacting carbon emission caps, greenhouse gas emissions in the U.S. have declined over the past few years. As oil prices reached record highs in 2008, demand for oil fell and CO_2 emissions declined as a result. The total decline in U.S. CO_2 emissions between 2007 and 2009 was nearly 620 million metric tons,[4] or a 10% decline over the two-year period.

However, the decline in greenhouse gas emissions in the U.S. occurred during a recession, when economic activity—and thus energy usage—declined. When the economy technically emerged from recession in mid-2009, demand for energy began to rebound, and total carbon emissions once again began to climb. Carbon dioxide emissions in 2010 were 240 million metric tons higher than in 2009, an increase of 4%.

Emerging CO$_2$ Emitters

While most developed countries saw their CO_2 emissions fall between 2006 and 2010, developing countries experienced sharp increases in CO_2 emissions over that time frame. In 2006, China displaced the U.S. as the largest global emitter of CO_2. Since then, China's annual CO_2 emissions have increased by 28%, or 1.8 billion metric tons.

In addition to China, some of the countries that experienced double-digit growth in CO_2 emissions between 2006 and 2010 include Peru (49%), India (40%), Vietnam (37%), Singapore (36%), and Saudi Arabia (28%).

The net result was that even as the U.S., Canada, European Union, Australia, New Zealand, Japan, and Malaysia all saw declines in total CO_2 emissions over the past five years, global emissions grew by 11% over the same time frame.

An examination of the past decade shows that economic development in the Asia Pacific region is the current driver behind growing CO_2 emissions. Over

---

[4] According to data from the BP *Statistical Review of World Energy 2011*.

the past decade, CO_2 emissions declined slightly in North America and the EU, but grew steadily across the Asia Pacific region, as shown in Figure 5-3. Further development of the region could see it become responsible for 50% of global CO_2 emissions within a decade (see Figure 5-4).

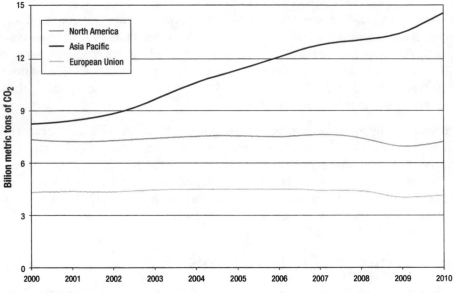

Annual CO_2 Emissions 2000-2010

Figure 5-3. Global CO_2 emissions over the past decade for Asia Pacific, North America, and the European Union (Data source: *BP Statistical Review of World Energy 2011*)

Did you know? If CO_2 emissions in the U.S. and the EU fell to zero, global emissions would still be at 1994 levels—and rapidly increasing.

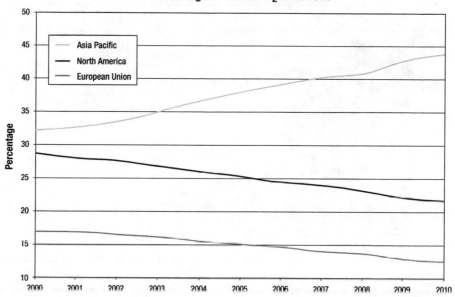

Figure 5-4. Percentage of global CO_2 emissions over the past decade for Asia Pacific, North America, and the European Union (Data source: *BP Statistical Review of World Energy 2011*)

Not only does the Asia Pacific region emit the most CO_2, it has the highest CO_2 emissions growth rate of any region. Other developing regions—the Middle East, Africa, and South and Central America—have much lower overall emissions than both the Asia Pacific region and more developed regions, but as Figure 5-5 shows, all developing regions are experiencing very fast growth in CO_2 emissions.

This is understandable, considering that the majority of the world's population lives in developing regions, and they seek to raise their standards of living. Developed countries have done that by burning fossil fuels, and developing countries seek the same modern conveniences—washing machines, televisions, computers, and cars—enjoyed by the developed world and which are currently powered mostly by fossil fuels.

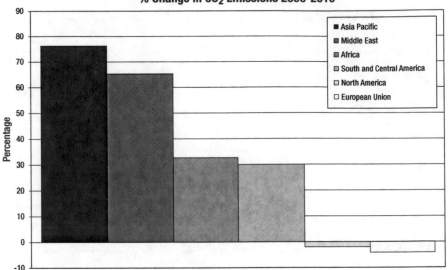

Figure 5-5. Change in CO2 emissions from 2000–2010 (Data source: *BP Statistical Review of World Energy 2011*)

Thus, due to growth in developing countries, global CO_2 emissions are likely to continue to increase just as they did in the past decade. If that trend is to be reversed, future development would need to take place without fossil fuels. This may be possible in theory, but no country has yet provided the blueprint to show that it can be done in practice.

Consider again the per capita emissions of the United States, China, and India. While the U.S. has heavily subsidized and incentivized renewable energy, per capita emissions in the U.S. are still more than 3 times those of China and over 13 times those of India.

It is one thing to imagine that developing countries could develop without increasing their use of fossil fuels, but the reality is that even the developed regions have not shown that it can be done. Thus, the developed world is in the poor position of asking developing countries to do something we ourselves have not done.

The U.S. consumes 9 times as much oil per capita as China, and 24 times as much as India—thus the U.S. is an order of magnitude beyond being able to demonstrate an appealing, low-fossil-fuel lifestyle for these countries. Imagine your life with one-tenth of the oil you currently consume, and you may see why I believe consumption in these countries will continue to climb.

Emissions and GDP

One of the ways to control carbon emissions would be to produce goods and services more energy efficiently. The amount of gross domestic product (GDP) produced per ton of CO_2 emissions is a function of

- The specific industries in a country.

- Which forms of energy those industries use.

- How efficiently those industries use energy. The energy efficiency of industries is influenced by government standards as well as the price industries must pay for energy.

For instance, countries with high levels of chemical, metal, or concrete manufacturing will generally have a high level of CO_2 emissions because these industries typically rely heavily on fossil fuels.[5] Thus, an oft-cited reason for the high per capita CO_2 emissions of the United States is that this is the result of the country's high GDP.

It is true that the U.S. has the highest GDP of any country in the world. However, many developed countries emit far less CO_2 per dollar of GDP. Switzerland and Sweden, for instance, produced nearly $7,000 per ton of CO_2 emissions in 2009, but the U.S. produced just over $2,000 per ton of CO_2 emissions.[6] India and China are even less efficient, producing $550 and $460 per ton of CO_2 emissions, respectively. The global average in 2009 was $1,300 per ton of CO_2 emissions.[vi]

However, these numbers do indicate that further economic growth is possible without increasing CO_2 emissions. If China and India simply improved to U.S. standards of energy efficiency, they could produce four times their current GDP without increasing their carbon emissions. If the U.S. can improve to the efficiency standards of Switzerland and Sweden, it could produce 3.5 times current U.S. GDP without increasing carbon emissions.

And in fact, over the past two decades, most countries have increased GDP per ton of CO_2 emissions. For example, the U.S. increased GDP by 51% per

---

[5] Iceland is a notable exception. Aluminum smelting is a major industry in Iceland and a heavy consumer of electricity, but Iceland derives most of its electricity from hydropower and geothermal power. However per capita oil consumption in Iceland is comparable to that of the U.S.

[6] Amounts are U.S. dollars per metric ton in dollars inflation-adjusted to 2000.

ton of CO_2 emitted, Switzerland increased by 24%, Sweden by 80%, China by 85%, and India by 19%.

Mitigation Options

Global CO_2 emissions increased by nearly 50% over the past two decades, while global GDP increased by 64%. Thus, while the world as a whole increased GDP per ton of CO_2 emissions over that time frame, the efficiency gains weren't nearly great enough to keep CO_2 emissions from growing.

One of the biggest reasons CO_2 emissions continue to grow is that many of the fastest-growing economies are also the least efficient at producing GDP. Thus, if developing countries improve their fossil fuel efficiency to the levels of the developed world, this would address the major contributor to growing carbon emissions.

But there are other tools for mitigating carbon emissions. Probably the most common method is through the establishment of carbon trading markets. With this approach, a governing body sets limits on the amount of carbon that can be emitted, and then distributes emission allowances equal to the emission limit set for a specific company (or cumulatively, a country). Firms may use their permits to emit up to their limit of CO_2, or they can emit less and then sell the extra allowances. The ability to sell unused allowances provides a financial incentive for a company to reduce their carbon emissions below their limit.

The world's largest carbon trading exchange is the European Union Emission Trading Scheme (EU ETS). The EU ETS was put into place to provide EU countries a way to help meet their emission reduction obligations under the Kyoto Protocol. Other mandatory trading exchanges exist in New Zealand and in Tokyo, Japan. In the U.S. trading exchanges do exist, but they aren't mandatory under federal law. California, however, did recently adopt the first state-administered cap-and-trade program in the U.S.[vii]

SULFUR TRADING MARKETS: MODEL FOR CAP-AND-TRADE?

In response to the acid rain caused by sulfur dioxide (SO_2) emissions from U.S. power plants, the EPA in 1990 established a market-based sulfur trading scheme. This sulfur cap-and-trade system has been cited as one of the major factors behind the steep decline in SO_2 emissions.

Some would argue that the sulfur trading markets in the U.S. provide an example of how such markets might bring carbon emissions under control. However, there are two significant differences between SO_2 emissions and CO_2 emissions. One is that sulfur is washed out of the air by rain (and in the process forms acid rain) and remains in the atmosphere only for a few days. That means that SO_2 emissions in China aren't going to result in a prolonged global increase in atmospheric sulfur. That is not the case with CO_2, which has a residence time in the atmosphere of years versus days for SO_2. Thus, a country's SO_2 emissions are more a localized problem.

Second is that the point sources for sulfur emissions are predominantly coal-fired power plants, and therefore pollution-control equipment could be concentrated there. There are far more point sources for CO_2 emissions, making them much more difficult to control.

Another class of emission reduction tools is carbon offsets. Carbon offsets typically involve projects that reduce carbon emissions by a specific amount to create a potentially tradable offset that another company could use to counter its own emissions. Certain carbon offsets qualify for trading on various emission trading schemes. For example, Company A could execute a project to reduce carbon emissions by one ton, and Company B could then buy the offset to compensate for one ton of its own emissions. Examples of carbon offsets that have been traded include those that have been generated from the planting of trees, from installation of renewable energy projects, and from energy efficiency improvements.

A more direct way to deal with CO_2 emissions is through a carbon tax. As energy becomes more expensive, people are more frugal with their usage and businesses invest more money into energy efficiency projects. The disadvantage of a carbon tax over emission trading schemes is that it is more difficult to predict the level of emission reduction at specified tax levels. The advantage of the carbon tax is that the costs are more transparent than when companies simply have mandates to reduce their emissions by a specified amount.

Summary

Carbon dioxide emissions from human activity have been increasing since coal began to be burned in large quantities during the Industrial Revolution. Since then, the atmospheric CO_2 concentration has increased from about 285 ppm to the present value of 390 ppm. Based on our scientific understanding of the greenhouse effect, this increase in atmospheric CO_2 concentration should cause the surface temperature of the earth to increase, and this has the potential to cause serious environmental damage.

My own view is that the earth is warming, and that human activity is contributing to that warming. However, even though greenhouse gases are at current levels primarily due to emissions from developed countries, future emissions are likely to be driven by developing countries. Because this problem is global in nature—and developing countries are starting out at such a low per capita level of CO_2 emissions (but rising rapidly)—it is hard to imagine a scenario in which CO_2 emissions stabilize in the near future.

Thus, I liken the issue of growing CO_2 emissions in developing countries to trying to stop a hurricane: we may see a hurricane headed toward landfall, but even if the results are projected to be devastating, we have no actual tools for stopping the hurricane. That is not to suggest that we therefore do not try; it is simply my prediction that we will continue to see growing CO_2 emissions for the foreseeable future because developed countries presently lack the tools (and moral authority) to prevent their growth in the developing world.

References

[i] Ipsos, "Reuters/Stanford/Ipsos Environmental Poll," September 16, 2011, http://www.ipsos-na.com/news-polls/pressrelease.aspx?id=5337; full report, "National Survey of American Public Opinion on Global Warming," available at http://www.ipsos-na.com/download/pr.aspx?id=10987.

[ii] National Energy Technology Laboratory (NETL), "Key Issues & Mandates: Climate Change - Frequently Asked Questions," accessed October 1, 2011, http://www.netl.doe.gov/keyissues/climate_change3.html.

[iii] Andrew A. Lacis, et al., "Atmospheric CO_2: Principal Control Knob Governing Earth's Temperature," *Science* 330, No. 6002 (October 15, 2010): 356.

[iv] Energy Information Administration (EIA), *Alternatives to Traditional Transportation Fuels 1994, Volume 2, Greenhouse Gas Emissions*, App. D, "Greenhouse Gas Spectral Overlaps and Their Significance," page last

modified January 10, 2008, http://www.eia.gov/cneaf/alternate/page /environment/appd_d.html.

ᵛ U.S. Geological Survey (USGS), *Volcanic Gases and Their Effects*, page last modified June 11, 2010, http://volcanoes.usgs.gov/hazards/gas/index.php.

ᵛⁱ International Energy Agency (IEA), *CO₂ Emissions from Fuel Combustion 2011* (Paris: OECD Publishing, 2011).

ᵛⁱⁱ Julie Cart, "California Becomes First State to Adopt Cap-and-Trade Program," *Los Angeles Times*, October 21, 2011, http://www.latimes.com /news/local/la-me-cap-trade-20111021,0,1125437.

Peak Oil

Myth or Threat to Civilization?

The peaking of world oil production presents the U.S. and the world with an unprecedented risk management problem. As peaking is approached, liquid fuel prices and price volatility will increase dramatically, and, without timely mitigation, the economic, social, and political costs will be unprecedented.

—Robert L. Hirsch et al., *Peaking of World Oil Production*

In the 1970s, it was thought that we were going to run out of oil and, of course, it turned out that there is a lot of oil. The theory today is that we're about halfway through the global endowment. Our view is that we're probably more like 20 percent, based on what we know today.

—Daniel Yergin, *The Prize*

Between 2000 and 2010, world oil prices advanced from approximately $25 per barrel to more than $100 per barrel. The price appreciation of oil over the decade was around ten times the rate of inflation.

By 2005, the idea that escalating oil prices were the result of an impending global peak in oil production—a phenomenon commonly known as "peak oil"—was receiving widespread attention. Many books and articles were published that argued that peak oil was the culprit behind the escalating price of oil, and an imminent threat to civilization. But others dismissed the idea of peak oil, instead offering up oil speculation, OPEC, growth in developing countries, or other geopolitical factors as the primary factors behind the advance in prices.

In this chapter I will examine the issue of peak oil in depth and weigh the risks posed to society.

What Is Peak Oil?

In simple terms, *peak oil* refers to the rate of maximum global oil production, after which oil production will begin a terminal decline when oil fields deplete faster than new production can be brought online. Oil production has already peaked and is in decline in numerous countries around the world.

I am personally not a fan of the term peak oil, for two reasons. First, there are a number of negative stereotypes associated with it, some of which are based on misconceptions (discussed in a later section) and some of which are based on the fact that there have been many incorrect predictions of the date of a global peak in oil production. There have also been many incorrect predictions—at least to this point—about the ramifications of peak oil.

The second reason I don't like the term peak oil is that it implies consequences will occur only following the peak of oil production, while I believe there will be serious "peak-like" consequences before a global peak necessarily occurs. We won't be able to confidently say that world oil production has peaked until several years after the production decline begins. Thus, a preoccupation with the timing of peak oil can diminish the sense of urgency that I believe we need in order to cope with a world whose countries are increasingly competing for the remaining oil supplies.

As a result, I prefer to discuss the subject as one of resource depletion. When I discuss the problem in terms of "peak oil," what I am really referring to is the inability of oil supply growth to stay ahead of oil demand growth. After all, this is the real implication of peak oil: insufficient supplies to meet demand, and rising prices and potential shortages as a result. This can take place even when oil production is rising, and in fact has been the case in recent years.

■ **Did you know?** "Peak oil," effectively, is the inability of oil supply growth to stay ahead of oil demand growth.

I do not know whether oil production peaked last year or might instead peak in five or even ten years. But I do know that oil production has struggled in recent years to meet surging demand. The worsening of this situation over time is what peak oil means to me, and is the context in which it is discussed in this chapter.

The Scientific Study of Peak Oil

The history of the scientific study of peak oil dates to the 1950s, when Shell geophysicist M. King Hubbert reported on studies he had undertaken regarding the production rates of oil and gas fields.[i] In a 1956 paper, Hubbert predicted that oil production in a particular region would approximate a bell curve, increasing exponentially during the early stages of production before eventually slowing, reaching a peak when approximately half of a field had been extracted, and then going into terminal production decline.

Hubbert applied his reasoning to oil production in the contiguous United States.[1] He estimated that the ultimate potential reserve of the Lower 48 U.S. states and offshore areas was 150 billion barrels of oil. Based on that reserve estimate, the 6.6 million barrels per day (bpd) extraction rate in 1955, and the fact that 52.5 billion barrels of oil had been cumulatively produced in the U.S. already, Hubbert estimated that oil production in the U.S. would reach maximum production in 1965.

Hubbert further calculated that if the U.S. oil reserve was 200 billion barrels, peak production would occur in 1970, a delay of five years from his base case. Hubbert's estimate of 1970 U.S. oil production based on the 200 billion barrel reserve case was 3 billion barrels, or 8.2 million bpd. Oil production in the U.S. did in fact peak in 1970 (see Figure 6-1), albeit at 9.6 million bpd.

---

[1] Alaska had not yet been granted statehood.

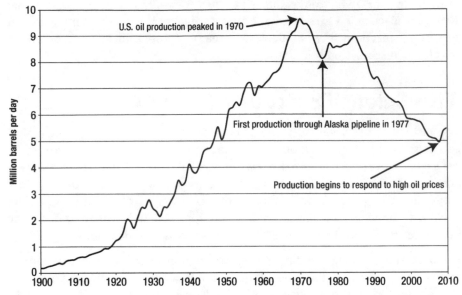

Figure 6-1. Historical oil production in the United States (Data source: Energy Information Administration [ii])

Through 2010, cumulative U.S. production stands at just over 200 billion barrels,[iii] with a remaining estimated reserve of 20 billion barrels.[iv] Even correcting for Alaska's cumulative 15 billion barrels of production and remaining 3.5 billion barrel reserve[v] that Hubbert didn't consider, the total reserve of the Lower 48 in 1955 was somewhat higher than Hubbert's higher estimate (200 billion barrels) of Lower 48 oil reserves.

■ **Did you know?** Hubbert's 1970 prediction of a U.S. oil production peak, which turned out to be correct, was based on a secondary case in which he assumed the U.S. oil reserve grew to 200 billion barrels. But he indicated skepticism that this was possible because it would require the U.S. to find additional oil fields equivalent to "eight East Texas oil fields."

Hubbert's critics argue that while his technique may have some utility, the methodology is simplistic and does not account for reserve growth, unconventional oil production, or geopolitical factors. Hubbert did address the issue of improved extraction techniques but argued that rather than significantly impacting the date of peak oil in the U.S., better extraction techniques would slow the rate of production decline—and thus skew the back half of the bell curve. And in fact, the average annual rate of decline in U.S. oil production since the 1970 peak has been under 1%—much lower than the natural decline rate of most aging oil fields.

However, Hubbert's critics do make some valid points. Hubbert's model was based on a presumed global reserve of 1.25 trillion barrels of oil, but the ultimate size of the reserve was vastly underestimated. Cumulative global oil production through 2010 is just over 1 trillion barrels of oil, and remaining proved reserves are estimated to be nearly 1.4 trillion barrels.[2]

PEAK OIL: IT'S ALL ABOUT FLOW RATES AND NET ENERGY

One of the fundamental mistakes that some peak oil critics make is to misunderstand the relationship between peak oil, the size of the oil reserve, and the rate of flow from the reserve. To illustrate the problem, let's presume that in fact the world has produced 1 trillion barrels per oil, and the remaining proved reserves are indeed 1.4 trillion barrels of oil. This would mean that the total reserve that would ultimately be produced is 2.4 trillion barrels, and the world is still 200 billion barrels from the halfway mark. At the current global production rate of around 75 million bpd (just crude oil plus condensate), 200 billion barrels will last over seven more years. Hence, this would imply that peak oil could be seven years away, and maybe more if more oil reserves are discovered.

There are two problems with this line of reasoning. The first is that peak oil is about flow rates, not about the size of the reserve. The easiest to extract oil has already been produced. A lot of the remaining oil falls into unconventional oil categories like oil sands and deepwater oil. The production rates for the remaining oil likely won't be ramped up as quickly as the production rates for the oil that was produced during the 20th century, and potentially not fast enough to keep up with depletion in existing fields. In this case, global oil production may start to decline even though less than half the reserve has been produced.

The second problem is that the amount of energy required to produce the remaining oil will be greater than the amount of energy required to produce the previous oil. This will be addressed in a later chapter, but it essentially means that the net energy obtained from one barrel of oil in the future will be lower than for one barrel of oil

---

[2] This includes unconventional oil such as oil sands that are technically recoverable and economical to produce at present-day oil prices.

produced in the past. The implication of this for the preceding example is that 1.2 trillion barrels isn't the effective halfway point, because the second 1.2 trillion barrels will provide less energy to society than the first 1.2 trillion barrels did, due to the higher energy requirements to produce it.

Based on his underestimate of global oil reserves, Hubbert estimated that a global peak in oil production would occur around the year 2000 at an annual production rate of 34 million bpd. While it is unclear whether global oil production has peaked, it is clear that it did not peak in 2000. The rate of global oil production by 2010 was 73.5 million bpd—which represents a slight decline from the 73.7 million bpd rate achieved in 2005.[3]

Hubbert's defenders point to his U.S. oil peak prediction as proof of the utility of his methodology, and his critics point to the missed global peak prediction and gross underestimate of global oil production in 2000 as evidence of the shortcomings of his model. In fact, Hubbert's method is not designed to predict reserve growth; a specific reserve size must be assumed. If the reserve size is accurately estimated, Hubbert's model would be expected to give a fairly accurate estimate of an oil production peak. Thus, in the U.S., where the oil reserve estimate was fairly accurate, Hubbert's model made a fairly accurate prediction on the peak.[4]

While global oil reserves appear to be more than twice what Hubbert estimated, the production rate has also been more than twice Hubbert's estimate. The result is that Hubbert's estimate for the year of global peak oil—44 years in the future at the time of his prediction—may not be grossly in error. In fact, the current peak for conventional oil stands at the year 2005, with many convinced that this peak will not be exceeded. If that peak were to stand, Hubbert will have missed the mark by only five years.

So what can the world expect as oil production begins to decline? It depends largely on the timing and the steepness of the decline.

---

[3] This represents crude oil plus lease condensate, according to the Energy Information Administration. Inclusion of "all liquids" increases the total to more than 80 million bpd and pushes the current peak forward to 2010.

[4] Of the two cases he modeled, the case with the higher estimate of U.S. oil reserves correctly predicted a 1970 peak, but at a somewhat lower bpd rate than was actually achieved.

Peak Oil Consequences

When oil production peaked in the United States, the primary consequence was a rapid increase in the volume of oil imported into the country. Between the peak year in 1970 and 1977, oil imports into the U.S. nearly tripled. As a result—and because the price of oil also sharply increased following the 1973 OPEC oil embargo—increasing amounts of money began to flow from the U.S. to oil-exporting countries.

Did you know?   In January 2000 the price of West Texas Intermediate crude was $25 a barrel. By January 2008, the price had reached $100—an annual average increase of 19%.

While this certainly didn't help the U.S. trade deficit, global oil production continued to rise and economies continued to expand. U.S. oil consumption continued to grow—from 14.7 million bpd in 1970 to the current peak consumption of 20.8 million bpd in 2005—and U.S. GDP continued to rise.

However, when world production peaks, global increases in oil consumption must necessarily come to an end. There are a number of implications and possible outcomes from this.

As the pie shrinks, countries will compete for the remaining slices. It may seem obvious that the wealthiest countries will bid against each other for available oil supplies, pricing poorer countries out of the oil market. However, that is not what has happened over the past few years as oil prices have risen. In fact, it is in the developed countries where demand has fallen in the face of oil prices. Developing countries have increased their consumption even in the face of higher oil prices.

The reason for this trend will be covered in a later chapter, but if this trend holds true, we may see oil consumption continue to increase in developing countries while developed countries continue to cut back. Developed countries will cut back by reducing discretionary consumption and by turning to alternative sources of energy. As the pie shrinks, the developed countries will go on a diet and try to find other pies.

The economic consequences are dependent on the timing of the production peak and the rate of the global production decline. If oil production peaks within the next decade, as many believe will be the case, it does not appear that liquid fuel alternatives can be scaled quickly enough to fill the supply gap that will develop. The results will be potentially much higher and more volatile oil prices, and great economic strain on oil-importing countries.

Industries that are heavily dependent on oil—such as the airline industry—will be particularly susceptible to bankruptcy (and many regional carriers declared bankruptcy when oil prices spiked in 2008). Goods that have long supply chains will experience significant cost increases, and because so much industrial and agricultural output is dependent on oil, there will likely be widespread inflation.

Military forces and critical services will be near the front of the line for receiving oil supplies, but higher oil prices for them may mean tax increases to pay for the higher costs, or a decline in military capabilities and reduced critical services.

Globally, political power will increasingly shift toward oil-exporting countries. Oil-importing countries will likely find themselves making concessions toward the oil exporters. Political stability within top oil-exporting nations like Russia and Saudi Arabia will assume greater urgency, and maintaining good relations with the oil exporters will be an increasingly important part of a country's foreign policy.

The liquid fuel shortfall will likely result in some scarcity, but as oil prices rise, some alternatives will begin to make a greater impact. Countries will increasingly turn to unconventional oil sources like oil sands and very heavy oils, and more countries will produce synthetic fuels from coal and natural gas.

The severity of the consequences will increase if oil production has already peaked, or peaks within the next two to three years. However, some of the implications of peak oil have already begun to be felt due to a scenario I have termed "Peak Lite."

"Peak Lite"

One implication of peak oil is that declining oil production will mean that there simply won't be enough oil to go around. In this case, the price will rise until supply and demand are back in balance.

Over the past ten years, oil prices made their impressive advance even though oil production increased by 10% over the same time span. A major driver of the price increase was the fact that oil consumption in developing nations grew sharply, while global production rose slowly.

In a world with ample spare production capacity and free markets, the price of oil will be correlated with the price of producing it. With excess oil production capacity, disruptions in supply can be managed by bringing excess capacity online.

But as the supply cushion diminishes—either because oil production declines or because demand grows faster than new supplies can be brought online (or both)—there will be upward pressure on oil prices and increasing volatility in the oil markets. The implications are that some people will be priced out of the market for oil, many other people will be forced to become more frugal with their oil consumption, and rationing of oil supplies may eventually occur. Erosion of excess capacity also strengthens the positions of oil cartels such as OPEC, because there are fewer suppliers able to bring oil onto the market if OPEC restricts supplies.

The scenario of rising production but eroding spare capacity because of increased demand prompted me to propose the idea of Peak Lite. It is "peak" because the symptoms will mostly manifest themselves as those of a true production peak: not enough supply to meet demand. In fact, we have already passed the point at which there was sufficient production to meet everyone's expectation of oil being supplied at $25 per barrel. But production can still grow in this scenario, which is why it is "lite"; it is not a true peak. Contrary to the case of falling oil production, however, the dangers of demand outpacing production growth may be underappreciated because rising oil production could convey a false sense that oil prices will soon return to "normal."

It is important to note that Peak Lite does not imply that peak oil will be a minor event. Rather, it is meant to convey that the world could begin to see some impacts of peak oil before we necessarily experience a physical peak. I envision a scenario in which global demand growth outstrips the growth in supply, so that even if supply can still grow, the market behaves as it would in a peak oil situation. So I used Peak Lite to denote "effective peak"—which is not to imply that the impact of peak oil would be "lite."

The Long Recession

Another implication of peak oil is the possibility of an extended economic recession or depression.

Historically, as economies grow, so does demand for oil. As long as supplies can keep pace with demand—and barring geopolitical factors—oil prices should be relatively stable. But when the demand for oil grows at a faster rate than new supplies can come online, higher prices are inevitable.

Spiking oil prices have historically contributed to recessions. Jeff Rubin, in his book *Why Your World Is About to Get a Whole Lot Smaller* (Random House Canada, 2009), wrote that four of the past five recessions were caused by spiking oil prices. This makes sense when we consider the impact of rising oil prices on consumers. As fuel prices rise, people have less money to spend on discretionary items. They start to cut back on purchases, and then companies have to cut back. Unemployment increases, and then fewer people are driving to work. If the rise in oil prices is steep and sustained, the result can be a recession.

In normal economic cycles, oil companies invest more money in oil production capacity when oil prices are high. Because demand normally declines in a recession, the combination of higher capacity and lower demand will cause oil prices to fall. Lower oil prices eventually ease the way to economic recovery.

But what if spare capacity can't be built, because oil production has peaked or because spare capacity can't be built quickly enough to outpace demand? In this case, even if spending begins to recover and economies emerge from recession, there will be greater pressure on oil prices because oil demand increases when economies begin to gain strength. Higher oil prices may in turn "restall" the economy, leading to another slowdown that just repeats the cycle every time the economy begins to recover. Borrowing terminology from James Kunstler's book *The Long Emergency* (Atlantic Monthly Press, 2005), I describe this sort of cycle as the Long Recession.

The Long Recession is a risk, particularly for countries that are heavily dependent on oil imports. Oil-exporting countries will benefit from an influx of cash during periods of high oil prices, and thus should be more resistant to oil-price-induced recessions. They will not be totally immune, as many oil-producing countries may see some of their other exports decline in the face of a global economic slowdown. But in general, those whose economies depend the most on oil imports will face the greatest economic challenges, and those whose economies depend the most on oil exports will thrive in the face of sustained high oil prices.

GOVERNMENT REPORTS ON PEAK OIL

Peak oil is a threat recognized by many government agencies around the world. In 2005, the United States Department of Energy released a report it commissioned, *Peaking of World Oil Production: Impacts, Mitigation, and Risk Management.*[vi] The report concluded that the peaking of oil production presents the world with an "unprecedented risk management problem" and that serious mitigation efforts would need to start 20 years prior to the peak to avoid supply shortages. The report warns that if the world waits until oil production peaks before initiating an emergency mitigation program, there will be a significant liquid fuel shortfall for more than two decades.

In a 2009 report, the Department of Energy and Climate Change in the UK warned the government that there would be "significant negative economic consequences" if peak oil occurs before 2015, and that mass deployment of alternatives would take time.[vii] The report further warns of the potential for oil price–induced inflation and stagnant economic growth as a result of peaking oil supplies.

A 2010 report from the U.S. Department of Defense warned that "By 2012, surplus oil production capacity could entirely disappear, and as early as 2015, the shortfall in output could reach nearly 10 MBD."[viii]

Also in 2010, a study on peak oil by a German military think tank revealed that the German government is closely studying the issue of peak oil, and is aware of the potential for serious consequences as oil production declines. The study warns of the potential for regional shortages, market failures, and a shift in political power toward those capable of exporting oil.[ix] The report lays out Europe's vulnerability toward Russia because of its continuing dependence on Russia for both oil and gas, and notes that Russia will be in a very strong political bargaining position as a result.

Peak Oil Misconceptions

In its simplest form, peak oil means that just as oil production in the United States peaked in 1970 and began to decline, so shall production for the entire world peak and decline (see Figure 6-2). Once you get past that basic premise—one in which there is near-universal agreement when people understand that is what you mean when you say "peak oil"—there are many different opinions of exactly how events will unfold.

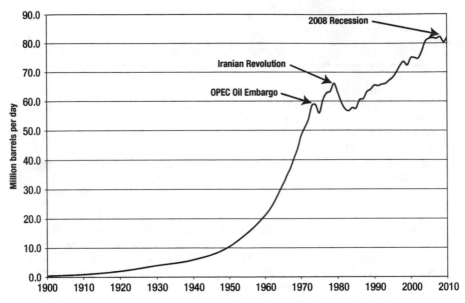

Global Oil Production 1900-2010

Figure 6-2. Is global oil production nearing a peak? (Data sources: Netherlands Environmental Assessment Agency[x] and BP *Statistical Review of World Energy 2011*[xi])

However, there are a number of misconceptions and negative connotations associated with the term "peak oil." The most common misconception about peak oil is undoubtedly that peak oil means that the world is running out of oil. Many would-be debunkers of peak oil make that assumption, and then respond with claims about the very large global oil resource and further argue that there is a lot of oil still left to be produced.

■ **Did you know?** An oil *resource* is the total amount of oil available in the ground. The oil *reserve* is the amount that is technically and economically recoverable, and is generally a small fraction of the resource.

Resource vs. Reserve

In fact, anyone concerned about peak oil will readily acknowledge that oil will continue to be produced for a very long time. Peak oil is not about how much oil is in the ground—it is about the speed at which that oil can be extracted. How much of the oil resource is ultimately produced will be a function of technology improvements and the price of oil, but some—and perhaps most—of the original oil in place will never be economically recoverable. So it is important not to confuse the resource—the total amount of oil in the ground—with the amount that will actually be recovered (the reserve).

Civilization Will Collapse

The second most common misconception about peak oil is probably that anyone who is concerned about peak oil believes that a collapse of civilization will inevitably follow. In fact, the beliefs among people who are concerned about peak oil cover a wide span. There are certainly those who believe that a global peak is imminent, followed by a catastrophic decline in oil production rates. Included in this group are people who have vocally and (to this point) wrongly predicted dates and catastrophic consequences as a result of peak oil. These people are the real targets of those who claim that peak oil is nonsense. What critics really mean—but perhaps don't say due to misconceptions about peak oil beliefs—is that the idea of imminent, catastrophic decline is nonsense. But that isn't the same thing as arguing that peak oil is nonsense.

But there are also people who believe peak oil will inevitably lead to cleaner environments, closer communities, and healthier food. Then there are those who believe that peak oil will lead to a dirtier environment as we become more desperate for energy and turn to more oil sands and coal to replace declining oil supplies. There are people who believe peak oil will be a minor inconvenience because there are plenty of sources capable of replacing oil, including an enormous reserve of unconventional oil. And there are those who believe certain elements of all of the above.

Peak Oil: Merely a Theory

Peak oil is sometimes referred to as a theory in a pejorative sense. Again, this paints with a very broad brush. When someone describes peak oil as a theory, they are likely referring to some of the worst expectations of the consequences of peak oil. Strictly speaking, there is a "Hubbert peak theory," which merely posits that oil-producing regions will tend to see production approximate a bell-shaped curve (as shown in Figure 6-1, earlier in the chapter). But this is an observation rather than a real scientific theory, as there are far too many factors that can skew the bell-shaped curve.

Peak Oil: Oil Company Manipulation

Another misconception is that oil companies dreamed up peak oil in order to convey a sense of scarcity to inflate oil prices. However, most of the major oil companies argue that oil production will not decline for decades. This has been the publicly stated view of ExxonMobil and the American Petroleum Institute. Within individual oil companies, there *have* been some executives who have publicly expressed concern that oil production could not grow to the levels projected by various agencies. I am unaware that this is the official position of any major oil company, but the CEOs of Total, BP, and ConocoPhillips have all expressed concern that oil supplies will not meet projected demand growth. I don't believe this is some ploy to drive up oil prices; rather, I believe they expressed concern because they *are* concerned.

Oil Companies: Peak Oil Deniers

A final misconception is the flip side of the previous misconception: peak oil is denied by oil companies because they are afraid that awareness would spur a major push to alternatives. The idea is that if oil companies acknowledge peak oil, governments will redouble their efforts to develop alternative fuels, hastening the end of Big Oil. I worked in the oil industry for several years, and from my experience I believe that there are two flaws to this reasoning. First, most people in the industry who deny peak oil do so either because they simply have never given it much thought or because they subscribe to one of the misconceptions. I frequently had conversations with people about peak oil in which their response was, "They have been saying that we are running out of oil my entire life."

The second flaw in this argument is that I have never heard anyone in the oil industry express any worry over alternative energy. They may be annoyed by mandates that force them to do something they don't want to do (like blend ethanol which takes away market share for gasoline), but rather than worry they can respond by getting into the alternative energy business themselves.

In fact, I have yet to encounter an alternative energy scheme that oil companies aren't already working on: algae, cellulosic ethanol, butanol, solar—oil companies have major efforts in every one these areas (and have been working on them for years). It's just that, in most cases, the general public doesn't hear about the specifics of those efforts because the oil companies aren't trying to raise funds. This is just a part of the basic research that oil companies do (and with which I have personally been involved). The scientists and engineers that work at oil companies aren't just basking in the final days of the age of oil—a very common misconception. They are thinking about what comes next, and investing to make sure that when it does come, the oil companies will be in the position to provide it and profit from it if they believe there is a viable business case.

Peak Oil Criticisms

There are legitimate criticisms of peak oil arguments. The primary criticism is one illustrated by Hubbert himself, and that is a tendency of peak oil proponents to underestimate the size of oil reserves. Hubbert estimated that the size of the U.S. reserve was 150 billion barrels, and as a result he predicted a U.S. peak would occur in 1965. Many peak oil advocates may be unaware that Hubbert's 1970 peak prediction was based on his assumption that the U.S. reserve might grow to 200 billion barrels, but he indicated his skepticism by noting that this would require the discovery of another "eight East Texas oil fields." Yet based on what we now know, even his optimistic 200 billion barrel reserve case was too low.

Similarly, Hubbert greatly underestimated the global reserve at 1.25 trillion barrels of oil. Current estimates of the total global reserve (produced and still to be produced) are in the range of 2.4 trillion barrels. Thus, while his method has shown to be fairly accurate when the reserve size is accurately estimated, the tendency among peak oil advocates to underestimate the reserve is common, and hence a major reason that incorrect forecasts have been made for production peaks of certain countries and the world as a whole.

There are a couple of reasons that the reserves tend to be underestimated. The primary reason is an underestimate of the impact of technology in increasing the recovery efficiency of existing fields, as well as in opening up fields that were previously inaccessible. Indeed, the "eight East Texas oil fields" that Hubbert skeptically indicated would be needed to push the reserve to 200 billion barrels were largely "found" in fields that were already known at that time.

Looking to the future, it is reasonable to expect that technology will continue to increase the size of the reserves, as long as oil prices continue to hold up. Unconventional oil will further add to reserves as high prices push resources such as oil sands and ultra-deepwater oil into the reserve category.

However, offsetting these increases will be strong growth in global demand driven primarily by developing countries. Strong demand growth is why even though Hubbert's estimate of global reserves was far too low, his prediction of the peak year may not be that far off because the rate of production has been much greater than he expected. In other words, the reserve was larger but has been drawn down at a faster rate. Continued strong global demand growth means that even potentially large reserve additions won't necessarily push peak oil off into the far future. It may simply mean a prolonged Peak Lite scenario.

Summary

Most of us can agree that, just as it did in the U.S. in 1970, global oil production will inevitably decline. The points of contention are the timing, the steepness of the decline, the impact on the global economy, and the ability of other energy sources to fill the supply gap. Some people believe it will be a nonevent, and some people believe it will be catastrophic.

Personally, I think that peak oil either has or soon will take place, but regardless, oil supplies will continue to struggle to keep up with demand. This will keep prices at recession-inducing levels, and make for a difficult transition to a post-peak economy. I think that we will probably eke out a bit more global production, but I will be surprised if the world gets past 90 million bpd. I believe that shale gas and oil sands production will continue to rise, that unconventional oil sources will become an increasingly important part of the oil supply mix, and that global carbon emissions will continue their upward march as a result.

References

[i] Marion K. Hubbert, "Nuclear Energy and the Fossil Fuels" (presented at the Spring Meeting of the Southern District, Division of Production, American Petroleum Institute, San Antonio, TX, March 7, 1956), Drilling and Production Practice (1956): 22–27, available at www.hubbertpeak.com /hubbert/1956/1956.pdf.

[ii] Energy Information Administration (EIA), *Crude Oil Production*, July 28, 2011, www.eia.gov/dnav/pet/pet_crd_crpdn_adc_mbbl_a.htm.

[iii] Ibid.

[iv] EIA, *Crude Oil Proved Reserves, Reserves Changes, and Production*, December 30, 2010, www.eia.gov/dnav/pet/pet_crd_pres_dcu_NUS_a.htm.

[v] Ibid.

[vi] Robert Hirsch, Robert Bezdek, and Robert Wendling, "Peaking of World Oil Production: Impacts, Mitigation, and Risk Management" (commissioned by DOE NETL), February 2005, *www.netl.doe.gov/energy-analyses/pubs /Oil_Peaking_NETL.pdf.*

[vii] Department of Energy and Climate Change (DECC), "Report on the Risks and Impacts of a Potential Future Decline in Oil Production," June 1, 2009, www.decc.gov.uk/assets/decc/What%20we%20do/Global%20climate%20cha nge%20and%20energy/International%20energy/energy%20security/1790-decc-report-2009-oil-decline.pptx.

[viii] U.S. Joint Forces Command (USJFCOM), "The Joint Operating Environment 2010," February 18, 2010, www.fas.org/man/eprint /joe2010.pdf.

[ix] Stefan Schultz, "Military Study Warns of a Potentially Drastic Oil Crisis," *Spiegel Online* (International edition), September 1, 2010, www.spiegel.de /international/germany/0,1518,715138,00.html.

[x] Netherlands Environmental Assessment Agency, History Database of the Global Environment, "Global Oil Production" (Excel table), accessed January 20, 2012, available for download at http://themasites.pbl.nl/en/themasites /hyde/productiondata/oil/index.html.

[xi] BP, *BP Statistical Review of World Energy 2011*, www.bp.com/ sectionbodycopy.do?categoryId=7500&contentId=7068481.

Nuclear Power

Practical Solution or Environmental Disaster?

It's ridiculous that time and time again we need a radioactive cloud coming out of a nuclear power station to remind us that atomic energy is extraordinarily dangerous.

—Pierre Schaeffer, French composer and engineer

Nuclear power will help provide the electricity that our growing economy needs without increasing emissions. This is truly an environmentally responsible source of energy.

—Michael Burgess, U.S. Congressman

When nuclear power was first commercialized in the mid-1950s, it was widely viewed as an almost magical solution for the electricity needs of a growing global population. One pound of uranium-235 can produce two to three *million* times as much electricity as one pound of coal or oil—but without producing any emissions. Scientists and the general public alike were enthusiastic about the abundance of cheap, clean energy that nuclear power promised.

But this was before issues like nuclear accidents, disposal of nuclear waste, or nuclear proliferation were part of the public discussion. Following accidents at Three Mile Island and Chernobyl, enthusiasm for nuclear power was replaced for many people with paranoia and mistrust. Nevertheless, nuclear power still offers the promise of abundant, emission-free power, and it retains many devoted advocates, but it also has many devoted opponents.

A Nuclear Renaissance

Prior to March 11, 2011, the future of the global nuclear power industry looked very bright. Due to growing concerns over climate change, the nuclear power option was gaining in popularity as a low-carbon alternative to coal-fired power plants. There had been no serious nuclear accidents since the 1980s, and attitudes toward nuclear power were improving.

HOW NUCLEAR POWER WORKS

Certain elements are capable of undergoing a fission reaction. Fission occurs when an atom splits into two smaller atoms and releases energy. This energy release occurs when a small amount of the atom's mass is converted into energy. Albert Einstein's famous equation for this mass–energy equivalence is $E=mc^2$, where "E" is energy, "m" is the mass that is converted, and "c^2" is the speed of light multiplied by itself. This is a very big number. The speed of light is just under 300 million meters (186,000 miles) per second, and c^2 is 90 quadrillion meters^2 per second^2. Therefore, a very small amount of mass can be converted into a huge amount of energy.

Most nuclear power plants are based on an isotope[1] of uranium called U-235. When U-235 absorbs a neutron, it splits into isotopes of two smaller atoms (some of the possibilities are isotopes of barium, cesium, krypton, and iodine) and releases energy, radiation, and more neutrons. If there is sufficient U-235 in the vicinity of the released neutrons, they may be captured by other U-235 atoms, and a chain reaction results that can be controlled to produce nuclear power.

The principle of a nuclear reactor is that as nuclear fuel undergoes fission, the heat that is released is used to produce steam, which is then passed through a turbine to produce electricity. Loss of cooling to a nuclear reaction results in a build-up of heat, and that can lead to a runaway nuclear reaction and ultimately a meltdown.

A quarter of a century had passed since the devastating Chernobyl nuclear accident resulted in many deaths from radiation poisoning or, ultimately, cancer. Chernobyl spread contamination across many countries in Europe, and left more than 1,600 square miles uninhabitable due to heavy radiation contamination. The Chernobyl disaster set the nuclear power industry back

---

[1] Isotopes are different versions of the same element. Each version has a different weight because the versions have different numbers of neutrons. Certain isotopes are radioactive.

many years (see Figure 7-1) as countries delayed or cancelled plans to construct new nuclear power plants.[ii]

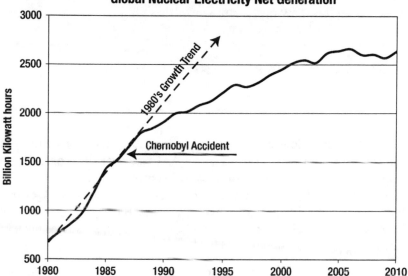

Global Nuclear Electricity Net Generation

Figure 7-1. The growth rate in global nuclear generation slowed substantially after the Chernobyl accident in 1986. (Data source: EIA[iii])

But over the subsequent 25 years, there had been no other major nuclear power plant disasters in the world, and many countries were facing difficult energy choices. Chernobyl began to look more like a fluke; a product of shoddy design from a bygone era. Ironically, a nuclear renaissance was sparked in part by developments in Russia and the Ukraine—the location of the Chernobyl disaster.

Following a series of disputes between Russia and the Ukraine over natural gas—a dispute that impacted gas supplies for many European countries and reminded Europeans of the tenuous nature of their energy security—many countries began to see nuclear power as a better energy option than Russian gas. The possibility of a gas shortage from Russia loomed for many as an imminent threat.

In 1987, Italy shut down its four nuclear power plants in the wake of the Chernobyl disaster. But by 2009, Italy began to reconsider that decision. Claudio Scajola, Italy's minister for economic development, stated that the gas crisis had "made the Italians understand the importance of energy security [and that] we must go back to nuclear power if we want to become less dependent on others' moods."[iv] They turned to France—the country that gets the highest percentage of its electricity from nuclear power—for help in constructing four new nuclear power plants.

■ **Did you know?**   France obtains 75% of its electricity from nuclear power, the highest percentage for any country.

Germany was also reconsidering nuclear power. In 2000, Germany's leaders had announced a plan to phase out Germany's 17 nuclear reactors. But in 2007, following a dispute between Russia and Belarus that shut down an oil pipeline and temporarily restricted oil imports into Germany, German Chancellor Angela Merkel began to question that decision, saying, "we have to consider what consequences there will be if we shut down nuclear power stations."[v]

Chancellor Merkel, who holds a doctorate in the sciences and had long supported nuclear power, viewed it as an effective way to reduce carbon dioxide emissions that are believed to be contributing to climate change.

Merkel argued that pro-nuclear policy changes in both Italy and the UK left Germany as the only country in the G8[2] to have anti-nuclear policies. She characterized the phase-out plan as "absolutely wrong." Michael Glos, the Minister for Economics and Technology in Merkel's cabinet, argued that "It is impossible to fulfill the Kyoto objectives[3] without using nuclear energy."[vi]

But an incident in Bulgaria in early 2009 is perhaps instructive. Bulgaria was one of the countries impacted when Russia curtailed gas exports in a dispute with the Ukraine, and they began to petition the European Union to allow them to restart an idled nuclear reactor because some towns had run out of gas during the crisis. The weather was below freezing at that time, and Bulgarian President Georgi Purvanov pleaded with the EU to allow the

---

[2] The G8 consists of Germany, France, Italy, the United Kingdom, Japan, the United States, Canada, and Russia.

[3] The Kyoto Protocol was an agreement by many countries—including Germany—to reduce their greenhouse gas emissions by an average of 5.2% compared to 1990 levels.

restart, stating that "a more critical situation is hardly possible.[vii]" (The EU turned down the petition.)

It turns out that President Purvanov may have been wrong about that. The reason the reactor had been shut down was because it was deemed to be dangerous. The U.S. Department of Energy once described the Bulgarian reactor as "one of the world's most dangerous nuclear installations."[viii]

But seemingly desperate times sometimes spawn desperate measures, and Bulgaria faced a choice of leaving some Bulgarians with no power in freezing weather or taking a risk with the idled nuclear power plant. The risk of restarting that idled reactor was acceptable in the mind of the Bulgarian president.

Assessing Risk

Whenever an energy project is being developed, a risk assessment is conducted. This is a systematic and rigorous process to identify risks, quantify the risk probability and the consequences, and mitigate the risk and/or associated consequences. Designing safety measures that would minimize the impact if an event were to take place is a key outcome of doing risk assessments.

We are all familiar with some level of risk assessments, as we constantly evaluate risk in our lives. Many risky situations are obvious; people are injured or even killed each year falling off of ladders. We recognize that risk, but we may not properly consider the probability of an accident, or the consequences if the risk actually goes against us. Failure to identify risks and/or consequences results in a great many preventable accidents each year.

Often, public expectation is that accidents related to energy production should never occur, but there are many reasons why that metric will never be achieved, the most fundamental of which is that we simply can't guard against every possible outcome.

Speaking as someone who has been involved in many safety studies and incident investigations, there is always the possibility that a series of incidents deemed low probability (or even not considered) in a safety study will combine to cause an accident.

For example, during a safety study, the risk of an employee pushing the wrong button on a control screen might have been considered. The risk of a leak in a certain process unit might have been considered. The risk of a fire in the process might have been considered. And appropriate mitigation may have been applied in each case. But the risk of all of these events occurring together may not have been considered. In fact, we often find out, after the fact, that accidents were caused by a series of low-probability events that no one considered happening simultaneously.

Risk assessments are done by people, and people have blind spots. People make mistakes. People cut corners. People sometimes underestimate consequences. (We more often overestimate risks and consequences that are considered in these risk assessments, but the impact of that is higher project costs—not damage to people and property.)

But if we accept that there are no risk-free energy options, we must then observe a very important rule of risk assessment: never accept a risk for which you can't afford the consequences.

Whether drilling for oil deep in the Gulf of Mexico, operating a nuclear power plant, or deciding not to carry homeowner's insurance, one has to be prepared to live with the worst-case scenario. The earthquake and subsequent tsunami that hit Japan in March 2011 reminded the world just what those consequences could be for a nuclear power plant.

Disaster and Aftermath in Japan

The Fukushima I Nuclear Power Plant located on Japan's east coast was certainly designed with safety in mind. Located on the coast in an earthquake-prone area, tsunamis were an ever-present possibility. Thus, the 4.7-gigawatt plant—the 11th largest nuclear power plant in the world at the beginning of 2011—was designed to withstand major earthquakes and a tsunami wave of 5.7 meters (18.7 feet).[ix]

The reactors were designed by General Electric, and the plant had DC batteries and emergency generators to keep the reactors under control in case of a power failure. The plant was subject to regular safety inspections, although Tokyo Electric and Power Company (TEPCO), the operator of the plant, has admitted to submitting some fake inspection and repair reports.[x]

▨ **Did you know?** At the time of the Fukushima nuclear accident, the Fukushima I Nuclear Power Plant was the 11th largest nuclear power plant in the world.

On March 11, 2011, a massive 9.0 magnitude earthquake took place under the ocean east of Japan. The Fukushima nuclear power plant was subsequently hit with a tsunami estimated to be 15 meters (49 feet) high—almost two and a half times the wave height the plant had been designed to withstand.

Immediately following the earthquake, the reactors did shut down as they were designed to do, and emergency generators were started to continue circulating water to cool down the reactors. When the tsunami actually hit the nuclear power plant, all power to the plant was lost. The emergency generators were flooded and they shut down. The back-up batteries provided power for less than a day, and once they were depleted, cooling to the reactors was lost.[xi]

On the first day of the incident, an evacuation order was given to 30,000 people living within 3 kilometers (1.9 miles) of the damaged nuclear power plant. About 24 hours after the tsunami struck the plant, the evacuation order was extended to anyone living within 10 km (6.2 miles) of the plant. By the end of the second day, that evacuation zone was increased to include everyone within 20 km (12.4 miles) of the plant, which Japanese officials later estimated to be over 80,000 people.[4] A voluntary evacuation recommendation was given to people living between 20 and 30 km from the plant.

As the world watched, workers struggled to regain control of the plant, but eventually three of the reactors reportedly experienced full meltdown. A *meltdown* means that the nuclear fuel gets hot enough to melt, and this has the potential to melt through the casing around the reactor and release radioactive material into the environment.

Also as a nuclear reactor heats up, zirconium, a metal alloy used in the construction of nuclear reactors, can initiate a reaction to break down water and release hydrogen.[5] Because hydrogen is highly explosive, as the reactors heated up and hydrogen accumulated, there were several associated hydrogen explosions.

Within a couple of weeks of the tsunami, high levels of the radioactive isotopes cesium-137 and iodine-131 were detected outside of the 30-km

---

[4] Reports immediately after the evacuations began put the number of impacted people at 200,000.

[5] Nuclear reactors have long been suggested as potential sources for hydrogen production should a hydrogen economy ever become a reality.

voluntary evacuation zone. Radiation above the designated national safety level was detected in spinach and milk produced near the crippled plant.[xii] Radioactive cesium at 520 times the government-designated limit was found in straw on farms near the plant, and contaminated beef from those farms was ultimately shipped across Japan and eaten by consumers.[xiii]

Tokyo Water Bureau officials temporarily recommended that people avoid the use of tap water for infants, because radioactive iodine was detected above the safe recommended drinking limits for that age group. Countries began to ban imports of Japanese food from near the restricted area.

■ **Did you know?** In the aftermath of the Fukushima nuclear accident, radiation exceeding government recommended limits was reportedly detected in beef, spinach, milk, and green tea originating from near the site of the accident.

About a week into the crisis, I was contacted by a reporter who told me that the Japanese people were being given much less information on the crisis than was being reported outside of Japan. The owners of the plant (TEPCO) and government officials tried to downplay the threat of harmful levels of nuclear radiation by assuring the public that "there is a low possibility that a massive amount of radiation has been leaked" or that there was a "low possibility of radioactive contamination."[xiv] But Japanese television programs began to openly question the lack of information about the crisis being given to the public.

Outside of Japan, the opposite was the case as speculation ran rampant. Some nuclear supporters tried to downplay the threat, while some nuclear opponents exaggerated the threat. One poll in the U.S. showed that nearly one-half of the people polled were concerned that the radiation could reach the U.S., while more than two-thirds believed the crisis would damage the U.S. economy.[xv]

The nuclear incident's long-term impact on Japan remains to be seen. In contrast to Chernobyl (and in contrast to thousands of people killed by the tsunami itself), at the time of this writing there have been no reported fatalities from radiation poisoning, although three workers reportedly received radiation burns. But many people were permanently displaced from their homes, and numerous lives were disrupted. The damage to the food production industry in Japan is incalculable. People in Japan will live in fear for years over how this incident will continue to impact them, as well as future generations.

The incident highlights the fact that on a very fundamental level, many people are fearful of radiation. A perfect example of this can be found in the attitudes toward food irradiation. Food irradiation can be used to kill potentially dangerous pathogens like *E. coli*, and it has the potential to save thousands of lives each year. But even though the treatment does not create radioactive food, the U.S. Department of Agriculture has reported that less than half of consumers would be willing to buy irradiated meat, citing concerns around the risks and safety of eating irradiated food.[xvi] When it comes to our food, it seems that the only radiation we are comfortable with is microwave radiation.

If consumers aren't willing to eat non-radioactive food that has been irradiated, the idea of experiencing elevated radiation levels[6] due to a nuclear accident is terrifying to many. Away from the immediate area of a nuclear accident—where radiation poisoning is likely a bigger concern—contamination of food and water is probably the single biggest fear related to a nuclear accident.

In this case, it didn't take long for fear to translate into actions.

Renaissance Interrupted

Within ten days of the accident in Japan, Germany signaled a reversal of its direction on nuclear policy, suggesting that the incident would force governments everywhere to reassess their policies. Angela Merkel had been pushing hard for wider acceptance of nuclear power to reduce the country's dependence on Russian natural gas, but within three months of the accident Merkel announced that all of Germany's 17 nuclear reactors would be closed by 2022. In announcing the closures, Merkel indicated that the consequences of the disaster were beyond her imagination: "After what was, for me anyway, an unimaginable disaster in Fukushima, we have had to reconsider the role of nuclear energy."[xvii]

---

[6] Background radiation is everywhere in our environment, and all of our food has some level of radioactivity. The human body itself is radioactive, albeit at very low levels that pose no threat.

■ **Did you know?** Prior to the March 2011 Fukushima nuclear accident, Germany's 17 nuclear reactors provided about a quarter of Germany's electricity.

Shortly after the decision in Germany, voters in Italy rejected a referendum proposal put forth by the government to restart the country's nuclear energy program. This vote nixed government plans to obtain 25% of Italy's electricity from nuclear power by 2020.

Anti-nuclear protests were held in many countries, calling for an end to nuclear power. Japan was one of the countries that held protests, and a poll taken there after the accident showed that 74% of those polled favored phasing out nuclear power.

The U.S. Congress held hearings on the accident to determine whether the lessons learned were applicable to U.S. nuclear power plants. A number of nuclear plants in the U.S. were determined to possess some of the same design characteristics that led to the escalation of the incident in Japan. One new rule instituted by the U.S. Nuclear Regulatory Commission was for nuclear plants to have the ability to operate for 72 hours on backup power.

However, polls taken in the U.S. after the accident showed that the percentage of people who favored building more nuclear plants in the U.S. wasn't that much different from what it was before the accident. These attitudes may reflect what happened during the first serious commercial nuclear plant accident in the world: Three Mile Island in Pennsylvania.

In that case, the core did melt down, but containment held. Thus, despite the close call, there was no permanent contamination of the environment. Nuclear power proponents point to this incident to show the efficacy of the safety measures in place that are designed to keep the nuclear fuel contained, but opponents argue that the situation could have easily been much worse.

THORIUM REACTORS AND FUSION POWER: THE FUTURE OF NUCLEAR POWER?

There are two nuclear power possibilities for the future that are viewed as inherently less risky than uranium-based nuclear power. Besides the generation of nuclear waste, one disadvantage of using uranium-235 as fuel for nuclear power plants is that it can also be used for nuclear weapons. When North Korea and Iran (among others) were known to be enriching uranium, each claimed that it was for the peaceful purpose of power production. Ultimately, however, the North Korean government admitted that it had used the enriched uranium to produce nuclear weapons. Much of the world suspects that Iran is in the process of doing the same thing.

Commercialization of power derived from thorium or controlled fusion reactions would dramatically reduce (although not totally eliminate) the risk of nuclear weapon proliferation. Thorium is abundant relative to uranium, and thorium does not have to undergo the enrichment process that uranium requires. Further, thorium reactors have little risk of melting down because climbing temperatures will decrease the power output, eliminating the runaway reaction possibility present in a uranium-fueled reactor. The primary disadvantage is that thorium reactors are still mainly at the experimental stage, and therefore commercial viability has not yet been clearly demonstrated.

Controlled nuclear fusion has been proposed for decades as a safe alternative to nuclear fission for power. Fusion reactions power the sun, and have been used on earth as the source of the destructive power of hydrogen bombs. *Fusion* is the joining together of two atoms to make a larger atom, which is accompanied by a large release of energy. However, attempts thus far to develop a commercial fusion reactor have not advanced past short-lived experiments because of the high temperatures and extreme pressures required to initiate and contain the fusion reaction. Thus, energy from controlled nuclear fusion remains a very long-term possibility.

Despite some protests in India, countries like India and China are expected to continue down a path of rapidly expanding their nuclear power production. The reason is the same reason Japan chose that path: the alternatives all have trade-offs that many consumers may not like.

Why the World "Needs" Nuclear Power

After the Deepwater Horizon spill in the Gulf of Mexico, someone said to me, "We have to stop all offshore drilling." In response, I asked what sacrifices the person was willing to make. The response indicated a belief that there wouldn't really be any sacrifices; to the contrary, the rewards would be a cleaner ocean, clean beaches, and healthy wildlife—and the only real impact would be a loss of profits to the oil companies.

This is often the case with people campaigning against the use of various forms of energy. They believe that the consequences will be all good (no more oil spills) with no real downside (like less energy available or higher energy costs). I have no doubt that we could live without offshore drilling or nuclear power, even though 20% of the electricity produced in the U.S. comes from nuclear power (see Figure 7-2). But I also have no doubt that energy costs would be greater—and perhaps far greater—than they are today. In some cases the alternatives would prove to be even worse. So once again we consider the trade-offs.

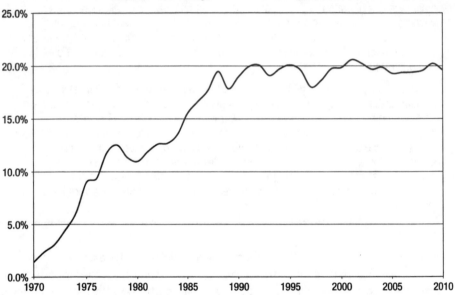

Nuclear Percentage of U.S. Electricity Generation

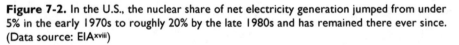

Figure 7-2. In the U.S., the nuclear share of net electricity generation jumped from under 5% in the early 1970s to roughly 20% by the late 1980s and has remained there ever since. (Data source: EIA[xviii])

The reporter I spoke with in Japan in the early stages of the Fukushima nuclear crisis told me that he couldn't help but notice that despite some rolling blackouts, Japan remained very much a country with all of the lights on.

This gets right to the heart of why we have nuclear power: we demand cheap energy, energy that is so cheap that we can afford to leave all the lights on all the time. Both coal- and nuclear-generated electricity are viewed as cheap and reliable relative to many other options—admittedly, this is debatable given various government subsidies and the occasional environmental calamity.

My response to the reporter was that I love to eat lobster, but I rarely eat it because of the high cost. My demand for lobster is moderated by the price of lobster.

But imagine the situation if everyone viewed cheap lobsters as almost a fundamental right, and they were willing to vote politicians out of office if they didn't deliver them.

Instead of telling us that cheap lobsters might result in lobster extinction, politicians would work to give us what we demand. We would see all sorts of lobster-related subsidies and programs designed to provide cheap lobsters to consumers (which would have to be paid through taxes and/or deficit spending). Consequences of our cheap lobster demands—higher deficits and possibly no more lobsters—would be pushed onto future generations.

This describes our energy dilemma. We demand cheap energy. Politicians strive to deliver or they lose their jobs. If energy prices rise despite their efforts, finger-pointing and congressional hearings follow to determine who is to blame. (These hearings never seem to conclude that consumers are to blame. But that's because consumers vote.)

Energy is subsidized in various ways to keep the *apparent* price as low as possible to consumers. Ultimately this means that our energy usage is so high that we "need" offshore drilling, tar sands, nuclear power, and coal power. Cheap energy perpetuates the careless consumption of energy, which diminishes resources and potentially spoils the environment for future generations.

The Path Forward

If people really want to be rid of nuclear power, it is important that they understand the consequences. Germany's decision to reverse course means that it is likely to rely more heavily on coal to meet the need for firm power. Is that a better option?[7] Other options—albeit fraught with political liabilities—are to make electricity so expensive that people greatly cut back on its consumption or, alternatively, to ration electricity.

---

[7] Interestingly, the radioactive emissions from a coal-fired power plant exceed those of a normally operating nuclear power plant because trace radioactive elements exist in coal.

Renewable energy can certainly make a contribution, but the present scale of our electricity consumption is simply too great for renewable energy to replace economically the firm power generated by nuclear (and, even more so, coal) power.

On the other side of the debate, nuclear proponents must have a clear understanding of the worst-case scenarios. The world can't afford more incidents like those at Chernobyl and Fukushima where large tracts of land have been rendered uninhabitable. We can't afford to look back with hindsight and say "I didn't know that could happen."

Those who build, own, and operate nuclear plants must do their utmost to engineer fail-safe systems. It is certainly true that designs become better after the lessons learned from accidents like Fukushima, but we can't lay waste to vast tracts of land before those lessons are learned.

It may be that fail-safe nuclear plants are possible. But there are still vexing political issues around the disposal and storage of spent nuclear waste. Just as many people don't want to live near a nuclear plant, many people don't want a nuclear disposal facility near their community, nor do they want nuclear waste passing through their community.

Summary

Nuclear power has long been an important part of the world's electricity generating mix, accounting for nearly 15% of global electricity production. Under normal operations, a nuclear plant produces no carbon dioxide emissions, and therefore nuclear power could be an important tool in the world's efforts to rein in carbon emissions.

But serious accidents involving nuclear power plants have convinced many people that nuclear power is inherently unsafe. These accidents have slowed the growth of nuclear power and have caused some countries to abandon it completely.

If history is any indication, the impact of the Fukushima incident will be to temporarily slow the global growth rate of nuclear power. But as history puts more distance between the present and March 11, 2011, many countries—just as they did years after Chernobyl—will again turn to nuclear power as an option that can provide cheap power with very low risk (but, as we have seen, potentially very high consequences).

Some countries will continue to develop without nuclear power. Others like Japan—which suffered the consequences when the risk went against them—and Germany will begin a long experiment of phasing out nuclear power. How well they manage that phase-out will show the rest of the nuclear countries what they are up against if they try to follow suit.

References

[i] European Nuclear Society, "Fuel comparison," accessed February 7, 2012, www.euronuclear.org/info/encyclopedia/f/fuelcomparison.htm.

[ii] Matthew Fuhrmann, "Nuclear Inertia," *Slate*, April 26, 2011, www.slate.com/articles/health_and_science/green_room/2011/04/nuclear_inertia.html.

[iii] U.S. Energy Information Administration (EIA), "International Energy Statistics," accessed August 14, 2011, www.eia.gov/cfapps/ipdbproject/IEDIndex3.cfm?tid=2&pid=27&aid=12&cid=ww,&syid=1980&eyid=2009&unit=BKWH.

[iv] Anna Momigliano, "Russian Gas Cutoff Energizes Nuclear Comeback," *Christian Science Monitor*, January 16, 2009, www.csmonitor.com/World/2009/0116/p06s01-wogn.html.

[v] Tony Paterson, "Germany May End Anti-Nuclear Policy," *The Independent*, January 10, 2007, www.independent.co.uk/news/world/europe/germany-may-end-antinuclear-policy-431488.html.

[vi] Dan Bilefsky, "Countries Part of the Kyoto Protocol Will Inevitably Switch to Nuclear Power," *International Herald Tribune*, January 10, 2007.

[vii] BBC, "Bulgaria Urges Return to Nuclear," *BBC News*, January 6, 2009, http://news.bbc.co.uk/2/hi/7814477.stm.

[viii] Ibid.

[ix] "Stabilisation at Fukushima Daiichi," *World Nuclear News*, March 20, 2011, www.world-nuclear-news.org/RS_Stabilisation_at_Fukushima_Daiichi_2003111.html.

[x] Agence France-Presse (AFP), "Operator of Fukushima Nuke Plant Admitted to Faking Repair Records," *Herald Sun*, March 20, 2011,

www.heraldsun.com.au/news/special-reports/operator-of-fukushima-nuke-plant-admitted-to-faking-repair-records/story-fn858jk3-1226024977934.

xi Nuclear Energy Agency (NEA), "Timeline for the Fukushima Daiichi Nuclear Power Plant Accident," last updated December 19, 2011, www.oecd-nea.org/press/2011/NEWS-04.html.

xii Fredrik Dahl, "Japan Mulls Fukushima Food Sale Ban: IAEA," *Reuters*, March 19, 2011, www.reuters.com/article/2011/03/19/us-japan-nuclear-food-idUSTRE72I1X120110319.

xiii Steve Herman, "Japan Acknowledges Radioactive Beef Sold to Markets, Restaurants," *Voice of America*, July 13, 2011, www.voanews.com/english /news/asia/Japan-Calls-Radioactive-Beef-Controversy-An-Isolated-Incident-125478143.html.

xiv Wieland Wagner, "Japanese Leaders Leave People in the Dark," *Spiegel Online*, March 15, 2011, www.spiegel.de/international/world /0,1518,751109,00.html.

xv Joe Cogliano, "Poll: Japan Nuclear Disaster Worries Americans," *Dayton Business Journal*, April 16, 2011, www.bizjournals.com/dayton/news /2011/04/16/japan-nuclear-disaster-worries-americans.html.

xvi Paul Frenzen and others, "Consumer Acceptance of Irradiated Meat and Poultry Products," *Issues in Food Safety Economics* (U.S. Department of Agriculture), Agriculture Information Bulletin No. 757, August 2000, www.ers.usda.gov/publications/aib757/aib757.pdf.

xvii Patrick McGroarty and Vanessa Fuhrmans, "Germany to Forsake Its Nuclear Reactors," *Wall Street Journal*, May 30, 2011, http://online.wsj .com/article/SB10001424052702303657404576354752218810560.html.

xviii EIA, "*Annual Energy Review*," October 19, 2011, www.eia.gov /totalenergy/data/annual/showtext.cfm?t=ptb0802a.

Risk and Uncertainty

Energy Security Challenges

We will do everything that must be done within OPEC to continue strengthening the price of our oil; $100 is a fair price for a barrel.

—Hugo Chavez

Access to affordable, stable energy supplies is critical for the economies and national security of developed countries. For developing countries, affordable energy often offers a pathway to a better quality of life. But there are a number of global threats with the potential for destabilizing the energy markets. In this chapter I will discuss some of those threats.

OPEC

The Organization of Petroleum Exporting Countries—commonly known by the acronym OPEC—is composed of 12 major oil-exporting countries. Over 77% of the world's remaining proved crude reserves are within OPEC countries, which were also responsible for 42% of the world's crude oil production in 2010. As a result, OPEC has a great deal of influence over global oil production—and therefore at present OPEC has a great deal of power over the global economy.

OPEC's function is viewed very differently from different perspectives. Among member countries like Iran, Saudi Arabia, and Venezuela, OPEC is viewed as an organization that helps safeguard the financial interests of the country by ensuring the best possible price for oil exports. A country with depleting natural resources is obviously interested in extracting the maximum possible value for the resource, as well as maintaining production of those resources for the longest possible period of time.

But many oil-importing countries have a different view of OPEC, because OPEC's pricing power has been wielded in ways that have harmed Western economies. The most famous example is the OPEC oil embargo of 1973. In response to a political disagreement over the West's support of Israel in the Yom Kippur War, OPEC's Arab member countries stopped supplying oil to the U.S. and Western Europe. As a result, there was an immediate global oil shortage, oil prices quadrupled, and the world was thrown into a recession.

This incident framed a view of OPEC by many in the West as a group whose interests often run contrary to those of the West, and who are willing to wield a powerful economic weapon in pursuit of those interests. For many, OPEC became forever a major culprit behind the reason for high oil prices.

Today OPEC wields the same kind of power over oil supplies that it did in 1973. Collectively, OPEC member countries have the power to cause global oil shortages; and they could essentially drive the price of oil to hundreds of dollars per barrel in a very short period of time. Within OPEC, there are countries that could do this unilaterally. Saudi Arabia produces about 10% of the world's oil, and if it suddenly stopped producing for any reason, the price of oil would likely rise past $200 a barrel very quickly.

Iran is the second largest producer in OPEC, responsible for just over 5% of global oil production in 2010. The dispute over Iran's nuclear program is a perfect example of the disproportionate hold OPEC countries have over the global economy. The simple threat of Iran cutting off oil exports has been blamed for oil price increases in 2011 and 2012. Military action against Iran would likely send oil prices much higher, and thus the global economy is potentially at risk due to the actions of one country.

So the first threat from OPEC is that it retains the power to throw the global economy into turmoil overnight. This is a serious risk for the economies of oil-importing nations.

The second threat is that OPEC countries need the money from oil importers to pay for their budgets. It is a common phenomenon that governments find ways to spend any extra revenue they take in, and as that revenue grows so do government budgets. As oil prices increase and the budgets of these oil-exporting countries grow, they require higher oil prices to maintain these budgets.

Did you know? Saudi Arabia stated that to balance its budget in 2011, it required an oil price of at least $80/barrel, an increase of $15/barrel since 2009.

At one time OPEC was content with oil at $40 a barrel. Then it became accustomed to oil at $70 a barrel, and today some OPEC countries have signaled that they believe $100 a barrel is a fair price. In truth, "fair price" is a moving target, and that target will always tend to rise because of their need to maintain growing government spending.

The ideal situation from OPEC's perspective is to keep oil prices at a level high enough to still allow global economic growth, but at a price that allows them to cover their growing government budgets. But from the perspective of the oil importers, this raises the distinct possibility of a slow strangulation of their economies as the money they spend for oil imports increases year after year.

There are also countries within OPEC whose interests are directly counter to those of many Western countries, and who would like nothing more than to increase their wealth and power at the expense of oil importers. I suspect that if Iran or Venezuela could unilaterally raise the price of oil to $200 a barrel tomorrow, it would do so, and it would be a bonus for them that this would weaken the economy of the United States.

Did you know? When oil prices are $100 a barrel, the value of OPEC's oil production is $1.25 trillion per year.

Of course, there are moderate countries within OPEC that are more concerned about the impact of high oil prices on global economic growth, because that has the potential to reduce demand and cause prices to collapse. But even if the wishes of those countries prevail, it is unlikely that prices will be lowered to the historical levels that enabled Western economies to grow robustly.

Thus, countries whose economies are dependent on imported oil face multiple threats from OPEC that can quickly derail economic growth, and yet they will likely continue to transfer wealth to OPEC countries.

OVERSTATED OPEC RESERVES?

A different sort of threat is the possibility that OPEC oil reserves are overstated. OPEC reserves are not subject to outside audit, and therefore the rest of the world is left with the official reserve estimates from OPEC.

But there are reasons to believe those reserves are overstated. In 1982, Saudi Arabia stopped allowing its oil and gas data to be scrutinized. Prior to that, outsiders had some access to information on Saudi Arabia's reserves. At the time that accessibility was shut down in 1982, Saudi proved oil reserves were estimated to be 165 billion barrels.

Also in 1982, OPEC introduced a system of production quotas based partly on the oil reserves in each country. Shortly after, a number of OPEC countries raised their reserves estimates sharply, as a larger reserve would increase their production quota. In 1983, Kuwait increased its reserves by nearly 40%, from 67 billion barrels to 93 billion barrels, and Iran added 34 billion barrels to its reserves. In 1984, Venezuela increased its reserves by nearly 100%, from 28 billion barrels to 55 billion barrels. In 1985, the UAE nearly tripled its reserves from 33 billion barrels to 97 billion barrels. In 1988, Saudi Arabia raised its reported reserve number by 85 million barrels over the previous year.

Over the decade of the 1980s, OPEC's stated reserves increased from 425 billion barrels of oil in 1980 to 763 billion barrels by 1990—an increase twice the size of Saudi Arabia's entire estimated oil reserves in 1982 (see Figure 8-1). By 2010, OPEC's stated reserves had further grown to 1.1 trillion barrels of oil and accounted for 90% of the global oil reserve additions of the previous 30 years.

Reserve growth is certainly not out of the question. New discoveries take place and extraction technologies improve. But there have been reports that called into question some of the OPEC increases in reserves.[i] Since there are no independent audits of OPEC's reserves, its official estimates are accepted, yet it is possible that future production that has been counted upon will never materialize.

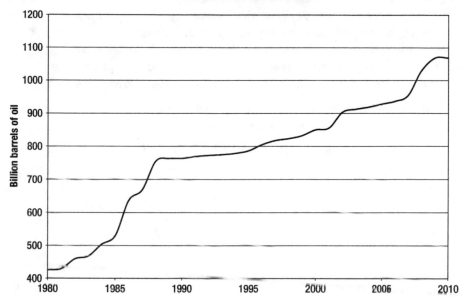

Figure 8-1. The growth of OPEC's stated oil reserves (Data source: BP *Statistical Review of World Energy 2011*[ii])

Developing Countries

Conventional wisdom may suggest that as oil prices rise, poorer countries will be priced out of the market as richer countries bid against each other for oil. But that is not at all what has happened over the past decade, and the trend implies a worrisome economic threat for developed countries.

From 2005 to 2010—as oil prices rose to record highs—oil consumption in the United States fell by 1.6 million barrels per day (bpd). The European Union saw oil consumption drop by 1.2 million bpd, and Japan registered a drop of 900,000 bpd.

Japan was the exception in the Asia Pacific region. Excluding Japan, the rest of the Asia Pacific region increased its oil consumption by 3.6 million bpd from 2005 to 2010 (see Figure 8-2). Africa increased consumption over this timeframe by 450,000 bpd, a 16% increase. Consumption in the Middle East increased by 1.6 million bpd, a 26% increase. Consumption in South America increased by 1 million bpd, a 19% increase over 2005 levels.

The trend was clear: As oil prices increased, developed countries reduced oil consumption, while regions that were significantly undeveloped or developing increased oil consumption. Perhaps unsurprisingly—since their revenues would have increased over this time period—oil-exporting regions experienced the greatest percentage increases in consumption. The Middle East and Venezuela both saw consumption increases of over 20%.

But why would developing oil-importing regions have also experienced consumption growth in the case of high prices?

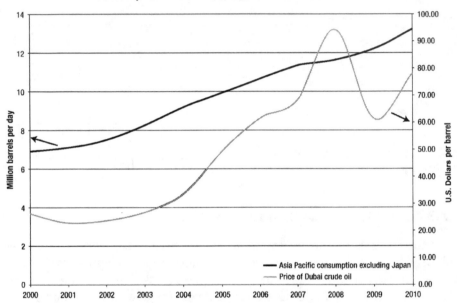

Consumption of Oil in Asia Pacific Versus Oil Price

Figure 8-2. Demand for oil in Asia Pacific showed strong growth in the face of rising oil prices. (Data source: BP *Statistical Review of World Energy 2011*)

Consider the change in the consumption habits of the United States and China over the past decade. In 2000, the U.S. consumed 19.7 million barrels of oil per day—25.5 barrels of oil per person per year. By 2010 the population of the U.S. had increased by 10%, but the country's oil consumption had fallen to 19.1 million bpd—22.6 barrels per person per year.

The trend in China was sharply in the other direction. In 2000, oil consumption in China was 4.8 million bpd, or 1.4 barrels per person per year. In 2010, consumption had grown to 9.1 million bpd, or 2.5 barrels per person per year.

The demand growth in China, in India, and across Asia and South America in the face of record-high oil prices may at first be counterintuitive. But consider the consumption patterns in developed countries. Developed countries consume a lot more oil than they really need to use because they have more discretionary consumption. So when oil prices rise, we make a few changes to our lifestyle—driving fewer miles, buying more fuel-efficient cars, using more mass transportation, etc.—and oil consumption falls.

Did you know? If per capita oil consumption in China was as high as it is in the U.S., China would consume more than 82 million barrels of oil per day—an amount equivalent to almost all of the world's oil production.

So the 22nd barrel of oil many of us in the U.S. consume each year isn't worth $100 to us, and we use a bit less when oil prices rise. If oil prices were sustained at $150 a barrel, we would use even less. But the vast majority of the world uses very little oil, and aspires to higher standards of living.

The average consumption of oil in the world—87 million bpd in 2010 divided by a population of approximately 6.8 billion people—is 4.7 barrels of oil per person per year. In other words, if everyone on earth was allocated an equal amount of oil, the 2010 allotment would have been 4.7 barrels per person. This is 79% lower than average U.S. consumption, and 54% lower than average EU consumption.

Developing countries are presently below the average 4.7 barrel allotment, but their consumption is rising. Chinese consumption has risen to 2.5 barrels per person per year, a 79% increase in the past ten years. At that growth rate—and assuming China's population remains constant—China will reach 4.7 barrels of oil per person in slightly over ten years.

But this would require another 8 million barrels of oil per day for China, which either must come from the allotment of other countries—most likely developed countries—or would require global oil production to rise another 10%. Bear in mind that this is only for China; other developing countries are also on growth trajectories that would see their demand for oil collectively increase by millions of barrels per day over the next decade.

The threat for developed countries is clear: As oil prices rise, consumption in developed countries is likely to continue to decline in response, but developing countries will continue to increase their consumption. To the extent that the decline in developed countries is a result of the adoption of alternative fuels and improved efficiencies, economic growth in developed countries may be able to continue. But if the decline comes as a result of people simply being unable to afford oil, economic difficulty in developed countries is practically assured.

What might this signal for future oil prices? A question I frequently encounter is, "How high can gasoline prices rise in the U.S.?" Because the oil markets are global, the answer to that question is, "It depends on how much value the people in developing countries place on increasing their oil consumption to two or three barrels of oil per year."

Or, an alternative way to think about it is, "If you were only allocated 3 barrels of oil per person per year, how much would you be willing to pay for those barrels?" The 20th barrel each of us in the U.S. consumes each year might allow us to drive that 12,000th mile. But the first barrel that someone in a developing country consumes might allow them to drive that very first mile and have heat in their home for the first time. They will be willing to pay a lot more for those initial barrels than we are for our excess barrels, and this explains why their consumption has increased even as oil prices have risen.

And if future oil prices are dictated by how much developing countries are willing to pay for their second or third barrel of oil per capita, this number may ultimately be much higher than $100 per barrel.

Declining EROEI

Two important—but largely misunderstood—concepts in the production of energy are energy return on energy invested (EROEI) and net energy. Here I will discuss how to use these concepts, why they signal a future threat, and some of the caveats that must be applied.

Understanding EROEI

The concept of EROEI is relatively straightforward. It is simply a measure of the energy that is produced relative to the energy that is consumed during the production of an energy source:

$$EROEI = \text{Usable Energy Output/Energy Consumed}$$

In other words, if 10 BTUs of energy are consumed to extract and refine 100 BTUs of oil into usable products, then the EROEI is 100/10, or 10 to 1.

The concept of net energy refers to how much energy is available for consumption after the energy inputs are accounted for. This equation is

$$\text{Net Energy} = \text{Usable Energy Output} - \text{Energy Consumed}$$

In our previous example, the net energy is 100 BTUs produced minus 10 BTUs consumed, or 90 BTUs.

Society operates on the basis of the net energy that is available for goods, services, transportation, etc. When the EROEI of an energy source is very high, it takes a relatively small portion of society to provide the energy for the entire society. For example, consider a world that requires 85 million barrels of oil per day. If the EROEI for oil production is 100 to 1 (which was the case in early days of the oil industry), solving the EROEI and net energy equations shows that total production need only be slightly higher than the required net. If the gross production were 85.86 million barrels of oil per day, 0.86 million bpd could be used as the energy to extract the oil at a 100 to 1 ratio. The net is then $85.86 - 0.86 = 85$ million bpd.

However, as EROEI declines, the implications are that it will require more time, effort, and money from society in order to maintain the net production. Historically, as the most accessible oil was produced, more energy had to be invested to produce a barrel of oil. Deeper wells had to be drilled, production moved offshore, and we began to process crude oil that was heavier and had more impurities. The EROEI of oil production fell from 100 to 1 a century ago to perhaps 20 to 1 today. Solving equations for an EROEI of 20 to 1, we find that global gross production would need to be 89.5 million bpd in order to net 85 million bpd for society.[1]

While the required gross production has not changed dramatically in these two cases, the curve does begin to change significantly as the EROEI continues to fall. Consider a society in which the EROEI is only 2 to 1 (see Figure 8-3). This is in fact the reported EROEI range of many biofuels. In this case, in order to produce a net of 85 million bpd for society, the gross

---

[1] The excess "barrels" required as energy to produce the oil will not necessarily be actual oil barrels. The energy can be the energy equivalent of the barrels of oil from other energy sources like coal, oil, natural gas, biomass, etc.

production must be 170 million bpd—twice the current global oil production rate! Half of that production would be consumed during the process, and half would be left for society.

This highlights one of the major challenges for biofuels as we use them to replace oil: replacing oil with biofuels (or any low EROEI source) requires significantly greater primary energy inputs, and this generally translates into more effort and higher costs. If the modern world could operate at an EROEI of 2 to 1, it would require a far greater portion of the economy to produce the energy needed by the rest of society. This is one reason that it is true that many renewable energy technologies create more jobs than fossil fuel technologies—it simply takes more people to produce the same amount of energy.

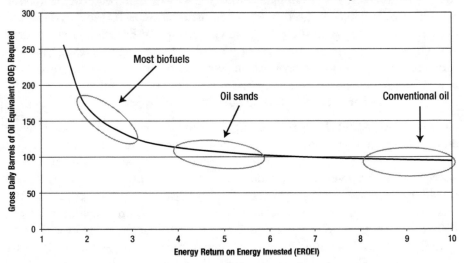

Figure 8-3. As EROEI declines, more primary energy must be produced just to produce the same amount of net energy.[2]

---

[2] This case considers production all the way to refined fuels. The EROEI of most conventional oil is still well above 10 to 1, but when refining is factored in, it drops below 10 to 1. Likewise, the EROEI for tar sands has been reported to be 6 or 8 to 1, but once the oil is refined, it drops to the 4 or 5 to 1 range.

EROEI Caveats

But there are some important caveats when using EROEI. First, the break-even figure for EROEI is 1.0. When the EROEI falls below 1.0, you have consumed more energy in the process than you got back from the process. But in some cases like this, it may make short-term economic sense.

An example of a process in which the EROEI is below 1.0 is the electrolysis of water to produce hydrogen, and then burning the hydrogen for power. The electricity required to produce the hydrogen will always be greater than the usable energy that can be obtained when the hydrogen is consumed for power. But, if the electricity used to produce the hydrogen is cheap—which could be the case if excess electricity is available at various times during the day—the hydrogen could be produced and used when needed. In this case, the hydrogen would be acting as a battery of sorts; storing the cheap electricity for later use.

The same is true of net energy—it can be negative and yet still make economic sense. But an important point here is that when the EROEI is less than 1.0 and the net energy is negative, the consumption of the primary energy inputs is accelerated. What a net negative energy return really says is that a process is not sustainable over the long term. This is like withdrawing money from a bank—at some point you have to make some deposits, or at least stop the withdrawals. If you consume 1 BTU of fossil energy to create less than 1 BTU of a derivative of that fossil fuel, this is a process that will speed up the depletion of fossil fuel reserves.

However, if the two forms of energy are not fungible (interchangeable), then economics can easily trump EROEI. For example, it might be economically attractive to consume 2 BTUs of coal to produce 1 BTU of ethanol (EROEI = 0.5 for this example). In that case the process speeds up the depletion of coal reserves, but economics (and potentially subsidies)—not EROEI—would dictate whether that process is commercialized because the coal has been turned into something of greater value.

On the other hand, if you consume one transportation fuel to produce another transportation fuel—as is mostly the case with corn ethanol (natural gas, diesel, and gasoline in; ethanol out)—then it may make more sense to just use the inputs directly as a transportation fuel *if the EROEI for the process is low.*

The other major caveat when using EROEI is that there is no time factor involved in EROEI calculations. Thus, it is possible for a lower EROEI process to be more attractive than a higher EROEI process if the former returns the energy over a shorter time interval. Think of it in terms of interest rate calculations.

Consider an investment that returns 3% on a daily basis versus one that returns 50% on an annual basis. The EROEI would simply say that the former is 1.03 to 1 and the latter is 1.5 to 1, but you would be far better off on an annual basis with the 3% daily yield. So, a process with a low EROEI— as long as it is still greater than 1—could be attractive if it produces the energy over a short time interval. An example of this could be a fermentation that can be done in 24 hours versus a different process that requires an entire growing season.[3]

Caveats notwithstanding, the threat from a declining EROEI is that we have to produce more gross energy just to produce the same net. This accelerates our consumption of fossil resources, and as EROEI continues to decline, a larger portion of our time, effort, and money must go into producing energy. This growing diversion of effort into energy production will potentially come at the expense of other sectors of the economy.

Miscellaneous Threats

While the three aforementioned threats are among the most glaring and potentially chronic concerns, there are other threats that can lead to short-term supply shortfalls. The 2011 civil war in Libya removed 1.6 million barrels of oil per day from the world markets, and oil prices responded by advancing back above $100 per barrel. There are numerous other oil-producing countries with the potential for civil unrest to remove oil from the markets.

Terrorism is an ever-present threat. There are a number of locations— particularly in the Middle East—where large fractions of the world's oil infrastructure are concentrated. There are also a number of oil transit chokepoints around the world where terrorism or military conflict could take a substantial fraction of the world's oil supply off the market.

---

[3] An obvious solution to this dilemma would be to standardize EROEI calculations on the basis of annual return in the same way financial interest is computed.

The Strait of Hormuz, located between Iran and Oman, is the world's most important chokepoint.[iii] In 2009, 15.5 million barrels of oil passed through the Strait of Hormuz, a third of all seaborne-traded oil. Another 13.6 million barrels of oil a day passes through the Strait of Malacca to supply oil to China and Indonesia.

Severe weather also has the potential to disrupt energy supplies. Americans see this directly when hurricanes force closure of oil rigs in the Gulf of Mexico, and occasionally the hurricanes are severe enough to result in fuel shortages. Hurricane Katrina in 2005 and Hurricanes Gustav and Ike in 2008 all resulted in temporary product shortages and higher prices.

Summary

There are a number of credible, serious threats with the potential to cause very high oil prices and dislocations in oil supplies. These threats exist presently, and appear likely to worsen as global demand for oil grows. In order to mitigate these threats, governments must first clearly understand the nature of the threats and how they might impact upon national and global economies.

Ultimately, countries that are high consumers of oil—and particularly high importers of oil—must engage in risk management that includes scenarios of declining oil supplies and much higher future oil prices. There are a number of potential energy policy options that could mitigate against these risks. These will be discussed in the next chapter.

References

[i] Energy Intelligence, "Oil Reserves Accounting: The Case Of Kuwait," *Petroleum Intelligence Weekly*, January 30, 2006.

[ii] BP, *BP Statistical Review of World Energy 2011*, www.bp.com/sectionbodycopy .do?categoryId=7500&contentId=7068481.

[iii] Energy Information Administration (EIA), "World Oil Transit Chokepoints," accessed December 16, 2011, http://205.254.135.7/countries/regions-topics.cfm?fips=WOTC.

Reducing the Risks

Policies to Enhance Energy Security

Let our advance worrying become advance thinking and planning.

—Winston Churchill

A sound energy policy should take into account the supply side, the demand side, and the possibility that projections will be wrong on one or both counts. Energy policy decisions must also factor in the impact on current and future generations, and they should be capable of weathering changing political climates. Unfortunately, when energy policy decisions fail to meet these criteria, the result is a dysfunctional, inconsistent energy policy.

While it will never be possible to satisfy everyone, the policy ideas discussed in this chapter attempt to find middle ground that can enjoy broad support. The purpose of the ideas in this chapter is to set in place energy policies that enhance energy security while attempting to satisfy concerns from those who hold very different opinions on energy policy.

Defining Common Ground

There are a few concepts on which people of very different political persuasion would probably find broad agreement, and upon which some sensible energy policies can be developed.

The first concept is that countries that are heavily dependent on other countries for their energy supplies face economic risks that are often beyond their control. As the dependence on energy extends into oil-exporting countries whose interests are counter to those of the oil-importing countries, the level of those economic risks increases. A country that imports energy also exports money out of the country and creates jobs outside of the country.

However, given the dominance of oil in the global transportation and manufacturing sectors, we probably can also agree that the world is likely to still be dependent on oil for at least the next two decades. Certainly the *level* of dependence is an issue that would be hotly debated, but the fact that we will need some oil for some years to come is something on which I think most would agree.

I think we would mostly agree that because fossil fuels are a depleting resource, there is a risk associated with being overly dependent on them even when supplies can be sourced domestically. For the past few years, that risk has manifested itself as very high oil prices that have helped drag down economies in the developed world. An economy built on depleting resources must eventually transition to other sources and/or decrease energy consumption as the resource depletes. Thus, *all other things being equal*, it would be preferable to eliminate wasteful energy consumption and encourage sustainable energy solutions.

Of course, all other things are never equal, and this is where we have to make choices. There is no free lunch in any of our energy choices. They all have costs, trade-offs, and risks associated with them, and this is the source of areas of disagreement. Certain costs are acceptable to some and not to others.

But on the basis of these premises—which boil down to a need to transition from oil while ensuring that secure oil supplies are available during the transition—I want to make three policy recommendations that would enhance the long-term energy security of any country. These recommendations address the demand side, the supply side, and the diversification of our fuel supplies.

Shifting Taxes from Income to Consumption

One way to encourage a transition away from oil is to send a strong signal to consumers that gasoline costs will continue to rise. But in order to get consumers and politicians to accept this, they need the following strong assurances:

1. The overall impact to a person's budget will be neutral.

2. A person will have the opportunity to make the impact to their budget favorable by making certain changes.

3. The change will improve the energy security for our children and future generations.

Some people still cling to the notion that gasoline prices will fall back to historically low levels (and politicians frequently make hollow promises to make this happen), and as a result they hesitate to make the changes that are necessary to reduce their level of oil consumption. My first proposal—a shift in taxation from income toward gasoline consumption—increases the certainty for consumers that they must become more fuel efficient.

Targeting Discretionary Consumption

I think most people can agree that in the U.S., a lot of gasoline usage is discretionary. We consume energy without too much consideration that it is a resource that our children and grandchildren might need. Many Americans are content to use up energy resources now and hope that there is an alternative solution right around the corner for future generations.

But what if there is no easy solution just around the corner for our fossil fuel dependence? What if you knew that unless we stretch our fossil fuel resources, our children will have to make far greater sacrifices? It seems prudent—given the risk to future generations—to make changes in our consumption habits to stretch those depleting resources.

■ **Did you know?** About two-thirds of the oil consumed in the United States is used for transportation, and about two-thirds of the oil used for transportation is gasoline (~45% of total U.S. oil consumption).

The most effective way to get people to consume less of something is to make it more expensive. We saw this in the U.S. the past few years in the face of record high oil prices. As oil prices climbed rapidly in 2007 and 2008, oil demand in the U.S. decreased by nearly 10%.

This of course brings up the obvious question: Why not simply let high prices in the marketplace rein in demand as they did following the price run-up from 2007 to 2008? The main reason is that extreme price swings can occur quickly, putting severe, unexpected pressure on personal budgets and contributing to economic slowdowns. In many cases, the demand that is curbed causes financial hardship for many. So I believe a proactive approach is preferable.

In addition, these price swings can be caused by the whims of nations whose interests are directly opposed to those of Western democracies. As a result of price spikes, wealth is transferred from oil importers to oil exporters. This ultimately weakens the U.S., the EU, Japan, Australia, and other countries that are dependent on oil imports. At the same time, it strengthens countries like Russia, Venezuela, Iran, and Saudi Arabia.

More Choice in Taxation

Very few people—including me—want to pay higher taxes. Politicians know this, which is why discussions to raise gasoline taxes go nowhere. When the subject arises, that is the end of the discussion for many people.

So I make it clear that my proposal is not to raise taxes, but rather to shift a portion of the tax burden from one kind of tax to another. My proposal is to increase gasoline taxes, but then to offset that tax increase with an income tax credit (or offset it by merely lowering income tax rates).

The idea I am putting forth is neutral with respect to overall tax revenues; it does not try to increase them or decrease them. But, what I am proposing would give people more choice in how much taxes they pay. I want to change the taxes people pay in a way that will benefit future generations by reducing our dependence on oil.

We pay numerous kinds of taxes, including income taxes, real estate taxes, sales taxes, and various kinds of consumption taxes. In the case of consumption taxes, people have a much larger degree of choice over the amount of taxes they pay. So when I pay taxes, I would rather be taxed on my consumption—which I can choose to reduce. If I don't like the tax on alcohol, then I can choose not to drink. But I still have the freedom to choose to drink, and voluntarily pay more taxes.

The same logic holds for certain other consumption taxes, such as gasoline taxes. I can choose to consume less, and the higher the price, the greater my incentive to make that choice. If the price is low, so is the incentive to conserve.

But I don't propose to simply give governments more tax money to spend, and therein lies the difference between my proposal and a simple increase in gas taxes.

Addressing Common Objections

There are two oft-cited objections to raising gas taxes. The first is a general objection to raising taxes, period. Many people believe that we are overtaxed, and some of them will not entertain the notion of higher taxes. But my proposal would not be a net tax increase, so that objection isn't relevant here. With my proposal, we would be taxing personal incomes at a lower rate, thus providing an even greater incentive to work—and taxing more of something we want to reduce—oil consumption.

The other frequent objection is that higher gasoline taxes are regressive, that they hurt lower-income workers the most. That's a fair criticism, but it can also be addressed. Let's consider an example for illustration.

An average family of five in the U.S. consumes about 2,000 gallons of gasoline a year.[1] If we phased in a federal gasoline tax increase of $0.20/gallon the first year, $0.30/gallon the second year, and then $0.50/gallon in each of the three

---

[1] In 2010, per capita consumption of gasoline for the entire U.S. population was 448 gallons per person per year. (Data source: Gasoline consumption data is from the Energy Information Administration and population data is from the *CIA World Factbook*).

following years, the total tax increase at the end of five years would be $2.00/gallon. Such an increase in the U.S. would still put gasoline prices at less than they currently are in Europe. But they should encourage serious conservation measures, while at the same time allowing people enough lead time to plan for the tax increase.

However, a $2/gallon tax would place an additional tax burden of $4,000 on this hypothetical family. In order to offset the burden of these higher taxes, I would propose that as a part of the package, a tax credit is available to offset the increased tax burden based on the average family's consumption. For this example, this would be $400 in the first year of the tax, and $4,000 by the time the last increase is phased in. The credit would be available to anyone who files a tax return (even if their income is below the threshold for paying taxes).

A family with a $4,000 income tax burden would see that burden reduced to zero, while a family with a tax burden of less than $4,000 in this scenario would qualify for a tax refund to offset their increased gasoline taxes.

Families that use less gasoline than average should actually see their overall tax burden decrease. Those who consume more than 2,000 gallons per year[2] would see an overall increase in their tax burden—and therefore would have a stronger incentive to reduce their fuel consumption. For those whose fuel usage is for farm or business use, the fuel taxes could be deducted against business income.

Since renewable fuels wouldn't be affected by this proposal, many options that are uncompetitive with gasoline at current prices would become much more attractive as the tax is phased in.

Benefits of the Proposal

Again, the intent is not to increase net tax revenues, but rather to discourage excessive consumption of a depleting resource. This is a practical measure to address our fossil fuel dependence from the demand side—without placing an additional tax burden on the average gasoline consumer.

---

[2] One consideration to make the idea more palatable is to given everyone a greater than average exemption initially, and reduce that over time. For example, in the first years of the program the exemption could be based on 500 gallons of gasoline per person per year—which is above the per capita average.

When gasoline prices are high, people start to embrace public transit, conservation, and vehicles with higher fuel economy. The advantages of having a higher gasoline tax would be many. They include:

- It would lead to conservation, which would help pre- serve our remaining fossil fuel endowment.

- It would encourage public transit (people flock to public transit when gasoline prices climb).

- It would make alternative energy candidates more com- petitive with fossil fuels, without picking specific tech- nology winners.

- It would enable people to do a better job of planning ahead, as opposed to the constant expectation that low gas prices are right around the corner.

- It should encourage more efficient city planning, and rein in the growth of suburban sprawl.

- It would make the price of fossil fuels more reflective of the negative externalities that are not currently priced in (air pollution, military expenditures, etc.).

Additional Considerations

There are admittedly many considerations beyond how this proposal might impact an average family. One consideration is the possibility that the net to overall tax revenues would be negative for the government. This is in fact what would happen if per capita gasoline consumption dropped—which is the objective. For instance, if the consumption for the example family of five fell to 1,000 gallons per year, their incremental gas taxes on that 1,000 gallons would be $2,000, but they would have gotten a tax credit of $4,000. But such a drop in consumption would be a success, and could be addressed by lowering the tax credits over time.

Another consideration is how to ensure that businesses that presently require high gasoline consumption won't be caused undue hardship by an increase in their fuel costs. Exemptions would need to be given to hospitals, fire and police departments, and numerous other critical services that are heavy consumers of energy. Some extra consideration may be required for those in commuter suburbs to allow sufficient time for public transit options to develop. In the longer term, everyone will have to become more efficient, but the low-hanging fruit is discretionary gasoline consumption by consumers.

The biggest challenge with the proposal, of course, will be politics as usual. As soon as someone makes a proposal such as this, some short-sighted politicians will say, "My opponent wants to raise your gas taxes"—while ignoring the revenue-neutral aspect of the proposal. This is the kind of selfishness and partisan behavior that has gotten the world into this energy predicament, but we will need to change our thinking to get out of it.

Drill—and Use the Proceeds to Curb Oil Demand

I consider myself to be an environmentalist, and like many environmentalists, I am concerned about the impact on our environment of continued fossil fuel consumption. But my thinking differs from that of many environmentalists in that I believe we will still need stable oil supplies for a number of years before we can fully transition away from oil.

My second proposal is designed to meet those petroleum needs during the transition phase, while using some of the proceeds to hasten the transition. In short, my proposal calls for governments to encourage domestic drilling while using the royalties and tax revenues to fund programs that reduce dependence on oil.

Ensuring Energy Supplies During the Transition

The objective of all of my proposals is that they should contain elements that people of very different viewpoints can support. In this case, a large number of people believe that domestic drilling is the answer to phasing out dependence on foreign oil, but a large number of other people believe that aggressive pursuit of alternative sources of energy is the only answer to eliminating dependence on foreign oil.

I believe that each viewpoint contains elements of the truth, and they can be combined into a powerful proposal. The thinking behind this proposal is that:

- As countries transition away from oil, they are still going to be dependent on oil for a number of years.

- To the extent that they can do so in an environmentally responsible manner, countries should satisfy as much of their oil needs as possible domestically to lower their economic risks.

Some critics will immediately complain that drilling merely ensures that we continue to be dependent on oil. But one element of my proposal specifically addresses this.

Environmentalists are generally vehemently opposed to opening up areas to additional drilling. They think there simply isn't a need to do so, and that it will just delay our transition to alternatives. They see oil companies—not ordinary citizens—as the primary beneficiaries of oil drilling.

Many environmentalists believe that if they can prevent further development of oil reserves, then alternative energy, public transit, and conservation will necessarily rise to the challenge and alleviate the dependence on diminishing fossil fuel reserves. But the risk in this approach is whether the alternatives can be delivered when they are needed, and whether they can cover severe shortfalls. What if they can't? What is Plan B? Shortages? Rationing?

On the other side are people who believe that underneath U.S. territory lies an ocean of oil, waiting to be tapped—if environmentalists would only get out of the way. They believe that energy independence is within our grasp if we aggressively develop our natural resources. But this notion suffers from a very similar risk as the position of environmentalists: What if the oil that is available simply can't cover any severe shortfalls? What if the expectations that these vast oceans of oil exist lead us to delay actions on alternatives? Again, what is Plan B? Military action? A continued transfer of wealth to OPEC?

Did you know?   In the past three decades, commercial oil production has taken place in 31 of the 50 U.S. states.[i]

The majority of us fall somewhere in between these two positions; we want to see some domestic development and some development of alternatives.

My proposal would enable one to fund the other, while giving both environmentalists and drilling advocates something they want. But each side would need to compromise a bit.

Both opponents and proponents of drilling would likely agree that our dependence on petroleum—and, specifically, imported petroleum—comes with risks. Among the arguments from both sides are that this dependence puts our national security at risk and that it poses risks to the environment. I think both sides would agree that a long-term solution to the problem of petroleum dependence could be a combination of conservation along with alternative options such as higher-efficiency vehicles, electric transport, and public transit. Where large numbers will start to disagree is whether this is achievable in the short term, or whether it is going to take a few more technological developments and more than a decade to see most of our petroleum dependence displaced.

HOW MUCH OIL?

In 2006, the Minerals Management Service (MMS) in the U.S. Department of the Interior estimated "that the quantity of undiscovered technically recoverable resources ranges from 66.6 to 115.3 billion barrels of oil and 326.4 to 565.9 trillion cubic feet of natural gas" below the offshore waters on the Outer Continental Shelf (OCS) of the U.S.[ii] Of that amount, the MMS estimated that 18 billion barrels of oil was off-limits due to a 1990 executive order that was signed into law by President George H.W. Bush.[iii]

The U.S. Energy Information Administration estimated in 2008 that there was another 10 billion barrels of technically recoverable oil within the coastal plain of the Arctic National Wildlife Refuge (ANWR) that was off-limits to development.[iv]

Based on 2010 U.S. petroleum demand of 19.2 million barrels per day (bpd), the 28 billion barrels of oil presently off-limits on the OCS and in ANWR is equivalent to four years of U.S. petroleum demand. In terms of the 9.4 million bpd of oil imported in 2010, 28 billion barrels of oil is equivalent to just over eight years of imports.

In dollar terms, 28 billion barrels of oil is worth $2.8 trillion at an oil price of $100/barrel—an amount equivalent to over $9,000 for every person in the U.S.

President George W. Bush lifted the ban on offshore drilling in 2008, and in March 2010 President Barack Obama announced his support for increased offshore drilling. However, this was prior to the Deepwater Horizon oil spill in the Gulf of Mexico, which galvanized resistance to drilling and led to a six-month moratorium on deepwater drilling. In December 2010 the Obama Administration announced that no drilling would be allowed in the eastern Gulf of Mexico or off the Atlantic coast for at least seven years.

I fall into the latter category, for a variety of reasons. I am familiar with a lot of the alternatives, and most are simply not competitive even at gasoline prices of $4 or $5/gallon—nor are they scalable. To illustrate that point, consider Europe, where gasoline prices in many locations are double the price in the U.S. Even at these prices, petroleum remains the dominant choice for transportation in Europe (albeit at lower levels of consumption than in the U.S.). But it is going to take more than price—or, at a minimum, much higher prices than Americans probably anticipate—to move us away from a very high level of dependence on fossil fuels.

Using Government Windfalls Wisely

So I propose a compromise. I propose that as we open up some of the more promising areas to exploration, governments earmark some or all of the royalties to funding fossil fuel alternatives. Leases on federal lands should also be structured so that governments share in any windfall if oil prices skyrocket. One of the problems with windfall profits taxes is that they discourage investment in projects with marginal economics. But oil companies don't plan projects with an expectation of $200/barrel oil; a lease that is structured to give governments an increasing portion of revenues at much higher oil prices will be unlikely to impact project economics for an oil company because the possibility of such high prices will be heavily discounted.

With the revenues, we could subsidize public transportation. We could provide a tax credit of $1,000 for each person who purchases a car that gets over 40 mpg. We could use these oil revenues to fund wind and solar power, freeing up natural gas that could then be used to displace petroleum in compressed natural gas (CNG) vehicles.

It is true that the oil won't flow from newly opened areas for perhaps a decade, but there is a risk that we will face oil shortages in a decade. Oil prices will probably be very high, which means the royalties from the oil would provide a lot of money for funding alternatives. By funding these alternatives, we are also buying insurance against the oil shortages that we hope to avoid.

This should be a compromise with attractive elements for both sides. If we don't agree to such a compromise, then what's going to happen is that as prices continue to rise, so will the pressure to drill, and governments will eventually cave in to this pressure. But by failing to earmark the money for alternatives, it will just postpone the inevitable day of reckoning for oil supplies.

That's a compromise I prefer. However, one that would have even greater support behind it would be to return an oil dividend to citizens (as Alaska has historically done). As noted in the sidebar ("How Much Oil?"), the oil that is currently off-limits to drilling in the U.S. is equivalent to over $9,000 for every person in the U.S. Thus, in this case one could propose to return 5% or 10% of the proceeds as an oil dividend back to U.S. citizens. That is tangible for people, whereas funding the alternatives may not be. However, while I think this compromise would find broad support among many people with stretched budgets, it does nothing to address the problem of oil dependence. That, in my opinion, must be part of any solution.

From an environmental perspective, the ideal situation would be that as we open up new areas to drilling, the incentives for alternative energy created through government lease revenue reduce the demand for oil to the point that extensive development is unnecessary. By using revenues from oil to transition away from oil, we move toward a more sustainable future while ensuring that domestic oil supplies are available if they are needed.

Open Fuel Standard

The reason the world originally became so dependent on oil is that it offered something that no alternative fuel did: enormous quantities of an ideal combustion fuel at a low cost. It certainly didn't hurt that as the automobile came of age, the U.S. was endowed with rich petroleum resources, which made driving affordable for the general public because oil was cheap.

Over time, a transportation infrastructure was built around oil, and decades of cheap oil influenced the choice of cars we drove and where we chose to live. But eventually oil became more expensive as demand grew and supplies depleted. However, because the transportation fuel infrastructure was built around oil, many countries simply paid more and more for oil—exporting greater and greater numbers of jobs and money—instead of building out a new infrastructure.

■ **Did you know?**   In 2009 there were just over 8 million E85 flex-fuel vehicles (FFVs) on U.S. roads, about 3% of the total U.S. vehicle population of 250 million.[v]

It wasn't as if there have never been economic alternatives to oil. Compressed natural gas and methanol, for instance, have both been cheaper than oil on an energy equivalent basis for many years (see the sidebar "The Price of Energy" for an explanation of energy equivalent basis). As I write this, conventional gasoline costs $24.61 per million BTU (MMBTU), methanol is $23.59 per MMBTU, and natural gas is $2.60 per MMBTU.[3] Ethanol is more expensive than both gasoline and methanol at $28.78 per MMBTU.

THE PRICE OF ENERGY

The price of energy has a strong influence on the energy choices governments and individuals make. I sometimes hear people ask, "Why are we still building coal-fired power plants?" or "Why don't we replace more petroleum with biofuels?" There are several reasons, but a major factor is simply price.

The price and convenience of energy sources are ultimately the keys to customer acceptance. Automobiles can be powered with gasoline, ethanol, natural gas, diesel, electricity, and a wide variety of unconventional fuels. If consumers have a choice and the supply is convenient, they will tend toward the cheapest energy source they can get—even though that energy source may have hidden costs that don't appear in the price at the pump.

In the following table I have compiled a list of prices for some transportation fuel options on an energy equivalent basis—the British thermal unit (BTU). A BTU is simply the amount of heat energy it takes to raise the temperature of one pound of water by 1°F. Everything has been converted into U.S. dollars per million BTU (MMBTU).

The Cost of Transportation Fuel on January 18, 2012 (Data sources: EIA,[vi] CME Group,[vii] and Methanex[viii])

Energy Source	$US per gallon	BTU/gallon	$US per MMBTU
Natural gas	NA	NA	$2.60
Brent crude oil	$2.58	138,000	$18.70
Ultra-Low-Sulfur Diesel	$3.06	139,000	$22.01
Methanol	$1.34	56,800	$23.59
Conventional gasoline	$2.83	115,000	$24.61
Corn ethanol	$2.19	76,100	$28.78

---

[3] While natural gas is by far the cheapest option, the cost of converting a vehicle to run on natural gas is much higher than the cost of converting one to run on an alternative liquid fuel.

The problem lies in the fact that consumers don't have the option of filling up with methanol, ethanol, or any of the other contenders to replace gasoline (all of which will be discussed in later chapters)—because the transportation infrastructure is incompatible and, more importantly, the cars on the roads are not designed to handle these fuels.

Thus, my third proposal calls for support of the Open Fuel Standard[4] that would require that a growing percentage of vehicles sold in the U.S. must be capable of running on fuels other than gasoline. I am not usually a big fan of mandates, because of the potential for unintended consequences, but in this case the additional cost to produce a vehicle that is flex-fuel capable is reported to be between $100 and $200. This would therefore only add around 0.5% to the cost of the average new car.[5]

The availability of more flex-fuel vehicles would remove one of the major obstacles for new fuels attempting to break into the transportation fuel market. Currently, there is no demand for methanol or mixed alcohols as transportation fuel primarily because the vehicles on the roads are not entirely compatible. If more vehicles were capable of operating on a wide variety of fuels with little added production cost, the market for domestically produced fuels would grow.

■ **Did you know?**   In 1994, 25% of the FFVs on U.S. roads used methanol for fuel and 2% used ethanol. In 2009, the percentage of FFVs using methanol had dropped to 0%, but the percentage using ethanol increased to 74%.[ix]

Anne Korin and Gal Luft, in their excellent book *Turning Oil into Salt: Energy Independence Through Fuel Choice*,[x] compare the situation today with oil to the situation with salt hundreds of years ago. Salt held a monopoly on food preservation, and was thus an important strategic commodity. Countries with salt mines derived wealth from their salt exports, and sometimes wars were fought over access to salt. But eventually salt evolved from a strategic

---

[4] A great deal of background information on the Open Fuel Standard may be found at www.openfuelstandard.org/.

[5] According to the National Automobile Dealers Association, the average price of a new car sold in the United States was $29,200 in 2010.

commodity into simply a commodity, because refrigeration broke salt's monopoly on food preservation. That is the goal of the Open Fuel Standard: to break oil's monopoly on the transportation system and convert it from its present status as a strategic commodity into simply a commodity.

Summary

There is still a lot of oil that will be produced in the coming years, but the world must begin planning for the end of the oil age. Further, countries that are heavily dependent on oil imports face special economic risks that should be mitigated against. To the greatest extent possible, we should begin to encourage a transition away from oil toward conservation and alternatives. I have suggested three proposals designed to accelerate this transition:

- A revenue-neutral scheme that would shift taxes from income taxes toward gasoline taxes

- Expansion of domestic drilling, with contracts written such that governments benefit increasingly from climbing oil prices, and a significant portion of those revenues dedicated to programs that decrease dependence on oil

- Support for an Open Fuel Standard that would diversify the fuel supply by enabling a wider variety of fuels easier access to the transportation fuel market

Trillions of dollars' worth of oil remains in the ground. We should leverage the remaining endowment of oil and some of those oil revenues to proactively wean ourselves from oil dependence. The realistic alternative to this is that we will simply continue to be highly dependent on petroleum until the end of the oil age, which will be met with price surges that crush global economies. Further, failure to act heightens the risk that a new generation of sons and daughters will march off to fight resource wars because of our failure to plan ahead.

References

[i] Energy Information Administration (EIA), "Crude Oil Production," release date July 28, 2011, www.eia.gov/dnav/pet/pet_crd_crpdn_adc_mbblpd_a.htm.

[ii] Minerals Management Service (MMS), *Assessment of Undiscovered Technically Recoverable Oil and Gas Resources of the Nation's Outer Continental Shelf, 2006*, February 2006, www.boemre.gov/revaldiv/PDFs/2006NationalAssessment Brochure.pdf.

[iii] EIA, "Impact of Limitations on Access to Oil and Natural Gas Resources in the Federal Outer Continental Shelf," *Annual Energy Outlook 2009*, January 2009, www.eia.gov/oiaf/aeo/otheranalysis/aeo_2009analysispapers /aongr.html.

[iv] EIA, *Analysis of Crude Oil Production in the Arctic National Wildlife Refuge*, Report No. SR-OIAF/2008-03, May 2008, www.eia.gov/oiaf/servicerpt /anwr/methodology.html.

[v] U.S. Department of Energy, Alternative Fuels and Advanced Vehicles Data Center (AFDC), "E85 FFVs in Use in U.S.," accessed January 25, 2012, www.afdc.energy.gov/afdc/data/docs/ffvs_in_use.xls.

[vi] EIA, Natural Gas Spot and Futures Prices (NYMEX), accessed January 25, 2012, updated weekly at www.eia.gov/dnav/ng/ng_pri_fut_s1_d.htm; EIA, Spot Prices, accessed January 25, 2012, updated weekly at www.eia.gov /dnav/pet/pet_pri_spt_s1_d.htm.

[vii] CME Group, CBOT Denatured Fuel Ethanol Futures, accessed January 25, 2012, real-time market updates at www.cmegroup.com/trading/energy /ethanol/cbot-ethanol.html.

[viii] Methanex, Methanol Price, "North America (Valid January 1 - 31, 2012)," accessed January 25, 2012, updated monthly at www.methanex.com /products/methanolprice.html.

[ix] U.S. Department of Energy, AFDC, "AFVs in Use: 1995–2009," accessed January 25, 2012, www.afdc.energy.gov/afdc/data/docs/afvs_in_use.xls.

[x] Anne Korin and Gal Luft, *Turning Oil into Salt: Energy Independence Through Fuel Choice* (BookSurge Publishing, 2009).

Investing in Cleantech

A Guide to Technical Due Diligence

The field of greentech could be the largest economic opportunity of the twenty-first century. There's never been a better time than now to start or accelerate a greentech venture.

—John Doerr, American venture capitalist, 2006

From 2004 to 2010, over $700 billion was invested globally in renewable energy projects by governments, private investors, private companies, and institutional investors (see Figure 10-1).[i] Of course, investing involves risks, and sometimes unforeseen factors cause an investment to underperform or even to fail. But, all too often, renewable energy investments have failed for reasons that should have been foreseen by investors had they done sufficient due diligence on the company and their technology.

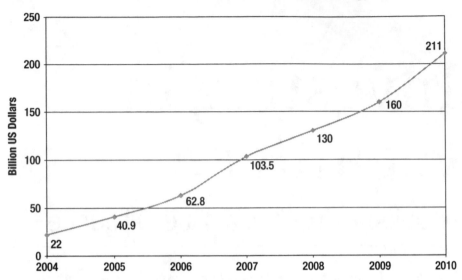

Figure 10-1. Global new investment in renewables 2004–2010 (Data source: *Renewables 2011 Global Status Report*)

Given the levels of investment at stake, it's a common occurrence for companies to announce that they have developed the key to solving the world's energy crisis. Maybe they claim they can convert any sort of waste biomass into gasoline at very low cost. Or perhaps they claim they can produce renewable electricity at a price competitive with that of producing coal.

■ **Did you know?** Solar photovoltaic (PV) capacity has increased by a factor of seven in the past five years.[ii]

In my experience, the vast majority of renewable energy startups are guilty of making exaggerated claims, and the reason they usually make such claims is that they believe it enhances their ability to raise money. These sorts of claims come in varying degrees of credibility, from outright fraud to misleading or misinformed statements to credible claims from companies with real potential. But exaggerated claims are exactly what you want to uncover as an investor interested in investing money in a technology. In order to sort what is real and credible from what is essentially hype, a certain level of due diligence must be applied.

Due diligence is the responsibility of those who are interested in becoming stakeholders in a process. Stakeholders could be private investors, corporations, institutional investors, or government entities. Journalists who wish to maintain journalistic credibility should also conduct due diligence as they report on new technologies. However, many people don't know where to start the process of performing due diligence. This chapter provides an overview of the due diligence process regarding potential new renewable energy investments. The same approach is generally applicable to investing in nonrenewable energy projects as well, but the focus of this chapter is on the relatively young field of cleantech[1] investing.

Understand the Hurdles That Come with Each Step

All projects begin with an idea, which is first subjected to preliminary screening. Following screening, a decision may be made to conduct some small-scale laboratory experiments to validate certain aspects of the idea.

But it is a huge challenge to take results that were achieved in a laboratory and scale them up through a pilot facility to a demonstration facility to a commercial facility (see Figure 10-2). Each of those steps is a gate, and each of those gates has the potential to halt a technology from advancing to the next gate.

Skipping steps—for instance, jumping from the lab to a demonstration facility—greatly lowers the probability of success while putting much more money at risk. For instance, if each step has only a 50% chance of successfully demonstrating the technology (and, in my experience, the probability of success is typically lower), then advancing the three steps from lab scale to pilot scale to a demonstration facility to a full-scale commercial facility has a probability of failure of nearly 90%.

---

[1] The terms *greentech*, which is short for "green technology," and *cleantech* are synonymous.

Figure 10-2. Common steps in the development of a project

This is why the least risky strategy for investors is to fund each step and only proceed if the results at that step are completely satisfactory. The disadvantage of this strategy for investors is that it takes more time and, if commercialization ultimately occurs, will have been costlier than if some steps were skipped.

To illustrate, presume that each step requires a tenfold increase in investment. If laboratory experiments cost $1 million, then the cost of the pilot plant would be $10 million, the cost of the demonstration plant would be $100 million, and the cost of the commercial plant would be $1 billion. The piloting and demonstration scale testing together may cost $110 million, but most of the time the decision will be made not to advance to the commercialization scale for various technical or economic reasons that are often uncovered at smaller scale. Jumping straight from the laboratory to commercialization could save $110 million in this case, but doing so would place the $1 billion commercial plant at much greater risk of failure. Thus, an investor is at far less risk to fund five different pilot plants, and then only proceed to funding a demonstration plant based on the most promising pilot plant trials. Passing through each gate greatly enhances the chance of success at the next stage of scale-up.

■ **Did you know?** Globally, there are over 80 publicly traded companies whose primary business is production of renewable energy.

Companies sometimes get large loan guarantees or grants from governments and then proceed to skip some of the steps because some of the financial risk has been shifted away from the private investors. It is not surprising that many of the companies that take this route eventually go out of business.

LEVELS OF SCALE

Technologies must be scaled up if they are to compete with petroleum and coal. As a facility grows larger in size, the cost per unit of product tends to decline for reasons commonly referred to as *economies of scale*. This cost decline is important in the low-margin commodity fuel business. Producing fuel at a pilot or demonstration scale is important for purposes of proving the viability of a technology, but a commercial facility will ultimately be required for producing competitively priced fuel.

How large is a commercial facility relative to a demonstration facility? There are no hard-and-fast rules defining the scale of these particular facilities; one person's commercial facility may be another person's demonstration facility. But for renewable fuel projects, I think of lab experiments as consisting of one aspect of a technology at scales of ounces or milliliters.

Piloting moves up into scales of pounds or liters per day and incorporates more pieces of the process into the experiments. Demonstration facilities reach the realm of barrels per day (1 barrel = 42 gallons) and typically are integrated facilities designed to demonstrate that all aspects of the technology work—in conjunction with each other—at that particular scale.

A liquid-fuel facility producing 10 barrels a day (150,000 gallons per year) is demonstration size; one that produces 1,000 barrels a day is on the low end of commercial size. To put those numbers into perspective, the average size of a corn ethanol plant in the U.S. is just over 4,000 barrels per day, and the average size of an oil refinery in the U.S. is 125,000 barrels per day.

Interviewing the Company

As you dig for information, generally the first people you will encounter are those who are promoting the company. The information they provide will be carefully controlled and very optimistic. What you really want to do ultimately is talk to an operator or technician who is involved in the day-to-day operation of the process. They are the people who can tell you about potentially significant issues.

The Secrecy Agreement

Before you even get to ask questions about a technology, you may be asked to sign a secrecy agreement or nondisclosure agreement. This is a legitimate and necessary step for companies that wish to protect against someone copying their technology and starting a competing company, or leaking proprietary information to competitors. Signing a secrecy agreement will give you access to information you might never obtain otherwise, and you will often find out very quickly that what companies tell you privately is different from what they state in their press releases.

On the other hand, many companies that are out promoting their technology and searching for investors will answer many questions before asking you to sign a secrecy agreement—and ideally you want to learn as much as you can before signing an agreement.

Of course, if you are a reporter doing an investigative story, you would not sign a secrecy agreement. You are just going to have to dig a little harder to find answers to your questions.

First Questions

The most important thing you want to learn is where the technology currently stands. The first question to ask is, "At what scale has this process been demonstrated?" But that's just a start, because you likely will get misleading and incomplete answers. You may not be told, for example, that the company only simulated some parts of the process. For instance, a biomass gasifier produces synthesis gas (syngas), but there can be problems with the gas quality because of tar formation. If a simulated syngas is used in lab or piloting experiments (e.g., bottled hydrogen and carbon monoxide are sometimes mixed together to produce the syngas), the tar issue can be conveniently ignored in the lab and yet be an intractable problem at a larger scale.

Did you know? There are approximately 500 biofuel companies in the world.[iii]

So you have to dig into the details. You want to know the scale of the process that has been demonstrated, and you also want to know how many consecutive hours it has been run, as well as whether runs have been repeated for confirmation. You want to find out the source of the raw materials and the composition of the final product.

Ask the company to provide an independent chemical analysis of the product. Often, what a company calls "renewable oil" or "renewable diesel" doesn't remotely meet the specifications for the petroleum counterparts. Ask about the nature of byproducts and waste products as well. Product quality issues and waste disposal issues have both bankrupted companies attempting to commercialize a process.

Know the Limits of Computer Modeling

Next you have to ask about the assumptions that are being used to model a commercial plant. What is the scale-up factor between what has actually been demonstrated and what a commercial plant will be? What are the production volumes in each case? How were the costs estimated for construction of a commercial plant? Have they attempted to skip steps in the scale-up process? (Going from lab or small pilot scale to small commercial scale with biomass-based processes, for example, is a red flag to me.)

If they are running at lab or small pilot scale and projecting their production costs for a commercial plant, I generally don't take those numbers seriously. There are just too many hurdles between the lab and commercial scale. Small lab-scale problems often become much bigger problems at demonstration scale.

You want to clearly distinguish between how much of the process has actually been proven and how much has been simulated with computer models. You also want to understand the basis of the model and how it was validated. Some companies will argue that you can prove a technology through modeling. In fact, the reverse is true: you prove a model by actually demonstrating that the process gives results consistent with the model. But some companies will present model results as if they represent reality.

THE CHALLENGE OF SCALING UP

Some readers may wonder why a process that works at a small scale would fail to work at a larger scale. This is really more specific to processes that require heating and chemical reactions, and biomass-based processes generally fall into this category. Scale-up is less technically challenging for a technology such as solar photovoltaics, which behaves essentially the same for 1 solar panel as it does for a system of 100 panels.

But processes that scale by creating larger and larger reactors are quite different. To illustrate, consider the act of cooking a single turkey in an oven. Heating elements surround the turkey and ensure a fairly uniform temperature profile within the oven. But now assume that you want to scale up this process to cook 1,000 turkeys per hour. If you were to duplicate this process in 1,000 different ovens, you would require mass production to produce very cheap ovens to keep capital costs low. This is analogous to the way solar power is scaled. But large industrial reactors are not mass-produced, so the analog to a biomass-based process would be to cook all of the turkeys in one large oven (which should be cheaper than 1,000 small ovens). The challenges then are easy to imagine. Turkeys of different sizes may cook at different rates. Some parts of the oven may be hotter than others. What could result in this case is a process that produces some turkeys that are overcooked, some that are just right, and some that are undercooked.

The same is true when trying to scale up a process to produce biofuel. As a reactor grows larger, the temperature and flow will start to deviate from those in a smaller reactor. There may be hot spots and cold spots within the reactor, and there may be locations that are better mixed than others. Any of these factors can lead to the production of undesirable byproducts (like overcooked and undercooked turkeys) and an ultimate failure of the process at a larger scale.

Models are merely guides that are used to help design processes at various stages of development; a model won't tell you whether a process will work or not. It will give you some guidance, but ultimately you have to take the results from the model and actually run the process. That is how you prove a technology (and validate a computer model). Boeing doesn't build a fleet of airplanes based on a model. It uses the model as guidance for building a prototype. Then it refines the model based on how the prototype performs, and then modifies the prototype—through several iterations if needed. In short, models provide feedback for testing, and the testing is fed back to validate and improve the model.

Feedstock, Economic Assumptions, and Energy Requirements

You need to ask about the presumed source, availability, and cost of the feedstock that will be used. Many biomass projects make unreasonable estimates of their future feedstock costs. Just because a lot of biomass ends up in municipal dumps each year, does not mean that this biomass is well-suited for the particular technology. Wood, grass, and municipal solid waste can behave very differently in specific processes.

An assumption of a long-term supply of cheap, free, or even negatively priced biomass is the most common assumption behind claims from companies that they can produce fuel for $1 or $2 per gallon. It is true that sources of free or cheap biomass do exist, but companies often fail to take into consideration (or don't disclose) the cost of processing that biomass when they make their estimates. For instance, there is a lot of standing wood in the U.S. that has been killed by the pine bark beetle which has been cited as "a plentiful and cheap feedstock,"[iv] but it still costs money to process those trees and move them to a facility for conversion into fuel.

You should ask a series of "What if?" questions, such as "What if the biomass costs $100 per ton?" Ask, too, about the project risks associated with a crop failure that drastically reduces the supply of biomass. It is important to understand whether the process can run on a wide variety of feedstocks; in my experience, companies always claim that their process can do so, but they don't have any proof. Ask to see test results. Do not accept an assumption that wood chips will behave the same as wheat straw.

However, some special considerations apply. For example, just a few years ago, polysilicon shortages threatened the economics of a number of solar power projects, but additional manufacturing facilities that subsequently came online alleviated this shortage and are presently the driving force behind falling solar panel prices. The problem wasn't a shortage of the raw material required to produce the polysilicon, but rather a shortage of facilities to turn the raw material into polysilicon. A company attempting to enter the market during the polysilicon shortage could have legitimately projected that its costs would fall, assuming it knew that additional manufacturing facilities would soon be completed.

Biomass projects have different dynamics. Unlike silicon, biomass has been grown and harvested with modern techniques for decades. The costs for purpose-grown biomass are fairly well-characterized. After all, people have been growing hay for livestock and trees for pulp and timber for a very long time. So I typically evaluate what the economics of the process look like by comparing the cost of the biomass to the cost of hay (i.e., purpose-grown biomass that is currently produced commercially).

The energy requirement for the process is a very important issue, but one that is not always easy to dissect. You want to know the types of energy inputs required by the process, as well as the energy balance for the process (how much and what kind of energy was consumed relative to how much energy was produced).[2]

Companies often omit all sorts of energy inputs when stating an energy balance. Some examples are the energy inputs required to grow and transport biomass, and the energy inputs required to move the fuel to the customer. Companies often assume that they will burn waste biomass in the commercial plant, and thus they assume low external energy inputs. When a company claims an energy return of five or ten to one for a renewable process, it's usually making those kinds of assumptions. Verify whether the company has actually shown that its waste biomass has been extensively tested to produce process energy.

Talk to Competitors and Former Employees

It is important to find out about predecessors and competitors. Very little is invented from scratch; almost everyone builds off of previous work. First ask the startup company you're evaluating questions such as "Who did similar work previously?" "Who is doing similar work now?" "How is your work better than that of others?" Then ask their competitors the same questions. This is a very effective tool for sniffing out problems. Competitors are always happy to tell you what is wrong with the other company's process. Many companies will insist that their process is so unique they have no competitors, but that is rarely true in practice.

Talk to former employees. If the company has skeletons in its closet, former employees may tell you where to look (especially if they are disgruntled). The difficulty here is that they may not be willing to go on the record, but they can provide leads. For instance, a former employee will likely be bound by a confidentiality agreement, but they may be free to point you to a specific bit of information in a patent that doesn't mesh with the company's public claims.

Bring up the company in casual conversation with industry sources and see where it leads. I did this on a recent trip, and a refinery manager relayed to

---

[2] The energy balance has to be understood in context. It may be economically attractive to consume 2 BTUs of coal to produce 1 BTU of liquid fuel even though the energy balance is poor.

me that many years ago he had worked for the company I mentioned. The company was claiming a new breakthrough in converting natural gas into gasoline, so I mentioned this process to him, to which he said, "Yes, it works, but the gasoline has a very high aromatic content." That was the first time I had heard that particular revelation, and it was quite important because many countries have gasoline specifications that require very low aromatic content. Hence, this was a potential show-stopper, and at the least a good bit of information to have as I continued to investigate the company.

Read Between the Lines and Use Common Sense

Parse each sentence in a prospectus carefully. Claims like "Ideally suited for landfill waste" could mean "Our economics only work if we are getting paid to take the biomass." A statement like "Perfect for co-locating with a power plant" could mean "We need cheap steam."

Determine if the company has patents or patents pending. If so, find out what the patent or patent application numbers are. Find out if "patent pending" means "Someday we hope to get around to filing for a patent."

A prospectus will often contain specific technical claims that may be outside of your particular area of expertise. For instance, a company may claim to be able to run a car on water. You may not have the technical foundation to scientifically evaluate the claim, but you can often find lots of information freely available on the Internet that breaks down the technical issues. You can also consult with someone who knows the field. Sometimes you can locate a free opinion. You may see a quote from a researcher who is skeptical of the process. Contact that person for further information.

Beyond the technical questions, there are obvious signs that you can look for when evaluating a company's claims. Does the company issue press releases for fairly trivial developments? Do the company's claims appear to be grandiose? If the answer to either question is yes, this is a warning sign. Most companies making grandiose claims do not deliver on those claims. Simply applying the maxim "if it seems too good to be true, then it probably is" can frequently identify questionable companies.

Summary

To break this chapter down into a short "cheat sheet," here is a summary of some important questions that potential investors in a new energy project should ask the company that is seeking investment in the project (the last two questions are specific to biomass facilities). Try to corroborate answers by talking to former employees or competitors.

1. At what scale has the process been actually demonstrated, and is the process currently running?

2. What is the source of raw materials for the process?

3. What was being done with the product produced previously? Was it being sold? (Ideally, you are looking for a product that has been shipped to and tested by customers.)

4. What are the primary energy inputs into the process, and what is the energy balance?

5. Will there be intermediate scale-up steps before a commercial facility is built?

6. What are the key assumptions for a commercial facility (e.g., size, cost of production, location, need for subsidies)?

7. What are the patent or patent application numbers relevant to the process?

8. What prior work is most similar to yours, and who are your perceived competitors?

9. What is the presumed source and cost of biomass for a commercial facility?

10. Has the process been proven on the specific biomass that is proposed for the commercial plant?

If you manage to get honest answers to those questions, you will be well on your way to burrowing through the hype to understand the true potential of the process.

References

[i] Renewable Energy Policy Network for the 21st Century (REN21), *Renewables 2011 Global Status Report (GSR)*, July 12, 2011, www.ren21.net/Portals/97/documents/GSR/REN21_GSR2011.pdf.

[ii] Ibid.

[iii] Advanced Biofuels USA, "Companies Involved with Advanced Biofuels and Biofuels," accessed January 26, 2012, http://advancedbiofuelsusa.info/resources/companies-involved-with-advanced-biofuels.

[iv] Mark Jaffe, "The Deaths of Lodgepole Pine Trees Have a Silver Lining," *The Denver Post*, April 27, 2010, www.denverpost.com/ci_14964107.

The Race to Replace Oil

Alternative Transportation Fuels

The Stone Age did not end for lack of stone, and the Oil Age will end long before the world runs out of oil.

—Sheikh Yamani, Saudi oil minister, 1962–1986

The above quote from the former Saudi oil minister is rather well known, and it is popular among those who believe that technology will inevitably solve the problem of oil depletion. In fact, the Stone Age ended because the Bronze Age began. Thus, the implication is that the Oil Age will end because of the rise of the Fusion Age or the Solar Age or the Biofuels Age.

This chapter examines some of the contenders that seek to displace oil's use as a transportation fuel either through suitable substitution or as a drop-in replacement.[1]

---

[1] An *oil substitute* is a substance whose chemical properties differ from those of oil but that can function in the same role as oil (e.g., ethanol and gasoline). Using this substitute may require some modification to engines and/or infrastructure. A *drop-in replacement* is chemically the same as the hydrocarbons it is replacing, and thus requires no special modifications (e.g., hydrocracked renewable diesel and petroleum diesel).

Petroleum Fuel Alternatives

Oil rose to prominence as the world's dominant transportation fuel for three key reasons: cost, convenience, and abundance. In the early years of the Oil Age, the cost to extract and refine petroleum was low enough that it was easily affordable for the general public. Oil had ideal characteristics as fuel for internal combustion engines and for aviation, and its relative abundance and affordability helped to spur demand as people began to enjoy unprecedented mobility.

As oil supplies have been depleted, some of the characteristics that made oil so attractive for so long have lost much or all of the advantage relative to some of the oil substitutes. There are numerous substitutes for the transportation fuels produced from a barrel of oil,[2] but they generally suffer from high cost, are inconvenient compared to oil, or simply aren't widely available. Even today, some substitutes are gaining appeal for use in cars and airplanes as oil prices increase, but many suffer from issues of insufficient scalability or negative environmental impacts.

As oil depletes, there are two broad transportation fuel categories that will need to be replaced: gasoline for spark-ignition engines, and distillates such as diesel and jet fuel. Let's first look at the candidates to replace petroleum-derived gasoline.

Petroleum Gasoline Alternatives

There are a number of potential gasoline alternatives. Some are not yet widely used, while others, such as ethanol, have grown immensely in importance over the past decade.

Ethanol

Ethanol is the most widely utilized liquid fuel gasoline substitute in the world. Ethanol is used as a 10% blend in literally hundreds of millions of vehicles worldwide, and over 20 million vehicles globally are capable of

---

[2] In addition to the transportation fuels—gasoline, diesel, and jet fuel—a barrel of oil produces heating oil, lubricants, waxes, petroleum coke, and gases that provide raw materials for the plastics industry.

running on either pure ethanol or a blend of 85% ethanol and 15% gasoline. If you own a vehicle in the U.S., it is almost certain that you have operated that vehicle on an ethanol blend at some point.

Global production of ethanol in 2010 was just over 23 billion gallons,[i] which was the energy equivalent of almost 1% of global oil demand.[3] Ethanol contains two carbon atoms and is the second simplest alcohol after methanol. Ethanol can be made from a wide variety of starting materials, including starches, sugars, or cellulosic biomass.

Ethanol has some key differences from gasoline. First, the energy density is only about two-thirds that of gasoline, which means that a greater volume of ethanol is required to travel an equivalent distance. Ethanol is also hygroscopic, meaning that it will absorb water from the air. This can be an issue when transporting or storing ethanol, as well as when using ethanol blends in boats.

On the plus side, the octane rating for ethanol is higher than for gasoline. *Octane rating* is a measure of the tendency of a fuel to preignite when it is compressed. Higher-octane fuels are more resistant to preignition, which allows them to be used in an engine with a higher compression ratio. Engines with higher compression ratios are able to attain higher thermal efficiency, and therefore the fuel efficiency penalty from using ethanol is potentially less severe than might be estimated based simply on the energy content. This will be discussed in more detail in Chapter 13, which covers corn ethanol.

Ethanol from Carbohydrates

Most of the ethanol produced in the world today is made from carbohydrates. In tropical countries like Brazil and India, the carbohydrate source is often sugar or byproducts of the sugar-manufacturing process. However, ethanol can be produced from a wide variety of starches and sugars—from things like fruits, potatoes, wheat, or sorghum.

---

[3] Per the *BP Statistical Review of World Energy 2011*, oil consumption was 87.3 million barrels per day. One barrel of oil has the energy content of 5.8 million BTUs; 1 barrel of ethanol has the energy content of 3.2 million BTUs.

■ **Did you know?** Ethanol that is used for fuel is chemically identical to ethanol that is in beer, wine, and hard liquor. In some countries, ethanol that is destined for use as fuel is rendered undrinkable (denatured) by mixing it with poisonous additives before it leaves the ethanol refinery.

In the U.S., most ethanol is made from starch contained in corn. When starch is the feedstock, it must first be converted to simple sugars by using enzymes.[4] The sugar solution is then fermented with yeast to produce a solution of ethanol in water and a carbon dioxide byproduct. When the ethanol is to be used as fuel, it is purified to remove the water and then usually blended with gasoline.

Ethanol from sugarcane has long been one of the most competitive biofuels relative to oil. A major factor in the production of low-cost sugarcane ethanol is that the fuel that powers the ethanol plant is essentially free. When sugarcane is processed, it is washed, chopped, and shredded so the soluble sugar can be removed. This leaves behind a fibrous waste product called *bagasse*.

As a result of the processing, the bagasse is relatively clean. This, plus the fact that the bagasse is a waste product from the sugarcane processing facility, makes it an ideal fuel for a biomass boiler. Use of the bagasse to produce process energy minimizes the fossil fuel inputs required to process sugarcane and subsequently produce ethanol, and the sugarcane ethanol production process is therefore less sensitive to petroleum price spikes.[5]

Thus, sugarcane ethanol is an attractive candidate to displace some gasoline supplies when produced in regions with sufficient sunlight and ample rainfall. However, the price of a fuel derived from a crop that has a competing use as food can have increased volatility due to changes in demand for the feedstock. This was the case in recent years with sugarcane ethanol as world sugar prices have surged since 2009. A greater portion of the sugarcane harvest was used to produce sugar for sale, and this in turn drove up the price of sugarcane ethanol—making it less competitive on world markets.

---

[4] An enzyme is a protein that speeds up a chemical reaction.

[5] There is no reason corn ethanol producers couldn't also use biomass for power, but as long as low-price natural gas is available, it will usually be a more economical option.

Ethanol from Cellulose

Cellulose is an important component of plants. It is made up of a long series of sugar molecules that are bonded together in a chain. In 1819, Henri Braconnot, a French chemist, discovered how to release the sugars from cellulose by treating biomass with sulfuric acid. Once the sugars are released, the solution can be fermented to ethanol in processes that are very similar to those used to produce corn ethanol or sugarcane ethanol. Ethanol production via this process is called cellulosic ethanol and was used by the Germans in 1898 to first commercialize cellulosic ethanol production from wood.

The technique came to the U.S. in 1910, when Standard Alcohol Company built a cellulosic ethanol plant in South Carolina to convert lumber mill waste into ethanol. Standard Alcohol later built a second plant in Louisiana. Each plant was capable of producing over 5,000 gallons of ethanol per day from wood waste, and both were in production for several years.

Many attempts have been made to commercialize cellulosic ethanol over the past century, but there has been little success in developing cellulosic ethanol as a cost-competitive energy option. Because of the extra steps involved relative to corn or sugarcane ethanol, capital and operating costs are higher for cellulosic ethanol than for ethanol derived from carbohydrates.

The yields per ton of biomass are also lower than when using a carbohydrate feedstock, and the ethanol that is produced from the cellulosic ethanol process is at a far lower concentration (i.e., it contains more water) than that of corn ethanol. That means that a greater quantity of energy is required in order to purify the ethanol.

Because of the low energy density of biomass and the energy required to produce ethanol from cellulose, I don't view cellulosic ethanol as an economical, scalable replacement for gasoline. But it might be produced economically in some niche situations. One could be a situation in which there is waste heat available—perhaps from a power plant—near a central source of cheap waste biomass. Another alternative could be if there is a cheap source of steam available that can't be better utilized in proximity to a source of waste biomass.

▨ **Did you know?** The two most popular methods for converting cellulose into sugars for fermentation to ethanol are chemical hydrolysis and enzymatic hydrolysis. The former typically uses an acid like sulfur acid and the latter uses enzymes such as those used by cattle to digest grass.

Regardless of the method used to produce it, ethanol can serve as a suitable replacement for gasoline in a combustion engine, and the volume of ethanol being utilized as transportation fuel is growing rapidly.

Methanol

Methanol is the simplest alcohol and one of the world's most widely used commodity chemicals. Global capacity of methanol is similar to that of ethanol at 24 billion gallons.[ii] Most of the world's methanol is produced from natural gas, but it can be produced from other materials, such as coal or biomass.

Methanol's strength is that it is cheap to produce relative to both gasoline and ethanol. It is not unusual for methanol to trade at a 20% or greater discount to ethanol and gasoline per equivalent unit of energy.

Methanol's disadvantages are similar to the disadvantages of ethanol relative to gasoline. Methanol has a lower energy density than gasoline (about 2 gallons of methanol are equal to the energy content of 1 gallon of gasoline), and it is more corrosive than ethanol (which is more corrosive than gasoline).

Methanol is also much more toxic than ethanol. Despite the toxicity, methanol is commonly sold in the U.S. as a windshield washer solution. Further, methanol degrades much more quickly than gasoline (which not only is toxic but also contains carcinogenic compounds) in the environment as it is quickly consumed by microorganisms.

Like ethanol, methanol has a much higher octane rating than gasoline and could benefit from running in engines with higher compression ratios. Methanol has been used in high-performance race cars in the U.S. for many years, and was tested extensively in California from 1980 to 2005 as a part of the California Methanol Program.

THE ZUBRIN EXPERIMENT: METHANOL VERSUS GASOLINE

Aerospace engineer and methanol enthusiast Robert Zubrin—author of *Energy Victory: Winning the War on Terror by Breaking Free of Oil* (Prometheus Books, 2007)—recently documented an experiment in which he ran his 2007 Chevy Cobalt on 100% methanol.[iii] The car was not a flex-fuel car, but Zubrin reportedly made only two modifications to the vehicle before conducting the experiment. He replaced a fuel pump seal with a material that is methanol compatible (retail cost was reported to be 41 cents) and he advanced the ignition timing to take advantage of methanol's high octane rating.

Zubrin reported that the car's fuel economy was 36.3 miles per gallon on gasoline (which contained 10% ethanol), 32.3 miles per gallon on a 60% methanol/40% gasoline blend, and 24.6 miles per gallon on 100% methanol. But because methanol is much cheaper than gasoline, his reported cost per mile was almost 30% lower on 100% methanol than on gasoline.

Zubrin also tested the vehicle emissions on both gasoline and methanol, and found that hydrocarbon and NOx (nitrogen oxides) emissions were substantially lower on methanol. Carbon monoxide was higher, but still well under the emission limit.

While Zubrin's experiment is encouraging for those who believe that methanol could be an excellent gasoline substitute, I would caution readers against attempting to replicate this experiment in a vehicle that isn't designed for methanol. Methanol can attack certain components of the fuel system over time, and therefore long-term use requires that compatible materials be used.

In response to the oil crisis of 1979, the state of California began to investigate gasoline alternatives. After considering ethanol, methanol, natural gas, electricity, hydrogen, and propane, the California Energy Commission (CEC) determined that "methanol stood out clearly as having the best potential for replacing petroleum on a widespread basis."[iv]

The state partnered with automakers to build a fleet of flex-fuel vehicles (FFVs) that could operate on M85 (a blend of 85% methanol and 15% gasoline). Major fuel retailers participated in the program to provide a limited fuel infrastructure for the vehicles.

By 1997 there were over 21,000 M85 FFVs in the U.S., most of which were in California. At that time, the state had over 100 methanol refueling stations providing fuel for light-duty vehicles as well as hundreds of methanol-fueled transit and school buses.[v]

While drivers were reportedly satisfied with the performance of the methanol FFVs, the limited fueling infrastructure proved frustrating for drivers attempting to keep the vehicles fueled. After 25 years and 200,000,000 miles of operation, California terminated the methanol program in 2005. This was also the year that the Renewable Fuel Standard was passed in the U.S., which shifted the advantage strongly to corn ethanol with a national mandate that methanol has never enjoyed in the U.S.

▓ **Did you know?** In the U.S., the number of ethanol FFVs overtook the number of methanol FFVs in 1999, and surpassed the number of compressed natural gas (CNG) vehicles in 2002.

Methanol is used as automotive fuel in China, but in the U.S. it has never had the widespread political support of corn ethanol. Thus, some of the issues—such as compatibility with automobiles and fueling infrastructure—have not been addressed sufficiently for methanol as they have been for ethanol. Still, with adequate political support, methanol could make a major contribution as a long-term substitute for gasoline.

An additional advantage for methanol is that it can be used to produce di-methyl-ether (DME), which can substitute for gasoline or diesel (and will be discussed in the section "Petroleum Distillate Substitutes" a bit later in the chapter).

Higher Alcohols and Mixed Alcohols

In addition to ethanol and methanol, a number of longer-chain alcohols (higher alcohols) are also suitable for use as fuel or as a blending agent for producing reformulated gasoline. These include propanol (with three carbon atoms, or C3), butanol (C4), pentanol (C5), and others, as well as mixtures of these alcohols.

Higher mixed alcohols[6] may offer some advantages over methanol or ethanol as fuel. Reported advantages include lower corrosion rates, higher energy content and octane rating, and more favorable combustion characteristics than for ethanol and methanol. I personally tested a mixed alcohol blend in my car in 2009, and the car experienced a noticeable boost in power.[7] The blend consisted of eight alcohols ranging from methanol through octanol (C8), and I tested it with no modifications to my car.

There are three primary pathways for producing higher mixed alcohols, two of which are strictly biomass-based. The first is a platform in which starches or sugars are fermented to alcohols. This is a similar process to corn or

---

[6] Mixtures that contain methanol, ethanol, and longer-chain alcohols.

[7] The fuel I tested was called Envirolene, supplied by Mark Radosevich from Standard Alcohol Company of America. The fuel was a 30% blend of the mixed alcohol with 70% gasoline.

cellulosic ethanol production, but different microorganisms can be used to produce longer-chain alcohols. Such a process was used to make butanol long before the petrochemical route was discovered. Cobalt Technologies is currently working on a fermentation process to convert waste biomass into butanol. Cobalt is targeting the use of butanol as jet fuel instead of gasoline, as it believes the economics for jet fuel are better than those for butanol as a gasoline replacement.

The second pathway is also a fermentation platform, in which naturally occurring microbes are used to convert cellulose into chemical intermediates, which can then be converted into mixed alcohols. I actually helped develop this technology as a graduate student working for Professor Mark Holtzapple at Texas A&M in the 1990s. We used microbes from the stomachs of cattle, which are efficient digesters of cellulose. Cattle eat grass—largely cellulose—and in their digestive system a combination of microbes works to convert the cellulose into acetic, propionic, and butyric acid that the cattle then use for energy. Those acids can also be converted into mixed alcohols—ethanol, propanol, and butanol (and trace amounts of higher alcohols)—in a process called the MixAlco process. A company called Terrabon was formed in 1995 to commercialize the MixAlco process.

The final platform is a thermochemical platform, and it is not limited to biomass. In this process, carbon-containing materials (e.g., biomass, coal, natural gas, oil) are first gasified (more on gasification later in the chapter), and then a catalyst is used to convert the resulting synthesis gas into mixed alcohols. The Dow Chemical Company carried out catalyst research on this process in the 1970s and 1980s. Dow was awarded a number of patents for its alcohol catalysts. Several companies continue to pursue mixed alcohol production via this route today.

Compressed Natural Gas

Natural gas primarily consists of methane, which is the simplest hydrocarbon. Methane has the chemical formula CH_4. That is one carbon atom bonded to four hydrogen atoms. (Methanol is one carbon atom bonded to three hydrogen atoms and one OH group. The OH group is what makes it an alcohol.) When methane is burned—which means that it is reacting quickly with oxygen—it produces carbon dioxide (CO_2) and water (H_2O).

Compressed natural gas (CNG) is an alternative to gasoline that is used in approximately 13 million vehicles around the world (and is even used in diesel engines). Natural gas vehicles (NGVs) are especially popular in developing countries.

Countries like Brazil and India are well known for their sugarcane ethanol production. Less well known is the fact that Brazil and India have two of the largest NGV fleets in the world. Brazil's fleet of 1.7 million NGVs represents 13% of the world's total and is larger than the combined NGV fleets of Europe and all of North America. India's NGV fleet is just over 1 million vehicles. Neighboring Pakistan has the world's largest NGV fleet at 2.7 million vehicles, while Iran and Argentina each have nearly 2 million NGVs.

THE PICKENS PLAN

Oil tycoon T. Boone Pickens has proposed a plan that he believes could nearly cut in half the amount of money that the U.S. spends on imported oil. His proposal calls for an enormous investment in new wind turbines, which would displace some of the natural gas that is presently being used to produce electricity. This would free up more natural gas supplies for use in NVGs.

The plan consists of private investment, government investment, and legislation to reduce the risks. One of the biggest challenges for wind power in the U.S. is that many of the best locations for wind are far from population centers and thus lack major electric power transmission lines.

The Pickens Plan would have private investments funding the wind turbines, which would benefit from favorable legislation providing continued incentives for the purchase of wind-generated electricity, as well as a government investment in the transmission lines.

The final part of the plan—conversion of fleets and buses to natural gas—would also benefit from legislation that provides favorable tax incentives for the conversions and the infrastructure.

By comparison, the NGV fleet in the U.S. is only about 115,000 vehicles (of a total fleet of approximately 250 million vehicles). Europe has 1.4 million NGVs, with Italy by far leading the way with 54% of Europe's total fleet.[vi]

Advantages of natural gas relative to gasoline are that it is much cheaper and emits fewer pollutants when combusted. The U.S. Department of Energy estimates that NGVs emit 60% to 90% fewer smog-producing pollutants and 30% to 40% fewer greenhouse gas emissions than petroleum-fueled cars. Thus, some CNG advocates have even argued that natural gas can do more in the short term to reduce carbon emissions than can renewables, since the technology exists today to deploy NGVs on a large scale (and to convert coal-fired power plants to cleaner, natural gas–fired plants).

There are several disadvantages to CNG. Some opponents object that it is not a suitable replacement for gasoline since natural gas is also a depleting fossil fuel resource. While natural gas can be produced from the anaerobic digestion of biomass such as sewage sludge and landfill waste, the vast majority of the world's natural gas will continue to come from fossil resources for the foreseeable future. Thus, someone concerned about global CO_2 emissions would need to weigh the merits of the NGV against available alternatives—as well as the estimates of the future availability of natural gas.

Another disadvantage is that it can be costly to convert vehicles to run on CNG. This is especially true in the U.S., where onerous licensing requirements generally push the cost of converting a gasoline-powered car to above $10,000 per car. With conversion costs that high, one would have to drive many miles before the savings from natural gas paid for the conversion. On the other hand, fleets that drive many miles a day may find that the payback time is acceptable. However, it isn't necessarily the technology that pushes the costs up so high. Certainly the presence of millions of NGVs in developing countries (see Figure 11-1) attests to the fact that they don't have to be expensive. It is possible that changes in government regulations could greatly lower the costs of NGVs in the U.S.

Figure 11-1. The author in a natural gas-powered taxi in India

The final disadvantage of CNG is that there is insufficient CNG fueling infrastructure in many locations. Thus, CNG suffers from the same problem as many other gasoline alternatives. Even though there is a price advantage, there isn't necessarily an easy pathway to fuel your car with this cheaper alternative.

Still, NGVs are on the roads today in large numbers, and thus no new technology is required for them to displace gasoline.

Drop-in Gasoline Replacements

The final category of petroleum gasoline substitutes consists of drop-in replacements for gasoline. In this case, all of the infrastructure in existence today would be compatible, because the fuel is still gasoline; it is just derived from different feedstock.

There are several methods for producing gasoline from biomass, but most are still in the development phase. Here I will discuss some of the more widely known approaches.

One route is via flash pyrolysis of biomass and subsequent upgrading of the pyrolysis oil that is produced. With flash pyrolysis, biomass is rapidly heated to over 900°F (500°C), and the products are pyrolysis oil (also called bio-oil) and char. The pyrolysis oil is then reacted with hydrogen to produce about 30% gasoline (by weight) and nearly 10% diesel. The other products of the reaction are light gases that can be used as fuel, as well as carbon dioxide and water.

Another route is being commercialized by Virent Energy Systems, whose technique involves breaking down biomass into sugars and then utilizing an aqueous-phase reforming process to convert those sugars ultimately into hydrocarbons that are appropriate for use as gasoline, jet fuel, and diesel.

Gasoline can also be produced from methanol in a process developed by Mobil (now part of ExxonMobil) in the early 1970s. The process involves production of methanol, which is first converted to di-methyl-ether (DME)—which will be discussed in the next section—and then the DME is converted over a catalyst to gasoline-type hydrocarbons.

This process has been practiced commercially in New Zealand, and additional projects are underway based on the methanol-to-gasoline (MTG) technology. The Jincheng Anthracite Mining Group (JAMG) in China started up a plant based on ExxonMobil's MTG technology in 2009. In the U.S., DKRW Advanced Fuels is developing a project based on this technology in Wyoming.

Other companies are utilizing a biological approach to produce gasoline from biomass. In most cases, genetically modified microorganisms or algae consume sugars and then convert them into long-chain hydrocarbons in the gasoline and diesel range. Most of the companies working on this approach are still in an early development stage.

Petroleum Distillate Substitutes

The replacement of oil also means the replacement of petroleum distillates, the class of petroleum products that includes diesel, jet fuel, and fuel oil. These account for almost 30% of worldwide petroleum consumption. As with gasoline replacements, renewable distillates may be categorized as substitutes or drop-in replacements. Substitutes include biodiesel and di-methyl-ether (DME), and drop-in replacements can be produced via hydro-treating or gasification plus Fischer-Tropsch (FT) technology. Let's take a closer look.

Biodiesel

Biodiesel is derived from reacting fats like vegetable oil (sources include soybeans, oil palm, or even oil from algae) or animal fats with an alcohol like methanol. The products of the reaction are biodiesel and glycerin. The chemical structure of biodiesel is distinctly different from that of petroleum diesel. Petroleum diesel is composed of only hydrogen and carbon (hydrocarbons),[8] but biodiesel also contains oxygen. This gives biodiesel somewhat different physical and chemical properties from those of petroleum diesel.

Did you know? Modern diesel engines are capable of running on straight (unmodified) vegetable oil (SVO), but over time this leads to carbon deposits in the engine.

---

[8] Some minor additives to diesel may contain additional elements.

A key difference between biodiesel and petroleum diesel is performance in cold weather conditions. Biodiesel starts to gel and freeze at higher temperatures than does petroleum diesel. This is a disadvantage when using biodiesel in cold climates, as it can cause fuel filters to plug if the biodiesel concentration is too high. Thus, biodiesel tends to be blended at much lower levels with petroleum diesel in cold weather. The cold-weather properties would also limit the use of biodiesel in aircraft that fly at high altitudes.

A major attraction of biodiesel is that it is easy to produce. Unlike many alternative fuel technologies, an individual with a minimal amount of equipment or expertise can learn how to produce biodiesel in a garage from widely available waste cooking grease. Most alternative fuel technologies have much larger capital expenditure and expertise requirements.

Biodiesel is produced and used in numerous countries around the world, and is the most commonly used biofuel in Europe. Many countries have biofuel mandates that encourage the use of biodiesel. Global production in 2010 was 5 billion gallons (19 billion liters).[vii] Some of the major producers include Germany, France, Brazil, Argentina, and the U.S.

Di-Methyl-Ether

One fuel that can fulfill multiple functions as a petroleum substitute is di-methyl-ether (DME). DME is a gas that is classified as nontoxic and non-carcinogenic. It is a common propellant in many consumer products. DME can be used in a diesel engine, as a mixture with liquid petroleum gas (LPG) in a gasoline engine, as a substitute for propane for cooking, and even as a refrigerant.

DME is a simple compound. DME can be thought of as two methane molecules with an oxygen atom separating them. It looks like this: CH_3-O-CH_3. Two hydrocarbon groups separated by an oxygen atom is an ether; in fact, DME is the simplest ether. Note that each methane group is missing one hydrogen, which allows it to form the bond with oxygen. But when DME is burned, the products are still carbon dioxide and water, just as when methane is burned.

DME is normally produced from natural gas or coal, in a process that first makes methanol and then dehydrates the methanol. As a transportation fuel, DME has some advantages over methanol, the biggest of which are that it is nontoxic and noncorrosive. A disadvantage is that DME is a gas at room temperature, but it is easily compressed to a liquid at modest pressure.

Most of the world's DME production is in China. The Chinese have been using DME for many years, and continue to increase their DME capacity. DME allows them to convert their coal reserves into something much more desirable for them—an LPG replacement for cooking fuel and transportation fuel.

The Swedes are also at the forefront of rolling out DME as automotive fuel. The BioDME project is a partnership between the Swedish companies Chemrec and Volvo, the French company Total, and the Danish company Haldor Topsøe that is converting pulp mills into biorefineries that produce DME from waste black liquor. Volvo has announced that it is conducting studies on the performance of DME in 14 of its heavy trucks, and that it is developing an engine optimized for DME.

While DME is a promising alternative to petroleum, it suffers from the same issue as many other options: there is no distribution network, and therefore vehicles aren't being built that are optimized for DME.

Drop-in Diesel Replacements

There are two major methods of producing a hydrocarbon drop-in distillate: hydrotreating technology, and gasification followed by a reaction called the Fischer-Tropsch process.

If the drop-in fuel is produced from biomass, it is sometimes known as "green diesel." Green diesel is chemically the same as petroleum diesel, but it is made from recently living biomass. Since green diesel is composed of hydrocarbons, it can be mixed with petroleum diesel in any proportion for use as transportation fuel. Green diesel technology is frequently referred to as second-generation renewable diesel technology.

Hydrotreated Renewable Diesel

One way to make green diesel uses the same kinds of feedstocks used to make biodiesel. Instead of reacting the feedstocks with methanol, they are reacted with hydrogen in a process called hydrotreating. The products of this reaction are diesel-length hydrocarbons—green diesel—and propane (as compared to glycerin as the biodiesel byproduct).

Hydrotreating and hydrocracking technologies have long been used in the petroleum industry to convert long and complex molecules into simpler molecules ranging from those suitable for LPG applications through those suitable for use as distillate fuels.

The primary advantage of hydrotreated green diesel over biodiesel is that since the product is chemically equivalent to petroleum diesel, it can be used in diesel engines in any concentration with no modifications. The disadvantage is that the capital costs of hydrotreating equipment are much higher than the equipment required to produce biodiesel, and thus the process requires larger scale to be economical.

A disadvantage for both biodiesel and hydrotreated green diesel is that in their presently practiced forms, both are reliant on fossil fuels for a major step in their production. Biodiesel production uses methanol, and hydro-treated green diesel uses hydrogen. Both are predominantly produced today from natural gas. There are other ways to produce both methanol and hydrogen, but these methods are not presently as economical.

There are a number of commercial plants worldwide that are producing hydrotreated green diesel. Neste Oil in Finland began developing its hydrotreating technology—called NExBTL technology—in 2002, and in May 2007 started up a plant with a capacity of 50 million gallons (170,000 metric tons) per year of renewable diesel fuel from a feedstock of vegetable oil and animal fat. In November 2010, Neste Oil commissioned the largest renewable diesel refinery in Singapore. The feedstock for this plant is palm oil[9] and the capacity is 245 million gallons per year (800,000 metric tons). Neste Oil also operates a renewable diesel refinery in Rotterdam, with a capacity close to that of its Singapore facility, and which is Europe's largest renewable diesel refinery.

Some of the other companies involved in developing hydrotreated green diesel include Italian oil company Eni, Brazilian oil company Petrobras, U.S. oil company ConocoPhillips,[10] and Honeywell's UOP—which is a major provider of refinery upgrading technology.

---

[9] The environmental controversy from the expansion of palm oil plantations in Southeast Asia is well known, but discussion of it is beyond the scope of this book.

[10] Full disclosure: I worked for ConocoPhillips from 2002 to 2008, which was during the time it developed the hydrotreating technology. I also own shares in Petrobras.

Diesel from Gasification

The second major method of making a drop-in diesel replacement involves gasification and then conversion of the gas into fuel. Gasification may be thought of as a partial combustion reaction. Whereas a complete combustion reaction of biomass results in carbon dioxide and water as products, the gasification reaction stops the reaction at an intermediate stage to produce hydrogen and carbon monoxide as the major end products.

This combination of hydrogen and carbon monoxide is commonly known as synthesis gas (syngas). Syngas can be used as the foundation for producing a wide variety of chemicals, including synthetic hydrocarbons, methanol, ethanol, mixed alcohols, and DME. Syngas may also be combusted directly for power, in either stationary power or transportation applications.

Gasification is carried out on materials containing carbon and hydrogen, such as coal, natural gas, or biomass. These processes are referred to as, respectively, coal-to-liquids (CTL), gas-to-liquids (GTL), and biomass-to-liquids (BTL), and the resulting product is called "synthetic fuels" or "XTL fuels." Of the XTL processes, BTL produces the only renewable fuel (green diesel).

Did you know?   The Fischer-Tropsch process for producing liquid hydrocarbons from synthesis gas was invented in Germany in the 1920s.

Gasification has been used to commercially produce liquid fuels for decades. CTL was used during World War II by the Germans, when they had limited access to petroleum but desperately needed fuel for their military. At peak production, the Germans were producing over 5 million gallons of synthetic fuel a day.

South Africa during Apartheid had a similar experience. With sanctions restricting its petroleum supplies, South Africa followed Germany's example and turned to CTL, using its large coal reserves to produce liquid fuel. Sasol (South African Coal, Oil and Gas Corporation) operates a number of gasification facilities, including the 160,000 barrels per day (bpd) Secunda CTL facility in South Africa. In total, about 25% of South Africa's liquid fuel is produced synthetically from coal.[viii]

Shell is also a major developer of GTL technology. Shell has operated a GTL plant in Bintulu, Malaysia, since 1993, with a current capacity of nearly 15,000 bpd. In 2011, Shell commissioned the 140,000 bpd Pearl GTL plant in Ras Laffan, Qatar—by far the largest GTL plant in the world.

Capital costs are an economic challenge for all of the XTL technologies. According to the U.S. Energy Information Administration's *Annual Energy Outlook 2006*, capital costs per daily barrel of production were estimated to be $30,000 for GTL,[11] $60,000 for CTL, and $120,000 to $140,000 for BTL (more than five times the capital costs for a conventional oil refinery).

Capital costs for BTL are higher than for GTL or CTL because biomass requires more processing than coal or natural gas prior to gasification. Nevertheless, work is being done to commercialize BTL technology. Rentech, a U.S. company, completed its 10-bpd BTL demonstration unit in 2011, and has several more projects in the pipeline. UOP is providing the upgrading technology for the project.

Summary

There are numerous substitutes—both renewable and fossil-based—for gasoline and distillates. These fall into the categories of drop-in replacements and substitutes. The biggest challenge for most of the drop-in fuels is that many are higher-cost options or are still early in development.

The biggest challenge for most of the substitutes is that much of the infrastructure for transporting, dispensing, and using the fuel may be incompatible with specific alternatives. This creates a chicken-and-egg problem in which vehicles won't be built without infrastructure for delivering the fuel, and the fueling infrastructure won't be developed unless there is a market for the fuel.

One final word about scalability. While some of these options are capable of operating on a fairly large scale—as some of the CTL and GTL plants demonstrate—the scale of global oil consumption is far too great for most of the alternatives to make a major contribution toward displacing oil consumption. Thus, what is needed to close the supply–demand gap as

---

[11] These costs are likely to have all been grossly underestimated. Shell's reported cost for the 140,000 bpd Pearl Facility was at least $19 billion—$136,000 per daily barrel of production.

petroleum depletes is an approach that combines some level of petroleum replacements with some nonpetroleum transportation alternatives and a healthy dose of conservation and increased energy efficiency.

References

[i] Renewable Fuels Association (RFA), "2010 World Fuel Ethanol Production," accessed January 5, 2012, http://ethanolrfa.org/pages/World-Fuel-Ethanol-Production.

[ii] Methanol Institute, "The Methanol Industry," accessed February 11, 2012, www.methanol.org/Methanol-Basics/The-Methanol-Industry.aspx.

[iii] Robert Zubrin, "Methanol Wins," *National Review Online*, December 1, 2011, www.nationalreview.com/articles/284560/methanol-wins-robert-zubrin.

[iv] Peter Ward and Jonathan Teague (California Energy Commission), "Fifteen Years of Fuel Methanol Distribution," presented at the XI International Symposium on Alcohol Fuels, 1996, www.methanol.org/Energy/Resources/Alternative-Fuel/CEC-1996-ISAF-Fuel-Meoh-Paper.aspx.

[v] L. Bromberg and W.K. Cheng, "Methanol as an Alternative Transportation Fuel in the US: Options for Sustainable and/or Energy-Secure Transportation," MIT Sloan Automotive Laboratory, November 28, 2010, www.afdc.energy.gov/afdc/pdfs/mit_methanol_white_paper.pdf.

[vi] Natural & bio Gas Vehicle Association (NGVA) Europe, "NGVs and Refuelling Stations in Europe," accessed January 6, 2012, www.ngvaeurope.eu/downloads/statistics/20110919/1-ngvs-and-stations-in-europe-june-2011.xls.

[vii] Renewable Energy Policy Network for the 21st Century (REN21), *Renewables 2011 Global Status Report (GSR)*, July 12, 2011, www.ren21.net/Portals/97/documents/GSR/REN21_GSR2011.pdf.

[viii] Ebbie Haan (Sasol Petroleum International), "Sasol Overview," presented at the Howard Weil Energy Conference, New Orleans, March 25, 2009, www.sasol.com/sasol_internet/downloads/Howard%20Weil%20Energy%20Conference%20-%202009_1238077992064.pdf.

Oil-Free Transportation

Alternatives to the Internal Combustion Engine

*Someone's sitting in the shade today because someone planted a
tree a long time ago.*

—Warren Buffett

Liquid fuels dominated the transportation sector in the 20th century and the
first decade of the 21st century, and they will continue to dominate that
sector for at least the rest of the present decade. Over time, petroleum-
based liquid fuels will relinquish their dominance, but there is no apparent
sustainable liquid fuel option with the scalability to replace even half of
global oil consumption. As noted in the previous chapter, ethanol is the
most widely used biofuel in the world, yet the energy supplied by ethanol is
less than 1% of the energy supplied by global oil production.

In most of the developed world, the functioning of societies and economies
depends on a continuing supply of affordable oil. In many countries, there
are at present no significant oil-free transportation alternatives for industry
and commerce. Thus, development of these alternatives is critical to
minimize the risk of oil-related price and supply shocks in the future.

There are a number of oil-free transportation alternatives, some of which
have been around as long as humans have, and others that are still in

development or are just taking the first tentative steps toward commercialization. This chapter will discuss some of the more promising options for shifting transportation away from oil or oil substitutes.

Transportation Electrification

One way to greatly reduce oil's role as the dominant transportation fuel is to utilize transport that is not based on the internal combustion engine. Electric vehicles use electric motors to provide power to the wheels. There are many different kinds of electric vehicles, including electric-assisted bicycles, electric cars, and electric trains, and there are also hybrid combustion/electric cars and trains.

Hybrid Vehicles

A hybrid vehicle uses an electric motor and a gasoline (or diesel) engine to power the vehicle. The electric motor is powered by batteries, which are charged by the engine and, frequently, also by recovering energy when braking the vehicle (regenerative braking). On shorter trips, the hybrid vehicle can be operated in electric mode by draining power from the batteries. On longer trips, power ultimately shifts from the electric motor to the engine, which greatly increases the range of the vehicle.

Because of the dual sources of power, hybrids tend to be more expensive than cars with just a combustion engine. However, their advantage is that they achieve far superior fuel economy, because the efficiency of an electric motor in converting energy into power is much higher than the efficiency of a combustion engine. Thus, the cost of fuel per distance traveled is much lower with a hybrid, especially on short trips where electric mode is the predominant source of power.

Hybrids were first mass-produced in the late 1990s, and for several years the market was dominated by the Toyota Prius and Honda Insight. At that time oil prices were low, so, except for those who drove a great number of miles each year, the extra cost of the vehicles would not be recouped by the fuel savings.

This situation began to change over the course of the past decade as oil prices started to climb (see Figure 12-1). Higher fuel prices lower the number of miles that must be driven to warrant the extra expense of the car. Therefore, the economics of buying a hybrid became more attractive to greater numbers of people as fuel became more expensive. Hybrid sales have declined somewhat since 2007, but this can be attributed to the recession, as well as fuel prices that declined after 2008 (but are on the way back up).

U.S. Hybrids Sold 1999-2010

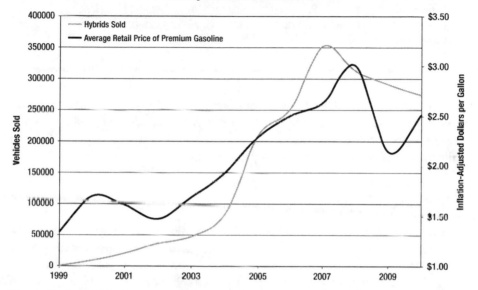

Figure 12-1. Hybrid sales grew rapidly as gasoline prices increased. (Data source: U.S. Department of Energy, Alternative Fuels and Advanced Vehicles Data Center)

From 1999 to 2003, Toyota and Honda offered the only hybrid options in the U.S. But in 2004, Ford introduced a hybrid version of the Ford Escape, and by 2010 there were almost 30 hybrid models available in the U.S. from a number of automakers. These models range from affordable options for the middle class to more expensive offerings from Lexus, Mercedes, and Porsche.

PLUG-IN HYBRIDS

Most hybrid vehicles combine gasoline engines and electric motors, although there are some diesel/electric hybrids on the market, with more in development. What these hybrids share in common is that the batteries must ultimately be charged by the engine (which includes regenerative braking).

Enter the plug-in hybrid electric vehicle (PHEV). A PHEV still has a combustion engine and an electric motor, but the batteries can also be charged by plugging into an electrical outlet. This can enable the vehicle to function as an all-electric vehicle for short commutes, and then the batteries can be recharged at home or at the workplace. This offers the potential to displace even more oil, and further save consumers money.

While some PHEVs have been available to consumers in Europe and China in the past decade, prior to 2010 most of the PHEVs on U.S. roads were from after-market conversions of the Toyota Prius. But in December 2010, General Motors began delivering the Chevrolet Volt to dealers in the U.S. While it is a common misconception that the Volt is an electric car, it is in fact the first mass-produced PHEV in the U.S.

Hybrid vehicles have become very much mainstream, yet they still comprise a small fraction of the auto fleet. But in the years ahead, rising oil prices will likely be enough incentive for greater numbers of people to opt for hybrids to insulate themselves from future price shocks.

Electric Cars

The history of electric cars dates back over 100 years. Prior to the rise of the gasoline-powered car, electricity was actually the preferred power source for an automobile. In 1900, electric cars outsold gasoline cars, but then electric cars nearly vanished for the next 90 years as gasoline-powered personal transportation took over.

Did you know?   In 1900, electric cars outsold gasoline-powered cars.

In the 1990s, as countries sought to reduce their carbon emissions and reduce demand for oil, they began to implement regulatory changes that improved the prospects for electric vehicles. Major automakers began to develop electric cars, and eventually models became available from General Motors (GM), Chrysler, Ford, Toyota, Nissan, and Honda.

All of these models were eventually withdrawn from the market, but GM's experience with its EV1 is probably the most well-known withdrawal, because it was featured in the 2006 documentary *Who Killed the Electric Car?* GM's official position was that it withdrew the EV1 from the market because it was simply too costly and was not expected to be profitable. This is reasonable considering the low cost of gasoline at that time and the higher price of the electric cars relative to gasoline-powered cars.

By the end of the 1990s, interest had shifted to hybrid vehicles, which dominated the alternative vehicle conversation for the next decade. During this time a few electric car models were available in Europe, but none to speak of in the U.S.

But development of electric cars continued, and in 2008 electric carmaker Tesla Motors began delivering the sporty (and pricey) Tesla Roadster to customers in the U.S. In December 2010, Nissan began delivery of the fully electric Nissan Leaf, which was the most affordable family-sized electric car in the U.S. in 2011. At a retail price of around $33,000 (which doesn't account for a $7,500 tax credit available for the first 200,000 electric car purchases in the U.S.), the cost is only about 10% higher than the price of the average new car in the U.S. (which was nearly $30,000 in 2011). In 2012 Mitsubishi began delivering its Mitsubishi "i" electric vehicle, which retails for around $5,000 less than the Nissan Leaf.

Unlike a plug-in hybrid there is no combustion engine providing back-up power for an electric car. The lack of a combustion engine lowers the cost relative to a hybrid, although it also limits the range of the vehicle. Further, some of the savings is lost in the cost of the batteries, which tend to be very expensive. But for those who have regular, short commutes, an electric vehicle could be a viable transportation option.

The fuel economy of an electric vehicle is far greater than for gasoline- or diesel-powered vehicles. The Alternative Fuels and Advanced Vehicles Data Center (AFDC)—a branch of the U.S. Department of Energy—reports that the fuel economy of electric vehicles is normally expressed as kilowatt hours per 100 miles (kWh/100 mi), and that a typical electric vehicle achieves 32 kWh/100 mi in city driving and 36 kWh/100 mi on the highway. One gallon of gasoline contains the energy equivalent of about 34 kWh, so these reported numbers for electric vehicles are akin to traveling 100 miles on a gallon of gasoline.

For most places in the U.S., this translates into a much lower cost per mile driven. In 2011, the average retail price of electricity to consumers (which can vary greatly) was 11.79 cents per kWh.[i] At 32 kWh/100 mi, this translates into a cost of $3.77 to travel 100 miles. In comparison, a reasonably fuel-efficient gasoline-powered car that gets 30 miles per gallon of gasoline and consumes $3.50/gallon of fuel (approximately the average price of regular gasoline in 2011) would require $11.67 per 100 miles traveled—over three times the cost per mile of the electric car.

Besides the improvement in fuel economy, another major advantage of electric cars is that the vehicles themselves emit no pollutants.[1] One of the major challenges in controlling carbon dioxide emissions and pollutants in general is that there are hundreds of millions of cars emitting pollutants in hundreds of millions of places. When electricity is used to power the car, the pollutants are relocated from the tailpipe to a central electrical generating plant. In this case, pollutants from the plant could be more easily controlled or captured than would be possible from numerous gasoline-powered cars.

FUEL CELL VEHICLES

In President George W. Bush's 2003 State of the Union address, he proposed $1.2 billion in funding for research into hydrogen-powered vehicles. Hydrogen can power a vehicle in either one of two ways: through direct combustion, similar to a compressed natural gas (CNG) vehicle, or via hydrogen fuel cells.

The direct combustion route is problematic because hydrogen has a very low volumetric energy density. That means that even a compressed tank of hydrogen would have a low range relative to most other fuels used in combustion engines.

Fuel cells, however, are much more efficient than combustion engines, and therefore have been proposed as a means of powering vehicles in the future. The fuel cell produces electricity by reacting hydrogen with oxygen. The electricity then charges batteries in the car in the same way that the electricity produced from the engine of a hybrid charges its batteries.

Hydrogen fuel cells are commonly used to produce electricity for spacecraft. They are also used in many stationary power applications. But the biggest challenge with the use of fuel cell technology in vehicles is that fuel cells are very expensive. A 2009 story in *Fortune* stated that the price of the hydrogen fuel cell–powered Honda Clarity was $300,000.[ii] Such high prices are commonly reported for fuel cell vehicles because the fuel cells themselves are expensive to produce.

After the Bush administration spent nearly $2 billion on research and development of hydrogen-powered vehicles, in 2009 the Obama administration announced that funding would be cut for the program because they did not believe that a hydrogen economy would materialize within the next two decades. So vehicles powered by fuel cells will likely remain a longer-term proposition.

---

[1] The emission profile is ultimately dependent upon the source of electricity used for powering the electric car.

This also raises the possibility of essentially pollution-free vehicles if renewable sources of electricity can be used. While today most electricity is produced from fossil fuels, production of electricity from renewable sources has grown rapidly. If renewable sources manage to displace significant fossil-derived electricity, then the emission profile for electric vehicles will decline.

Some critics have argued that in places that are heavily dependent on coal for electricity, increasing the numbers of electric cars on the roads will actually increase pollution as more coal power will likely be the source of the electricity for the cars.

One study compared the well-to-wheels (WTT)[2] emissions from the Tesla Roadster electric car to those of a similar car, the Lotus Elise.[iii] The author examined the way electricity is produced today in five different countries (Australia, China, New Zealand, U.S., and UK) and concluded that in four of the five countries, the Tesla would actually be dirtier than the internal combustion Elise because of the amount of electricity originating from coal In each country. New Zealand was the one exception in which the study concluded that the Tesla would have fewer overall emissions because of the large amount of renewable electricity produced in New Zealand.

Other studies have reached different conclusions. A 2007 paper from the Massachusetts Institute of Technology (MIT) concluded that based on the electricity generation mix in the U.S., the WTT carbon dioxide emissions from an electric vehicle would be 40% lower than those from an internal combustion engine.

In any case, there are regions today such as New Zealand where renewable sources like hydropower and geothermal are major sources of electricity. Adoption of electric cars in these areas would be expected to greatly lower net emissions from transportation. But more importantly, electric cars offer a transition pathway to cleaner energy transportation in the future while maintaining the same transportation infrastructure—even in regions that today predominantly obtain their electricity from fossil fuels.

Perhaps the biggest issue for electric carmakers to overcome is so-called range anxiety—the fear of being stranded by the vehicle. Range anxiety is a

---

[2] A well-to-wheels analysis would consider the entire life cycle of the car and the fuel used to power the car—from production to combustion to applying power to the wheels to disposal (if applicable).

particular concern when driving in cold weather or in hilly terrain, as the range of the vehicle can be lower in these circumstances.

Fear that the vehicle will leave a driver stranded with no way to easily charge it has led some to argue that electric vehicles will be predominantly used for niches like short, regular commutes and that hybrids rather than fully electric vehicles will continue to be a far more common personal transportation option.

It is too soon to project whether consumers will embrace fully electric cars. A 2010 report from J.D. Power and Associates[iv] projected that global sales of hybrids, plug-in hybrids, and battery-electric vehicles (BEVs) would total 5.2 million units in 2020—or just over 7% of the passenger vehicles projected to be sold worldwide in 2020. Nissan-Renault Chief Executive Officer Carlos Ghosn was more optimistic, projecting that electric cars will make up 10% of global sales by 2020.[v] The actual figure will ultimately be strongly influenced by oil prices.

First-year sales figures for the Nissan Leaf and the pricier Chevy Volt hybrid were both below forecasts, but in the case of the Leaf, some of the problem was due to the March 2011 tsunami in Japan that disrupted production for several months. Nevertheless, 2011 sales for both cars combined exceeded 17,000 vehicles, which is greater than first year combined sales for the Honda Insight and Toyota Prius a decade ago.

One little-known (but developing) concept that could have a major influence on the future development of electric vehicles is the potential for them to provide backup power to the electrical grid.[3] In the same way that some homes can draw power from the grid, but then also feed excess power back into the grid from solar panels (for example), the concept would allow a limited amount of electricity to be drawn from the batteries of vehicles connected to the grid. This would be net-metering, with the vehicle batteries acting as temporary power storage in the mix.

The way in which the idea is envisioned to work (and is currently being tested) is that a participant would indicate how much of their battery may be used on a particular day, and then the electric utilities could draw on that as needed. For example, if I indicated that my battery could be drawn down to 75% charge—presuming that was more than enough to cover my

---

[3] Full disclosure: my company is one of several working on this concept.

commute the next time I needed the car—the electric utility could draw it down to that level as needed. But then when excess electricity was available, the battery would be charged back up. The system could be managed by software, and in this example in the worst case I would make my commute with a 75% charge, but in the best case the battery would be fully recharged.

Imagine numerous electric cars, all plugged into the grid, from which power plants could draw electricity during periods of high demand. This would essentially be like a large battery backup for the grid, and it could reduce the need for new generating plants. It could also help smooth out the intermittency from renewable sources like wind and solar power.

A December 2010 report from business research firm Global Data estimated that the global market for vehicle-to-grid could pay $40 billion to owners of electric cars by 2020.[vi] Development of such a market would be a strong driving force for the future adoption of electric vehicles, as earnings from supplying power back to the grid could further offset the cost of ownership of an electric car.

Electric Rail

Nearly 50% of the oil consumed in the U.S. is for gasoline used by automobiles and light trucks. Diesel fuel—used mostly for heavy trucking, but also for diesel locomotives and barges—is the second largest category and accounts for another 20% of U.S. oil consumption.

Transporting freight by rail can be three to nine times as efficient as transporting it by truck, and thus simply shifting more freight from trucking to rail would reduce oil consumption. However, an even greater reduction in oil consumption would occur if rail transport were electrified and if greater numbers of people were to opt for electrified passenger rail over gasoline-powered personal transport.

The passenger and freight rail systems are already electrified across most of Europe and the large population centers of Southeast Asia, but in the U.S. the Northeast Corridor is the only major electrified rail line. This is partially a function of the population density; many European and Asian countries with extensive electric passenger rail networks have a population density five to ten times that of the U.S. Nevertheless, areas of California, Florida, Texas, and the Upper Midwest have population densities comparable to that of the Northeast Corridor's service area and could feasibly support electric passenger rail systems.

▓ **Did you know?** Fuel cell–powered vehicles are also in development for locomotives. As of this writing, the world's largest fuel cell vehicle is a hybrid locomotive.

Passenger rail is more competitive where population density is higher, so the top priority for increasing acceptance of passenger rail is simply to ensure that areas of high population density have access. The second priority would be to pursue policies that encourage people to use rail over highways. This could be done simply by shifting income taxes to fuel taxes, as discussed in Chapter 9. Finally, in order to save the most oil, routes should be electrified to the greatest possible extent.

But much of the U.S.—and indeed the world—comprises large areas of low population density. The appeal of traveling by even high-speed passenger train begins to drop off for trips longer than 300 miles, and the market share of passenger rail for trips 500 miles and longer is very low. Thus, for longer distances, passenger rail will have a more difficult time competing with other modes of transportation.

However, freight is still transported across these wide, open spaces, and the value of express freight service increases with distance. Reliably delivering vegetables from Fresno, California, to New York City in under 40 hours would attract virtually all of the market. But to do so would require some system upgrades to allow higher freight rail speeds.

Freight railroads in the U.S. already carry essential goods such as food and critical materials (over 15% of fruits and vegetables, and growing), but they are dependent on diesel fuel. Line and terminal capacity improvements plus electrification of major corridors would greatly reduce rail diesel usage. More importantly, it would allow freight currently carried by truck to be shifted to oil-free transportation. A double-stack container train could replace 280 trucks and move freight across a continent at 90 miles per hour.[vii]

Much of the freight carried by rail is essential for even minimal economic functioning. Rail quite literally "keeps the lights on" and can "put food on the table." Transforming one of the priority uses of oil—long-distance freight—to oil-free transportation using minimal amounts of domestic energy would be a major improvement in national security as rail becomes less dependent upon imported oil.

There is precedence for such a shift. During World War II, the United States faced a critical shortage of rubber, gasoline rationing, and the overseas deployment of a large number of trucks. As a result, 90% of truck freight was diverted to rail.

A DEVELOPING NATION

Many years ago there was a developing nation that had about 100 million people, was about half rural, and had an economy of 3% to 4% of current U.S. GDP. It had limited access to advanced technology.

Yet, despite these limitations, this nation managed to build subways or elevated rail lines in all of its major cities—and streetcar or tramlines in over 500 cities, towns, and villages—all in just 20 years.

The name of that developing nation? The United States of America.

Between 1897 and 1916, cities as diverse as Pine Bluff, Arkansas, Flint, Michigan, and Honolulu, Hawaii, all built light passenger rail powered by electricity.

Many of these rail systems operated for decades, but eventually the rise in popularity of the automobile, the impact of the Great Depression, and, in some cases, a nudge from automakers resulted in the closure of most of the rail lines.

But is it conceivable that with the resources and technology of today, these successes could be repeated in an emergency? If so, a viable oil-free transportation system in our cities and towns is a real possibility.

China has been expanding its electric rail system to decrease its dependence on oil and the vulnerabilities associated with oil dependence. By 2010, China had more high-speed railway track than Europe, and it is expected to have more than the rest of the world combined by 2012.[viii]

Human-Powered Transportation

In 2008 and 2009, I lived in the Netherlands. For the first time in my adult life, I managed to live for an extended period of time without a car. There were several reasons that I was able to do this. First, Europe has excellent high-speed passenger rail connections between central train stations in major cities, and it has slower trains that connect smaller stations. There are extensive, affordable bus networks and subway systems that I could use to move around large and small cities. Finally, many cities are designed with bicyclists and pedestrians in mind.

Within the city in which I lived—Arnhem—there was a large area in the city center that was accessible by pedestrians and bicyclists only. Numerous restaurants, small shops, and boutiques were contained within this pedestrian zone, which was easily accessible from my home via foot, bus, or bicycle. I was also able to bike (which is a very popular pastime in the Netherlands) to work in about 10 minutes on a bicycle path from my home to the front gate of the factory where I worked.

But much of the United States developed during the automobile age, and as a result many Americans have moved into the suburbs and have to drive everywhere—to the grocery store, to the doctor, to school, to work. Furthermore, many cities have failed, and still fail, to build sidewalks and bike paths, which discourages walking and biking by making them much riskier activities.

But some areas are planning for the future.

Bicycling

There are around a billion bicycles in the world, with about 40% of them located in China. While many people in China aspire to trade their bicycles for cars, they would be wise to keep their bicycles well maintained as they offer an excellent option for oil-free transportation. This will provide an insurance policy against much higher oil prices and/or oil shortages in the future.

Copenhagen and the rest of Denmark started making bicycling safer and easier in the late 1970s as a way to reduce oil consumption. Later they started to give bicycling and walking a higher priority than driving. Copenhagen's goal is for 40% of urban trips to be made by bicycling by 2012 (with walking, subways, commuter trains, and buses supplying most of the rest) and 50% by 2015.[ix] These goals are realistic because of four decades of steady improvements in infrastructure as well as a change in culture that steadily evolved over decades.

ELASTICITY OF TRANSPORTATION SUPPLY

Sometimes the world changes quickly. But how quickly can we adapt to these changes? Some modes of transportation can adapt quickly—others much more slowly—as the price and availability of oil change.

A commuter who drove to work today could bicycle to work tomorrow if the Strait of Hormuz was blocked overnight—provided there is a bicycle in the garage and safe and easy bike paths from home to work.

In an oil-supply emergency, it may take a few days to stagger work hours and adjust the schedule of the local urban rail to carry every commuter that suddenly wants to ride oil-free transportation to work. The ride may be packed with people for several hours in the morning and evening, but oil would be saved. More rail cars could be ordered immediately and delivered within a year or two, relieving the worst of the overcrowding. More rail lines could be built in four or so years in an emergency.

On the other hand, it would be a decade or so before enough electric cars could be produced to meet a sudden change in market demand. Most other alternatives would take just as long.

These are issues that political leaders should consider when evaluating transportation alternatives.

An example of a country that more recently decided to promote bicycling is France, whose goal in 2000 was to increase bicycling from 1% of urban trips to 10% in 2010. While France increased bicycling to "only" 6% of urban trips by 2010, this increase laid the foundation for substantially greater increases in the future—and created an elasticity of oil-free transportation supply in case of an oil-supply emergency.

In the U.S., the city of Portland, Oregon, has developed a comprehensive bicycling plan as a part of an overall initiative to create a more sustainable city. Its "Portland Bicycle Plan for 2030"x is intended to make bicycling safer and more accessible so that it is a preferred option for trips under 3 miles. The plan calls for an additional 681 miles of bikeways over the next 20 years at an ultimate cost of $613 million. (The annual cost for all transportation projects in the Portland metro area is reportedly around $630 million per year.)

An auxiliary benefit identified in the Portland plan is the impact on health. That plan's authors noted that a greater shift to bicycling would be expected to reduce rates of obesity and lower health care costs for treating obesity-related illnesses.

Some critics of Portland's plan have argued that it simply isn't reasonable in the car-centric culture of the U.S. to expect most people to opt for a bicycle for a three-mile trip. As someone who traveled between two worlds for two years—Texas and the Netherlands—I do believe it is possible, but the cultural mindset in the U.S. will somehow need to shift. In the Netherlands, practically everyone rides a bike, and when I was there I did the same. In Texas, few people bike, and neither did I (except as occasional exercise around the neighborhood). Part of the reason for the difference is that bicycling in most Texas cities simply isn't convenient or safe. Where I lived, there were no bike paths, and I certainly couldn't bike to the store or to work safely on the streets.

But if a U.S. community were to build extensive bike paths and persuade people to treat biking as a normal, or even preferable, way to get around—I do believe that large numbers of people would migrate toward biking for short trips. Portland's bicycle plan will provide a test of that hypothesis.

In any case, if communities can convince people to take up biking via policies that make it easier and safer, then this would be an attractive, medium-term option for oil-free transportation as oil prices rise. It can deliver results quickly, has an excellent oil reduction return on investment (perhaps the highest), superb elasticity of transportation supply, and a surprisingly high long-term potential.

Walkable Communities

Walking is the oldest form of transportation, but it is still just as effective today as it was when humans took their first steps. In addition to the two years I lived in the Netherlands, twice I lived in small villages in Europe—once in Germany and once in Scotland. In each case the village had a grocery store, a bakery, a butcher shop, a post office, a pharmacy, and a place to get my hair cut—all within a quarter mile of my house. The sidewalks from my house to the village shops were clean and well maintained, and therefore walking was a convenient (and healthy) means of transportation.

In fact, prior to the 20th century, almost all cities functioned as walkable cities. But the situation changed in many cities that grew over the past century. Numerous communities were built that put walking at a distinct disadvantage to other forms of transportation. A suburb in the U.S., for instance, often contains no stores or shops and is far removed from places of employment. Thus, there is no real alternative but to find other means of transportation to buy household goods and to travel back and forth to a job.

Did you know? There is already a wide variety of cities in the U.S. with neighborhoods that are walkable communities, including Seattle, Washington; Austin, Texas; Albany, New York; New Orleans, Louisiana; Pensacola, Florida; Milwaukee, Wisconsin; and Arlington, Virginia. Go to www.walkscore.com to find the walkability score for U.S. neighborhoods.

But if the long-term future brings persistently higher oil prices—as I believe it will—then walkable communities offer a proven way of reducing the vulnerability to price and supply shocks.

There are a number of characteristics that walkable communities should ideally possess in order to make them desirable places to live:

- The vicinity of the town center should contain the goods and services most people require on a weekly basis. This would include things like a grocery store, pharmacy, hardware store, and restaurants. An open, public space where children can play and people can meet would also be a plus.

- The highest population density neighborhoods should be adjacent to the town center, to give the largest number of people access to the town center. Neighborhoods that are further out should be connected to the city center by public transportation.

- The city center should be free of traffic, but if traffic is allowed, the speed limits should be kept low while also allowing an orderly flow of traffic at a safe distance from bicyclists and pedestrians.

Beyond merely the fact that they reduce oil consumption, properly designed walkable communities can be very pleasant places to live. Thus, it makes sense when making planning decisions for communities to make at least a portion of the community walkable. Even better would be to make planning decisions with future expansion of the walkable areas in mind—just as planners take into account future highway expansions when building a new highway.

Summary

The sheer scale of our oil consumption implies that it will be very difficult to replace it with sustainable sources of energy. Therefore, prudent planning would suggest that we replace today's cars and trucks—to the greatest degree practical—with oil-free transportation.

There are a great many options with varying degrees of potential for replacing oil-based transportation. Some of the options—such as hybrids and electric cars—offer a similar level of mobility to what we enjoy today. Another option would be to shift more freight to electrified rail, which would be transparent to most people.

Still other options require a higher level of forward planning. Cities that can be easily traversed by foot and by bike don't simply happen in today's car age without the input of forward-thinking individuals into long-range city planning. But these are the types of cities that will be sorely needed in the post-oil age.

References

[i] Energy Information Administration (EIA), "Average Retail Price of Electricity to Ultimate Consumers," accessed January 10, 2012, www.eia.gov /electricity/monthly/excel/epmxlfile5_3.xls.

[ii] Michael Copeland, "The Hydrogen Car Fights Back," *CNNMoney*, October 14, 2009, http://money.cnn.com/2009/10/13/technology/hydrogen _car.fortune/.

[iii] Clive Matthew-Wilson, "The Emperor's New Car," *The Dog and Lemon Guide*, 2010, www.dogandlemon.com/articles/emperors-new-car.

[iv] J.D. Power and Associates, "Future Global Market Demand for Hybrid and Battery Electric Vehicles May Be Over-Hyped; Wild Card is China," October 27, 2010, http://businesscenter.jdpower.com/news/pressrelease .aspx?ID=2010213.

v Dave Lee, "Nissan-Renault Head Carlos Ghosn's Zero Emission Goal," BBC World Service, February 9, 2010, http://news.bbc.co.uk/2/hi/business /8501348.stm.

vi Dan Ferber, "Vehicle-to-Grid: A New Spin on Car Payments," *Miller-McCune.com*, October 31, 2011, www.miller-mccune.com/environment /vehicle-to-grid-a-new-spin-on-car-payments-36697/.

vii Gil Carmichael, "Railways Fast and Cheapest Freight Transportation System," *Cargonews Asia*, December 15, 2008, www.cargonewsasia.com /secured/article.aspx?id=38&article=17935.

viii Michael Robinson, "China's New Industrial Revolution," *BBC News*, August 1, 2010, www.bbc.co.uk/news/business-10792465.

ix Sustainable Urban Transit Project, "Copenhagen- A Modern Transport Policy for a Sustainable City," accessed February 13, 2012, www.sutp.org /index.php?option=com_content&task=view&id=2777.

x Portland Bureau of Transportation, "Portland Bicycle Plan for 2030," adopted February 11, 2010, available at www.portlandonline.com /transportation/index.cfm?c=44597.

Corn Ethanol

Past, Present, and Future

By increasing the use of renewable fuels such as ethanol and bio-diesel, and providing the Department of Energy with a budget to create more energy efficiency options, agriculture can be the backbone of our energy supply as well.

—John Salazar, former U.S. Congressman

Today, about 40 percent of all U.S. corn—that's 15 percent of global corn production or 5 percent of all global grain—is diverted into the corn ethanol scam in order to produce the energy equivalent of about 0.6 percent of global oil needs.

—Robert Bryce, author

In order to examine the pros and cons of biofuel policies—and how they might be improved upon—this chapter considers the case of corn ethanol in the United States. Politicians, particularly those in farm states, love corn ethanol. The idea that the U.S. could begin to replace oil with domestic fuel by having farmers do what they do best contains many elements of a compelling story.

However, corn ethanol has had its critics—myself included—for a number of reasons. Some criticisms have arisen due to concerns about turning food into fuel and driving up food prices. Others have voiced concern about various environmental implications of corn ethanol. My own concerns have always centered on two issues in particular:

- The relative sustainability of the process—that we may be simply replacing one unsustainable fuel for another.
- That some U.S. ethanol policies are counterproductive.

In this chapter I will look at the past, present, and possible future of the corn ethanol industry, explore some of the controversies and challenges, and offer some suggestions for moving the corn ethanol industry toward a more sustainable long-term alternative to oil.

Corn Ethanol Policies: Past and Present

In an effort to spur development of a domestic renewable fuel industry, wean the U.S. off of foreign oil, and provide additional markets for farmers, the U.S. government introduced tax credits for ethanol usage with the Energy Tax Act of 1978. The tax credit was an exemption to the Federal Excise Tax on gasoline, and amounted to $0.40 for every gallon of ethanol blended into gasoline at the 10% level. This tax credit was increased to $0.60 per gallon in 1984, decreased in stages to $0.45 per gallon by 2009, and finally phased out completely at the end of 2011.

■ **Did you know?** 2012 marks the first year since 1978 that corn ethanol will not be directly supported by U.S. federal tax credits.

During the 1980s, in addition to increasing the tax credit to $0.60 per gallon, the U.S. government made government-backed loans available to ethanol producers for plant construction, and implemented an import fee to help protect domestic ethanol producers from cheaper ethanol imports. Despite these measures, the U.S. ethanol industry struggled to make headway. The majority of the ethanol plants that were built in the early 1980s were bankrupt by the mid-1980s.

However, the plants that were able to stay in business increased production from under 200 million gallons per year in 1980 to 900 million gallons per year in 1990. Production slowly continued to grow, reaching 1.6 billion gallons by 2000 and 3.9 billion gallons by 2005 (see Figure 13-1). But there were still two glaring problems at that point.

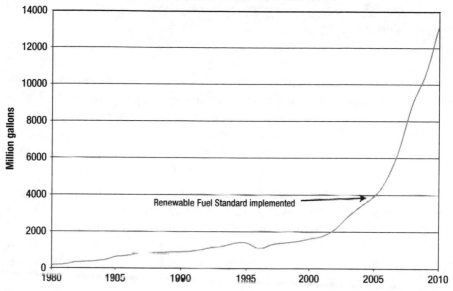

Figure 13-1. Three decades of corn ethanol production in the U.S. (Data source: Renewable Fuels Association[i])

First, while production had grown substantially between 1978 and 2005, ethanol still amounted to a tiny fraction of U.S. gasoline demand. Ethanol production expanded by 3 billion gallons per year from 1990 to 2005, but U.S. gasoline demand grew by 30 billion gallons—to 140 billion gallons per year. Petroleum imports grew by 87 billion gallons per year (5.7 million barrels per day). Clearly, if the purpose of U.S. biofuel policy was to reduce dependence on petroleum imports, ethanol was having very little impact up to that point.

The second glaring problem was that ethanol could not compete head-to-head with gasoline on price. Despite all of the financial incentives for ethanol, the average annual price of ethanol had exceeded the price of gasoline in every single year on record through 2005.[ii] Not only was ethanol more expensive on a per-gallon basis, but since ethanol contains only two-thirds the energy content of gasoline, consumers were also sacrificing fuel economy when using ethanol blends.

▓ **Did you know?** Ethanol became a mandated component of the U.S. gasoline supply with the Energy Policy Act of 2005.

The result was that the cost per mile for consumers when using ethanol in their fuel was higher than the cost when using straight gasoline. However, with a 10% ethanol blend (E10), the impact of the higher cost was diluted such that it was likely not overtly obvious to most consumers. But for gasoline blenders, ethanol at equal to or higher than the cost per gallon of gasoline was not a price that would compel them to buy ethanol.

So the U.S. government decided to force the issue by mandating ethanol usage in the Energy Policy Act of 2005. One of the provisions of the new energy policy was the Renewable Fuel Standard (RFS). The RFS started with a mandate of 4 billion gallons of ethanol in 2006—just about the amount that was being produced at that time—and initially increased each year to 7.5 billion gallons of ethanol by 2012.

THE MTBE PHASE-OUT

Ethanol demand also received a boost due to the phase-out of a blending component that was popular with oil refiners. The Clean Air Act Amendments of 1990 stipulated the use of oxygenated gasoline in certain areas with high levels of specific air pollutants. Oxygen-containing components in fuels (oxygenates) help to enable a more complete fuel combustion, and therefore help to reduce tailpipe emissions from gasoline engines.

The oxygenate of choice for many gasoline blenders was methyl tertiary butyl ether (MTBE). Blenders had already been using MTBE as an anti-knock alternative to tetraethyl lead, which was ultimately phased out of gasoline in the U.S. in 1995.

MTBE production ultimately rose to over 3 billion gallons per year as its popularity as an oxygenate increased, but it began to be implicated in groundwater contamination through leaking gasoline tanks. Unlike most gasoline blending components, MTBE is soluble in water, and gives water an unpleasant taste at very low concentrations. As reports of contamination began to surface, some states began to ban the use of MTBE in gasoline.

Ultimately, refiners moved to completely phase out MTBE usage when the Energy Policy Act of 2005 failed to shield MTBE manufacturers from liability for water contamination. The only real alternative oxygenate that could replace 3 billion gallons a year of MTBE was ethanol, and so oxygenate demand shifted from MTBE to ethanol in 2005–2006.

Although the U.S. Environmental Protection Agency (EPA) formerly lifted the oxygenate requirement in 2006—with the stipulation that refiners must still produce gasoline that meets Clean Air Act standards—ethanol remained a popular choice for boosting octane in gasoline. The sudden increased demand from the MTBE phase-out resulted in regional shortages of ethanol, which caused a short-term price spike and an increase in ethanol imports. But it also provided incentive for growth in the ethanol industry, and was one factor in the explosive growth in ethanol production that began in 2005.

The ethanol mandate and MTBE phase-out (see sidebar) quickly achieved what nearly 30 years of subsidies did not: explosive growth of ethanol usage, and ethanol prices that finally dropped below the price of unleaded gasoline (see Figure 13-2). An ethanol gold rush ensued, capacity was overbuilt, and suddenly the industry found itself in financial trouble as ethanol supply exceeded the mandates.

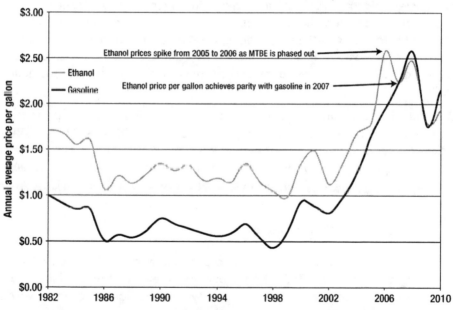

Figure 13-2. Average annual wholesale prices of ethanol and unleaded gasoline in Omaha, Nebraska (Data source: Nebraska.gov, Official Nebraska Government Website)

Again, the government came to the rescue by increasing and accelerating the mandates in the Energy Independence and Security Act of 2007. Instead of mandating 7.5 billion gallons of ethanol in the fuel supply by 2010, the new mandate was for 12 billion gallons of corn ethanol in 2010 and 15 billion gallons by 2015.[1]

One of the controversial aspects of the Renewable Fuel Standard was that Congress did not eliminate the ethanol subsidy when it put the mandate in place. The gasoline blender—typically an oil company—collected the subsidy as an incentive to purchase ethanol, but when the mandate was enacted, the blender was compelled by law to buy specific quantities of ethanol. Thus, gasoline blenders were being paid to comply with the law, a situation akin to paying someone to obey traffic laws, which was an ineffective usage of tax dollars.

In addition to the tax credit and mandate, domestic production was protected from ethanol imports by a tariff of 2.5% tax plus $0.54/gallon. The stated justification of the tariff was that ethanol imports were eligible for the ethanol tax credits, so the tariff was a way to ensure that foreign ethanol companies did not collect incentives intended for domestic ethanol production. However, the tariff was set at a higher value than the domestic tax credit, so foreign ethanol producers were at an economic disadvantage relative to domestic ethanol producers. By contrast, U.S. policies concerning crude oil do not give domestic producers the benefit of protective tariffs.

But did U.S. ethanol policies—the tax credits, mandates, and protective tariffs—create a viable, sustainable alternative to oil? Are U.S. ethanol policies a good model for creating an alternative energy industry? Answers to those questions vary greatly depending on whom you ask, because different people look at different metrics of success.

Metrics of Success

If the goal of U.S. ethanol policy was to produce a lot of domestic ethanol, the program has succeeded well beyond most expectations. Ethanol currently supplies about 10% of the fuel by volume for gasoline-powered

---

[1] There was also a requirement for cellulosic and advanced biofuels that pushed the total biofuel mandate to 36 billion gallons by 2022.

vehicles in the U.S. The program has also particularly benefited the U.S. Midwest, as billions of dollars flowed into the Midwest to buy the more than 12 billion gallons of ethanol produced in the region.

But some opponents of U.S. ethanol policies would argue that the success of the program for the Midwest comes at the expense of the rest of the country, as the mandate is essentially a government-imposed transfer of wealth into the ethanol-producing regions.

Others have argued that the increase in corn production has contributed to higher rates of soil erosion and more runoff of herbicides, pesticides, and fertilizers into waterways.

Still others suggest that while corn ethanol has somewhat improved the energy security of the U.S., it is a solution that is presently barely more sustainable than is usage of petroleum. The reason for this is that the production of corn ethanol is dependent on fossil fuels—particularly natural gas.

The truth is more complex than either ethanol proponents or opponents might acknowledge, because there are trade-offs with ethanol just as there are with all of our energy sources. Ethanol does provide a portion of the motor fuel for the U.S., and ethanol policies have created jobs and a robust economy in the Midwest.

But there have been costs as well, and there are risks associated with the use of corn to produce ethanol. For example, consider the risk of a major drought in the Midwest. If one year the corn crop comes in much lower than normal, consumers would likely have to contend simultaneously with much higher food and fuel prices, and potentially shortages of both. This risk is a trade-off, but one that may only be obvious if a disastrous drought occurs.

The question that must be asked and answered about U.S. ethanol policies—and for that matter energy policies in general—is whether the trade-offs we are making are ultimately beneficial to society as a whole. Certainly, some people benefit and some do not, but the proper measure of success should be the net benefit to society.

Challenges and Opportunities

Currently, U.S. ethanol producers face several challenges that threaten the future growth of the industry. In this section I describe those challenges, and make some suggestions for how to overcome them.

The Blend Wall

The most pressing challenge is that Congress has mandated levels of ethanol blending that are at odds with EPA regulations. In 1979, the EPA granted a gasohol waiver that put the legal maximum ethanol limit for general usage in gasoline engines at 10% by volume.

But as a result of high oil prices, demand for gasoline in the U.S. declined to less than 140 billion gallons in 2010, which meant that the 10% limit imposed by the EPA would create a "blend wall" well before 15 billion gallons of ethanol could be blended into the gasoline supply. The U.S. Energy Information Administration (EIA) has reported that the 10% limit was reached in the summer of 2011.[iii]

There are several possible solutions to this dilemma. The most obvious is to simply change the Renewable Fuel Standard to lower the volumes of ethanol that are legally required to be blended. However, given the political support that ethanol enjoys, this solution is unlikely to be seriously entertained. It would also be severely detrimental to the ethanol industry.

The solution favored by the ethanol industry is to have the EPA raise the maximum legal limit for general usage to 15% by volume. In March 2009, the ethanol lobbying group Growth Energy and a coalition of ethanol producers filed a request with the EPA to allow ethanol blends above the 10% limit. After conducting testing in conjunction with the Department of Energy, the EPA first approved (but did not mandate) the use of 15% blends (E15) in 2007 and newer light-duty vehicles in 2010, and then in January 2011 expanded that approval to 2001 and newer light-duty vehicles.

E15 Meets Resistance

However, the EPA's decision was met with resistance from many groups, including automakers, who sued to have the decision reversed. Their stated reason was that their automobiles were not designed for E15 service, and some indicated that they would not honor warranties for vehicles fueled with E15. They were further concerned that, because the EPA waiver allowing E15 usage did not cover all model years, putting E15 into nonapproved vehicles was inevitable.

Underwriters Laboratories (UL) also weighed in with results from tests on fuel-dispensing equipment.[iv] The purpose of its testing was to expose various pieces of fuel-dispensing equipment that were UL-approved for 10% ethanol blends (E10) to 15% ethanol blends (E15) to assess compatibility.

The results of the UL testing were that only three of eight categories of new dispensing equipment tested—fewer than 40% of the categories— passed all compliance tests. When used equipment was examined—that is, the equipment currently in service in the U.S. fuel infrastructure system— none of the categories was found to be fully compliant, and some pieces of equipment showed "a reduced level of safety or performance."

Did you know? Iowa contains less than 1% of the U.S. population and about 1.5% of the land area of the U.S., but it is responsible for 27% of U.S. ethanol production.

Gasoline retailers also had reason for concern. Given EPA's limited approval of E15 only for 2001 and newer light duty vehicles, retailers not only would have to buy additional equipment to store and dispense E15, but would also have to ensure, for liability reasons, that customers do not put E15 into nonapproved vehicles. In addition, because the EPA *allowed* E15 but did not specifically *mandate* E15, it was not clear to retailers that demand would justify the expense and hassle of selling E15. As a result, E15 sales were nonexistent.

Ethanol Exports

Ethanol producers have thus far dealt with the blend wall issue by exporting their excess ethanol production. The U.S. ethanol industry exported approximately 1 billion gallons of ethanol in 2011, well over double the export level of 2010. The industry has also advocated for a dedicated pipeline capable of shipping ethanol from the Midwest to the East Coast, where it could then be easily exported.

However, exporting ethanol undermines one of the main reasons for U.S. ethanol policy—to reduce dependence on foreign oil. In fact, ethanol that is exported actually increases dependence on foreign oil because some oil is used in the production and export of the ethanol, but no fuel is displaced domestically. Thus, while exporting ethanol may help the industry continue to grow, this is not the best long-term solution with respect to U.S. energy policy.

Long-Term Solution: Midwestern Sustainability

I have advocated a different, potentially long-term solution that would enable the future growth of the U.S. ethanol industry, and that is to aggressively grow the Midwestern market for 85% ethanol blends[2]—(E85).

One reason I have often spoken out against certain ethanol policies is that I didn't see regions actually becoming more self-sufficient as a result of those policies. What I saw was a delusion of self-sufficiency. Yes, more ethanol was being produced, but the oil dependence of those ethanol-producing regions continued to be very high—in some cases growing even as ethanol production soared.

The Midwest provides a perfect example. The United States is divided into five Petroleum Administration for Defense Districts (PADDs). These districts were created during World War II, and the Energy Information Administration (EIA) collects and reports statistics for the different PADDs. Most Midwestern states are contained within PADD 2. The states in PADD 2 are Illinois, Indiana, Iowa, Kansas, Kentucky, Michigan, Minnesota, Missouri, Nebraska, North Dakota, Ohio, Oklahoma, South Dakota, Tennessee, and Wisconsin.

PADD 2 is responsible for approximately 95% of all ethanol production in the United States.[3] Ethanol production in PADD 2 grew from 1.6 billion gallons in 2000 to 3.9 billion gallons in 2005 to almost 12.5 billion gallons in 2010. The region has been very successful in rapidly increasing ethanol production.

Despite this success, demand for conventional gasoline in PADD 2 has remained strong. In 2000, demand for conventional gasoline in PADD 2 was 2.1 million barrels per day (bpd). Demand increased slightly by 2004–2005 to 2.2 million bpd before slightly declining to the 2010 demand level of 2.14 million bpd.[v]

---

[2] E85 is 85% ethanol and 15% gasoline. E15 is 85% gasoline and 15% ethanol.

[3] Ethanol production is actually even more concentrated in a handful of PADD 2 states, as some PADD 2 states produce little or no ethanol.

E85 CASE STUDY: IOWA

Iowa is to corn ethanol what Saudi Arabia is to oil. In 2011, Iowa produced 3.7 billion gallons of ethanol, which is 27% of the U.S. total. This is due to the large amount of corn production in Iowa, enabled by ample rainfall and rich topsoil.

But Iowa differs from Saudi Arabia with respect to energy production in one very important detail: Saudi Arabia satisfies its own energy needs with the oil it produces, and it exports the excess. Iowa, on the other hand, exports the vast majority of the ethanol it produces while importing gasoline as motor fuel.

Gasoline consumption in Iowa is around 1.6 billion gallons per year. This is the energy equivalent of 2.4 billion gallons per year of ethanol. But only 100 million gallons of Iowa's ethanol production —less than 3%—is consumed within the state. Perhaps even more surprising is that Iowa—seemingly the state most ideally poised for biofuel self-sufficiency—ranks in the top ten consumers of gasoline per capita in the U.S.

Iowa is a state that by all accounts should be able to satisfy its own liquid fuel needs with ethanol, and still have some left for export. Iowa is perhaps unique among U.S. states in that respect. Instead, petroleum continues to supply over 90% of the motor fuel in Iowa and virtually all of the fuel used in the farm equipment for growing all of that Iowa corn.

Ethanol prices in Iowa are generally more competitive than in other states, with E85 sometimes selling at a 30% discount to gasoline. Iowa also has widespread—and growing—availability of E85 across the state. The biggest impediments to wide-spread adoption are that the percentage of flex-fuel vehicles on the roads is still small—under 5%—and the price spread between gasoline and E85 is inconsistent.

In other words, ethanol production soared in the Midwest by some 700%, but that production increase did not translate into reduced conventional gasoline demand.[4]

So, even though the Midwest produces about 95% of the ethanol in the U.S., it exports 70% of that ethanol out of the Midwest. At the same time, it imports gasoline that is the energy equivalent of 37 billion gallons of ethanol. If gasoline demand in the Midwest could be shifted to demand for E85, every drop of ethanol produced in the Midwest could be consumed in the Midwest instead of using energy to export the ethanol and import gasoline.

---

[4] Gasoline demand did decline slightly, but this phenomenon was seen throughout developed countries in response to much higher oil prices.

Further, this would greatly enhance the energy security of this important food-producing region.

What, then, are the obstacles to establishing the Midwest as a self-sufficient area utilizing locally produced ethanol as its primary fuel? There are three key issues:

- The price of ethanol relative to gasoline

- The availability of vehicles designed to run on E85

- Development of E85 infrastructure

Closing the E85/Gasoline Price Gap

The most pressing obstacle to large-scale adoption of E85 in the Midwest is that of price. Despite the enormous improvements ethanol has made relative to gasoline pricing, it is still not normally cheap enough to compensate for the loss of fuel efficiency relative to gasoline. In recent years, E85 in the Midwest has generally traded at a discount from 10% to 20% relative to gasoline.[5] When oil prices rise, the price differential between gasoline and ethanol tends to increase. While gasoline and ethanol are considered fungible (interchangeable) fuels, the primary fossil fuel input into ethanol production is natural gas. If natural gas prices remain low and oil prices rise, E85 can become more competitive against gasoline (barring major spikes in the price of corn).

Clearly, if E85 is to become the dominant fuel in the Midwest, the price differential will have to properly reflect the fuel economy difference of E85 versus gasoline. E85 contains about 25% less energy than gasoline on a volumetric basis. Owners that experience a 25% reduction in fuel economy will expect to pay 25% less for their fuel. In fact, they may expect to pay 30% less because they have to refuel more often.

The most promising way to reduce the price differential is to develop engines that have the potential to reduce the mileage penalty for E85. Several of these engines are in development. Because ethanol has a high octane rating, it is more resistant to preignition[6] than is gasoline. Thus, an

---

[5] Historical E85/gasoline price spreads are available at http://e85prices.com/.

[6] Preignition is ignition of the fuel mixture prior to the spark plug firing, leading to reduced engine performance.

engine can be designed with a higher compression ratio, which could then extract more useful work from ethanol. This is the principal behind diesel engines, which have higher compression ratios than gasoline combustion engines, and thus reach engine efficiencies of around 45%, versus 25% to 30% for gasoline engines.

Several automakers have been working on engines that are specifically optimized for ethanol. It may be possible to eliminate most or all of ethanol's fuel economy penalty in engines that are optimized for performance on ethanol. The disadvantage is that these engines will no longer be optimized for performance on gasoline, and in fact may be incapable of running on gasoline due to the high compression ratios and gasoline's greater tendency to preignite. Thus, automobiles based on these engines may not be flex-fuel, but rather ethanol-exclusive.

Nonetheless, in areas that are capable of producing substantial supplies of ethanol, engines that minimize the mileage penalty will also lower the significance of the ethanol/gasoline price differential—provided the engines themselves are not exorbitantly expensive.

Vehicles and Infrastructure

The other obstacles to large-scale adoption of E85 in the Midwest are the availability of flex-fuel vehicles (FFVs), and limited infrastructure. According to U.S. government statistics, only about 8 million of the 250 million registered highway vehicles on U.S. roads are FFVs.[vi] However, this represents an increase of 2.5 times the number of FFVs available five years earlier. So the number of FFVs on the roads is growing rapidly, but is still a very small percentage of the total number of vehicles.

Infrastructure for E85 has also grown rapidly. Iowa, for instance, currently has 180 stations across the state that sell E85, and there are nearly 3,000 stations across the U.S. that sell E85. The number of stations selling E85 has grown rapidly, but as in the case of FFVS, the number still represents a small percentage of overall service stations.

But the dual problems of lack of availability of FFVs and E85 would be quickly resolved if E85 were consistently a cheaper option per mile than is conventional gasoline. In that case, people would demand both the vehicles and the ability to purchase E85. Thus, achieving competitive pricing is the most important issue.

Competitive pricing may ultimately be achieved simply due to continued increases in oil prices. But this process could be accelerated. Money that is currently dedicated to shipping ethanol out of the Midwest—and money that goes toward importing oil into the Midwest—could be better spent ensuring that Midwestern ethanol is used closer to the source by further development and deployment of ethanol-optimized engines, as well as the continued build-out of E85 infrastructure to ensure E85 compatibility.

States with a lot of ethanol production may benefit from passing statewide tax incentives designed to incentivize local use of ethanol. In Chapter 9, I discussed the potential benefits of shifting federal income taxes to gasoline taxes. This could also be carried out on a state level. Iowa, for instance, has a state sales tax, an income tax, and property taxes. If the state could implement a higher tax on gasoline, it could keep the tax burden constant by lowering any or all of the other taxes. The benefit would be to make E85 in Iowa more consistently price competitive with gasoline, which would make the state more energy independent. The local economy would also be more resilient as more dollars that are spent on fuel would stay in the state, supporting local farmers, ethanol plants, and related businesses.

The addition of blender pumps is also an option for increasing the market penetration of ethanol. Blender pumps give consumers a choice of how much ethanol they want in their gasoline, and does not limit them to either regular gasoline (generally E10) or E85. Consumers could choose to have 20%, 30%, or 50% ethanol in their fuel. Some consumers who aren't immediately comfortable with the idea of E85 could first experiment with lower blends to determine optimal performance for their vehicles.

Summary

U.S. ethanol policy has resulted in the development of a large corn ethanol industry in the Midwest. While corn ethanol has been criticized on several points, it enjoys great support among Midwestern lawmakers, and will therefore be a part of U.S. energy policy for many years to come. So the best course of action is to pursue policies that address some of corn ethanol's shortcomings.

Current U.S. energy policy results in a little bit of ethanol being distributed across the U.S. It is inefficiently transported from the Midwest to coastal states, while at the same time oil imports continue to flow into the

Midwest. A portion of these imports comes from places like Venezuela and the Middle East, who are not necessarily sympathetic to U.S. interests.

My view is that instead of exporting ethanol from the Midwest to New York and California (or even out of the country), we should make sure that E85 dominates the local Midwestern markets and backs out crude oil from unstable and hostile suppliers. If ethanol is a true alternative to oil, then there is no reason that it shouldn't out-compete oil in its own backyard.

References

i Renewable Fuels Association (RFA), "Historic U.S. Fuel Ethanol Production," www.ethanolrfa.org/pages/statistics#A.

ii Nebraska.gov, Official Nebraska Government Website, "Ethanol and Unleaded Gasoline Average Rack Prices," accessed December 17, 2011, www.neo.ne.gov/statshtml/66.html.

iii Energy Information Administration, "Ethanol Blend Wall: Are We There Yet?," *This Week in Petroleum*, November 23, 2011, www.eia.gov/oog/info/twip/twiparch/111123/twipprint.html.

iv Kenneth Boyce and J. Thomas Chapin, Underwriters Laboratories (UL), "Dispensing Equipment Testing with Mid-Level Ethanol/Gasoline Test Fluid," November 2010, www.nrel.gov/docs/fy11osti/49187.pdf.

v Energy Information Administration (EIA), "Midwest (PADD 2) Product Supplied of Conventional Motor Gasoline," accessed December 25, 2011, www.eia.gov/dnav/pet/hist/LeafHandler.ashx?n=pet&s=mg4up_r20_2&f=m.

vi U.S. Department of Energy, Alternative Fuels and Advanced Vehicles Data Center (AFDC), "E85 FFVs in Use in U.S.," accessed January 25, 2012, www.afdc.energy.gov/afdc/data/docs/ffvs_in_use.xls.

U.S. Energy Politics

The Elusive Goal of Energy Independence

Fool me once, shame on you. Fool me twice, shame on me. Fool me eight times . . . I must be an idiot.

—Jon Stewart, *The Daily Show*

The current U.S. president and the past seven U.S. presidents—five Republicans and three Democrats presiding over a span of over four decades—have publicly declared that U.S. dependence on foreign oil is a national security risk. They have all stressed the need for a comprehensive energy policy to reduce U.S. dependence on foreign oil and improve U.S. energy security. The result? Oil demand and oil imports climbed mostly unabated across the terms of those eight presidents.

In this chapter I will examine the energy policy initiatives of those eight presidents and explore the reasons for the disconnect between what those presidents sought to achieve and what they actually achieved (or failed to achieve).

Forty Years of Growing Dependence

This chapter's introductory quote by my favorite comedian, Jon Stewart, comes from a brilliant segment he did following the Deepwater Horizon oil spill in April 2010. The segment, called "An Energy-Independent Future,"[i] has Stewart playing video clips from President Obama and the past seven presidents in which each of them voices concern that U.S. dependence on imported oil is a pressing problem that must be solved and offers up their proposed solutions.

They all had a plan. As Stewart noted, "Counting Barack Obama, the last eight presidents have gone on television and promised to move us toward an energy-independent future." How did they fare? Figure 14-1 tells the tale (numbers 1–12 along the Imports line are explained in the following section).

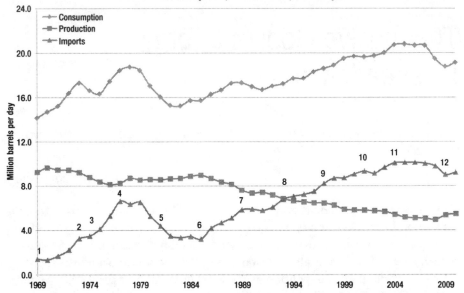

Figure 14-1. U.S. oil consumption and imports through four decades of U.S. presidents (Data sources: BP *Statistical Review of World Energy 2011* and the Energy Information Administration)

U.S. Presidents and Oil Production and Consumption: A Chronology

As previously noted, above the Imports line in Figure 14-1 is a series of numbers, 1–12. These numbers represent the inauguration dates for President Obama and his seven predecessors, including second terms where applicable. The following chronology coincides with those dates and briefly describes what happened with domestic oil production, consumption, and imports during each term:

1. Richard Nixon is inaugurated as the 37th president on January 20, 1969. When President Nixon took office, U.S. oil production was nearing its peak after over 100 years of increasing production. Imports made up 10% of U.S. consumption. In 1970, U.S. oil production reached 9.6 million barrels per day and began a long, steady decline.

2. Richard Nixon begins his second term on January 20, 1973. U.S. oil production had declined to 9.2 million bpd while consumption had increased by 3 million bpd from the first year of Nixon's first term. As a result, oil imports would more than double during Nixon's presidency, and American citizens would learn the danger of the dependence on imports with the OPEC Arab oil embargo of 1973.

3. Gerald Ford is inaugurated as the 38th president on August 9, 1974 after Nixon resigns in disgrace. During President Ford's term in office, domestic oil production continued to decline. Consumption and imports continued to grow, and both were at all-time highs during Ford's last year in office.

4. Jimmy Carter is inaugurated as the 39th president on January 20, 1977. Recent trends in consumption, production, and imports all reversed themselves during President Carter's presidential term. Consumption fell by 2%, U.S. production increased by 6%, and imports—after initially rising to record highs during his first year in office—were a fraction of a percentage lower at the end of his term than during Ford's last year in office. Factors beyond Carter's control—such as the Iranian Revolution and the Iran–Iraq War—heavily influence the oil markets.

5. Ronald Reagan is inaugurated as the 40th president on January 20, 1981. Oil consumption continued to decline during most of President Reagan's first term,

and oil production crept back to levels that had not been seen in a decade. Oil imports fell by 35% during his first term.

6. Ronald Reagan begins his second term on January 21, 1985. The trends from his first term all reversed themselves, as consumption rose 10%, domestic production fell by 8%, and oil imports increased by 49%.

7. George H. W. Bush is inaugurated as the 41st president on January 20, 1989. Consumption fell slightly during his term, but domestic production fell even more—down 12%. Imports increased by 19%, back above 6 million bpd for the first time since the 1970s.

8. Bill Clinton is inaugurated as the 42nd president on January 20, 1993. During his first term, consumption increased by another 7%, domestic production fell by 10%, and imports increased by another 23%— exceeding 7 million bpd for the first time in U.S. history.

9. Bill Clinton begins his second term on January 20, 1997. His second term trends were almost identical to those of his first term: consumption rose by another 8%, domestic production fell by another 10%, and imports increased by an additional 21%. Consumption and oil imports were at all-time highs, and production had fallen 40% from the 1970 production peak.

10. George W. Bush is inaugurated as the 43rd president on January 20, 2001. During his first term, consumption climbed above 20 million bpd for the first time in the nation's history. Imports also reached new highs, above 10 million bpd. Domestic production continued to fall.

11. George W. Bush begins his second term on January 20, 2005. During Bush's second term, consumption began to decline as the nation entered a recession and oil prices reached record highs, and imports fell

back to below 10 million bpd. The decline in domestic production continued, albeit at a slower rate of decline than during his first term. During Bush's last year in office, the level of imports reached just over 50% of U.S. consumption.

12. Barack Obama is inaugurated as the 44th president on January 20, 2009. The economic sluggishness continues, and consumption and imports both initially declined before heading back up. Domestic production grew in each of President Obama's first three years in office, increasing 14% from Bush's last term in office.

Synopsis

While there was certainly variation across the terms of these presidents, the general trend was one of increasing consumption, decreasing domestic production, and increasing imports. Over the course of four decades, consumption increased from 14 million bpd to above 20 million bpd, domestic production fell from 9.6 million bpd to 5 million bpd, and imports grew from 1.4 million bpd to over 10 million bpd. Imports increased during this span of time from 10% of overall consumption to 50% of overall consumption, pushing the U.S. ever further from the stated goal of energy independence.

Of course, there were many factors contributing to the changes in consumption and production that went well beyond the policies of different presidential administrations. There were price spikes, recessions, wars, and supply gluts—all of which influenced demand for oil. Production from the largest field ever discovered in the U.S.—Prudhoe Bay in Alaska—began in 1977 following the completion of the Alaska Pipeline, and this reversed the oil production decline in the late 1970s. Improvements in oil recovery technologies slowed the rate of decline in U.S. oil fields.

The population of the U.S. increased by 52% between Nixon's first term and Obama's first term, and U.S. gross domestic product (inflation-adjusted) more than tripled. Since oil consumption only increased by a little over 40% over that time, energy efficiency clearly improved in the U.S. The energy required to produce a unit GDP in the U.S. fell by more than half over the past four decades.[ii]

In addition to the many factors impacting upon oil supply and demand, the impact of one president's policies often extends into future presidential administrations.

Let's now examine some of the energy policy highlights of the past eight presidents.

Richard Nixon

Let us set as our national goal, in the spirit of Apollo, with the determination of the Manhattan Project, that by the end of this decade we will have developed the potential to meet our own energy needs without depending on any foreign energy source.

—President Nixon (November 7, 1973)

When President Nixon took office in 1969, concerns about energy were not high on the list of American priorities. That would change dramatically during Nixon's presidency. Beginning in 1971, the Nixon administration began a series of price-control measures designed to combat rising inflation. By the summer of 1972, there were long lines at gasoline stations in some regions as shortages of gasoline were dealt with by rationing.[iii]

■ **Did you know?** President Nixon instituted the first price controls in 1971, which led to long gas lines and rationing in the summers of 1972 and 1973—before the OPEC oil embargo.

But the defining energy event for the administration would not happen until October 1973. In that month, OPEC dramatically increased the posted price of oil, and in response to U.S. support for Israel during the Yom Kippur War, the Arab members of OPEC announced an oil embargo against the U.S. The embargo was ultimately expanded to a number of other countries, and the result was a rapid quadrupling in the price of oil.

In response, Nixon instituted additional price controls and began rationing oil to states based on 1972 levels of consumption. On November 7, 1973, Nixon announced Project Independence, the stated goal of which was energy independence for the U.S. by 1980 through conservation and alternative energy initiatives. That same month, Nixon increased funding for mass transit, and he authorized the Trans-Alaska Pipeline by signing legislation that cleared away legal challenges from those opposed to the pipeline. Soon after, the National Maximum Speed Law was passed, reducing the maximum speed limit nationwide to 55 miles per hour.

Did you know? There were a number of notable environmental accomplishments during the Nixon years (although not all were attributable to him). The Environmental Protection Agency was established, the Clean Water Act and Clean Air Act were passed, Earth Day was first observed, and National Arbor Day was standardized as a national holiday.

The oil crisis emphasized the risks from increased dependence on imported oil. The sharp run-up in price contributed to a deep economic recession in the U.S., and it represented the initial stages of what would become a massive transfer of wealth from the U.S. to oil-exporting countries. Despite Nixon's goal of energy independence by the end of the decade, the level of oil imports by 1980 was more than 50% greater than during his last year in office.

Gerald Ford

I am recommending a plan to make us invulnerable to cutoffs of foreign oil. It will require sacrifices, but it—and this is most important—it will work.

—President Ford (January 15, 1975)

Gerald Ford was nominated to be vice president under Nixon on October 12, 1973. This was less than one week before the OPEC Arab oil embargo began, so Ford had a high-profile seat from which to watch events unfold.

When Ford became president in August 1974—following Nixon's resignation—addressing the U.S. loss of energy independence was high on his list of priorities. In his 1975 State of the Union address, he stated, "Our growing dependence upon foreign sources [of petroleum] has been adding to our vulnerability for years and years, and we did nothing to prepare ourselves for such an event as the embargo of 1973."

In his address, Ford proposed a number of specific initiatives designed to re-duce growing dependence on foreign oil. He promoted expanded use of coal and nuclear power, development of synthetic fuels and shale oil resources, and he proposed tax credits to help homeowners with the cost of installing insulation. He set forth goals to reduce oil imports by 1 million bpd by the end of 1975 and by 2 million bpd by the end of 1977. But he also pushed out to 1985 Nixon's goal of energy independence by 1980.

However, Ford faced a hostile Congress that sometimes openly questioned the political legitimacy of his presidency since he had ascended to the vice presidency and the presidency without having been elected. When Ford moved to increase import fees on petroleum imports, Congress passed a law delaying implementation of the fee increase (which Ford then vetoed).

Two Ford proposals for eliminating the federal ceiling on domestic oil prices were rejected by Congress, and Ford vetoed a proposal to extend the ceiling.

But Ford did have some energy policy successes. In December 1975, the Strategic Petroleum Reserve (SPR) was established when the Energy Policy and Conservation Act (EPCA) was passed by Congress. The law was designed "to reduce the impact of severe energy supply interruptions" such as the interruption from the OPEC embargo. EPCA also extended the Emergency Petroleum Allocation Act of 1973—which had established price controls on petroleum—and for the first time set federal standards for fuel efficiency in new cars.

Some of the policies from Ford's tenure have had a lasting impact. Fuel effi-ciency in cars initially rose rapidly following implementation of the Corporate Average Fuel Economy (CAFE) standards in 1978. A 2002 study by the National Academy of Sciences concluded that motor vehicle fuel usage was 14% lower in 2002 than it would have been in the absence of fuel efficiency standards.[iv]

The SPR is also still an important tool of energy policy today, and has been utilized several times to stave off supply disruptions. However, it has also been used for political purposes in an attempt to manipulate the price of crude even in the absence of a supply disruption (as discussed later in the chapter, in the sidebar "Political Games with the SPR").

But even though Ford's tenure was shorter than the normal four-year presi-dential term, crude oil consumption and imports both rose sharply between his first year and last year in office. Thus, despite the best efforts of Nixon and Ford, the next president took over a nation that was more dependent on foreign oil than ever before.

Jimmy Carter

In little more than two decades we've gone from a position of energy independence to one in which almost half the oil we use comes from foreign countries, at prices that are going through the roof. Our excessive dependence on OPEC has already taken a tremendous toll on our economy and our people. This is the direct cause of the long lines which have made millions of you spend aggravating hours waiting for gasoline. It's a cause of the increased inflation and unemployment that we now face. This intolerable dependence on foreign oil threatens our economic independence and the very security of our nation. The energy crisis is real. It is worldwide. It is a clear and present danger to our nation. These are facts and we simply must face them.

—President Carter (July 15, 1979)

Of the past eight presidents, President Obama included, perhaps Jimmy Carter was the one most openly vocal about the need to reverse growing U.S. dependence on foreign oil. He was brutally honest with the American people about the need to act, and about the consequences if we did not. But his message was not entirely well received.

When Carter took over as president in 1977, oil imports had increased by 370% from Nixon's first year in office, 1969. Oil consumption was at an all-time high, and domestic production was down 14% from the 1970 peak.

Only three months into office, Carter delivered a major speech in which he described the energy situation as "the greatest challenge our country will face during our lifetimes" outside of preventing war. He predicted that the problem was going to get progressively worse through the end of the century.

But Carter underestimated the amount of oil still to be produced. At the time of his 1977 speech, the world consumed 60 million bpd. He noted that demand was increasing by 5% each year, and that—due to production declines in existing fields—just to maintain production at 1977 levels would require "the production of a new Texas every year, an Alaskan North Slope every nine months, or a new Saudi Arabia every three years." Carter stated that this obviously could not continue, but then oil production continued to expand for the next 30 years (albeit not at 5% per year).

The goal Carter set forth was that the U.S. would never again use more foreign oil than it did in 1977. He proposed initiatives such as insulating 90% of U.S. homes and all new buildings, establishing a six-month supply of oil in the SPR, placing import quotas on foreign oil, increasing usage of solar power, and increasing production of coal.

In August 1977, Carter signed into law the Department of Energy Organization Act of 1977, which created the Department of Energy (DOE). The DOE was established as a cabinet-level department originally designed to consolidate several energy-related government agencies, including the Federal Energy Administration and the Federal Power Commission.

In a much-maligned speech in July 1979 (commonly referred to as Carter's "national malaise" speech), Carter acknowledged that these programs would cost a lot of money, and urged windfall profits taxes on oil companies to pay for them. His justification for these taxes was that if oil price controls were gradually ended—as he also proposed—oil companies would receive "huge and undeserved windfall profits" as oil prices began to rise.

In 1980, Carter signed into law the Crude Oil Windfall Profits Tax Act, which imposed a 70% tax on the price of oil above a $12.81 per barrel threshold. The tax was forecast to raise $178 billion to $277 billion over 13 years, but by the time it was abolished in 1988 it had raised only $40 billion.

Did you know? The Three Mile Island nuclear power plant core meltdown in Pennsylvania took place in 1979, Carter's third year in office.

Many of Carter's proposals were advanced with the Energy Security Act (ESA) of 1980. Included within the ESA were programs to increase the production of gasohol (gasoline/ethanol blends) via loan guarantees for biomass and alcohol fuels projects.

The ESA also included the U.S. Synthetic Fuels Corporation Act, which established the Synthetic Fuels Corporation (SFC)—a government-funded corporation with the purpose of developing a synthetic liquid fuels industry. But technical challenges and cost overruns ultimately doomed the SFC to failure, and this failure is sometimes cited by critics as an example of why the government should leave the energy business to the free markets.

A cursory look at the oil production and consumption trends under Carter would suggest that his proposals were highly successful. U.S. consumption and imports both fell during his term, and domestic production reversed a six-year decline. However, it is important to note other world events that were taking place during his term, and that impacted world oil markets.

Beginning in 1978, protests in Iran—which ultimately culminated in the Iranian Revolution—reduced Iran's oil production from 6 million bpd to 1.5 million bpd. This resulted in a dramatic increase in world oil prices. The situation worsened when Iraq invaded Iran in 1980, and by 1981 the combined output of the two countries had fallen by 5.6 million bpd from 1978 levels.

The result is known as the 1979 oil crisis. It was the first major oil crisis to impact the U.S. since the 1973 OPEC embargo. The price of oil increased by 160% in two years, from $14.55 in 1978 to $36.00 in 1980. A sharp increase in prices generally has an impact on consumption, and this is at least part of the reason consumption and imports were down during the Carter administration.

Carter was also fortunate enough to be in office when the Prudhoe Bay oil field began production in 1977 upon completion of the Alaska Pipeline. Thus, the energy policy decisions made by previous administrations to approve the pipeline manifested themselves as increased oil production during the Carter administration. Excluding Alaska, production in the Lower 48 U.S. states declined by over 10% during Carter's term.

Carter was perhaps ahead of his time, as many of his energy policy ideas still have a great deal of support today. He was thoroughly engaged on energy issues throughout his presidency, and he understood the growing risks from dependence on foreign oil. But Americans were frustrated with high inflation, high oil prices, and a stagnant economy, and so they voted Carter out of office in 1980 in favor of someone who had very different ideas about the direction the country needed to go.

Ronald Reagan

> *Our national energy plan should not be a rigid set of production and conservation goals dictated by government. Our primary objective is simply for our citizens to have enough energy, and it is up to them to decide how much energy that is, and in what form and manner it will reach them. When the free market is permitted to work the way it should, millions of individual choices and judgments will produce the proper balance of supply and demand our economy needs. Overall, the outlook for this country's energy supplies is not nearly as grim as some have painted it, although our problems are not all behind us.*

—President Reagan (July 17, 1981)

When Ronald Reagan took office in 1981, crude oil prices were still hovering near all-time highs. But Reagan took a very different approach from Carter's proactive attempts to deal with the energy issue. Reagan believed that the free market was the best solution to the energy crisis, and his policies reflected that.

He accelerated the phase-out of the price controls on domestic oil production, let the tax credit on solar power expire, abolished the U.S. Synthetic Fuels Corporation, and repealed the Crude Oil Windfall Profits Tax Act that had been signed into law under President Carter. Reagan also famously removed from the White House the solar panels that Carter had installed during his term.

Did you know? The Chernobyl nuclear disaster in the Ukraine took place in 1986, prompting President Reagan to sharply criticize the secrecy the Soviet government originally attempted to maintain about the incident.

Reagan was a strong supporter of developing domestic energy, and he pushed to have more federal resources opened to exploration and development. He unsuccessfully advocated for the opening of parts of the Arctic National Wildlife Refuge (ANWR) for development.

Reagan was also an advocate of nuclear energy, signing several pieces of legislation during his tenure. Nuclear production overtook hydropower to become the second largest provider of electricity in the U.S (behind coal) while Reagan was in office.

The Strategic Petroleum Reserve was viewed by Reagan as an important part of emergency preparedness, and he supported the government's role in stocking the SPR with crude oil. The SPR reached the 250 million barrel mark during Reagan's first term and the 500 million barrel mark during Reagan's second term.

POLITICAL GAMES WITH THE SPR

The OPEC oil embargo of 1973 emphatically demonstrated the vulnerability of the U.S. to disruptions in oil supplies. In 1975, President Ford signed legislation that (among other things) would establish a petroleum reserve of up to 1 billion barrels of crude oil. The Strategic Petroleum Reserve was the result, and oil began to fill the SPR two years later.

The Energy Policy and Conservation Act (EPCA) states that oil can be released onto the market from the SPR if the President determines that there is a "severe energy supply interruption" or if the President declares that a condition "exists that constitutes, or is likely to become, a domestic or international energy supply shortage of significant scope or duration."

Oil has been released from the SPR under those conditions three times.

In 1991, President George H. W. Bush announced that the U.S. would release a portion of the SPR to stabilize the oil markets as military action began against Iraq; 17.3 million barrels were released.

In 2005, President George W. Bush authorized a release in the wake of Hurricane Katrina, which sidelined oil production in the Gulf of Mexico. The total release—which included emergency loans as well as direct sales—was 20.8 million barrels.

In 2011, President Obama authorized a release of 30 million barrels in response to the loss of production during Libya's civil war. The release was coordinated with the International Energy Agency (IEA), whose member countries also released 30 million barrels.

But many politicians have sought to use the SPR for political purposes. In 1996—an election year—President Clinton used the SPR in an effort to reduce oil prices. Senator Chuck Schumer lobbied to have the SPR tapped in 1999, when he cited oil's "meteoric ascent to nearly $25 per barrel" as justification for withdrawing oil from the SPR. As gasoline prices reached $1.33 a gallon, Schumer declared that this was a "crisis" and he introduced legislation to make it easier to use the SPR as a tool against high oil prices.

In 2011, Congressman Ed Markey introduced similar legislation that called for a release from the SPR to combat rising prices. The irony in Markey's request is that he is one of the most outspoken members of Congress on the need to reduce CO_2 emissions. Demand for oil had fallen sharply in the U.S. due to high prices (and hence, oil-related CO_2 emissions had also fallen), but Markey wanted to use the SPR to lower oil prices—which would result in higher demand and higher CO_2 emissions. Hence, his two positions were inconsistent: he wanted lower CO_2 emissions and lower oil prices.

In any case, use of the SPR to control oil prices puts the U.S. government in the role of an oil speculator. It is hard to imagine that oil prices today would have been materially different had the government released oil in 1999 in response to the "crisis" of $25/barrel oil. In all likelihood, the oil would have been replaced at a higher price than $25/barrel—a bad deal for taxpayers.

Higher oil prices do not constitute an oil supply emergency. They are an inconvenience. Supply disruptions such as the 1973 oil embargo—the spark that caused the SPR to be created in the first place—can result in no fuel at the service station. That can be an oil supply emergency, and the SPR should be saved for those sorts of events. If we end up draining the SPR in a series of futile attempts to control oil prices, then how will we cope with a true supply emergency?

During Reagan's first term, oil production continued the expansion that began under Carter, primarily driven by increasing production from the Prudhoe Bay oil field. Imports and consumption continued to fall throughout Reagan's first term, primarily in response to continued high oil prices and a recession that began during his first year in office.

However, the trends in domestic production, consumption, and imports reversed themselves during Reagan's second term. Years of high prices had brought online substantial oil capacity outside of OPEC and had reduced demand for oil. Prudhoe Bay was also reaching peak production. Despite OPEC's best attempts to cut production to hold prices up, an oil glut developed and oil prices collapsed in 1986—dropping more than 50% from 1985 levels.

Low oil prices provided a disincentive for domestic production, and Prudhoe Bay production peaked in 1988. Thus, the decline in U.S. production that had reversed itself as Prudhoe Bay ramped up continued, and it would not reverse direction for the next 22 years.

But low prices also spurred demand, and when Reagan left office, imports and consumption were starting to trend higher. Both were at the highest levels of Reagan's presidency when Vice President George H. W. Bush was elected to the presidency.

George H. W. Bush

> *But we are, I will be the first to concede, a long way from total energy independence. Our imports of foreign oil have been climbing steadily since 1985 and now stand at 42 percent of our total consumption. Too many of those oil imports come from sources in troubled parts of the world.*

> —President Bush (February 20, 1991)

George Bush had been in the oil business in Texas before entering politics. As president, oil would play a major role in his foreign policy decisions, the most notable of which culminated in the Persian Gulf War.

Following its war with Iran—which also corresponded to the global collapse in oil prices—Iraq was in desperate financial shape and deeply in debt to Kuwait and Saudi Arabia. Iraq partially blamed Kuwait for depressed oil prices, accusing it of overproducing its quota. Iraq further claimed that Kuwait was stealing Iraq's oil by slant drilling into oil fields in Iraqi territory.

Did you know? In 1989, the Exxon Valdez oil tanker ran aground and spilled hundreds of thousands of barrels of oil in Alaska's Prince William Sound.

Saddam Hussein's saber rattling with Kuwait finally led to action as Iraq invaded and overran Kuwait in August 1990. U.S. troops were immediately deployed to Saudi Arabia at the request of Saudi Arabia's King Fahd to deter Hussein from advancing into Saudi Arabia.

On August 8, 1990, Bush addressed the nation, demanding that Iraq immediately withdraw from Kuwait. Bush cited the potential economic threat from Iraq's invasion:

> *Iraq is already a rich and powerful country that possesses the world's second largest reserves of oil and over a million men under arms. It's the fourth largest military in the world. Our country now imports nearly half the oil it consumes and could face a major*

threat to its economic independence. Much of the world is even more dependent upon imported oil and is even more vulnerable to Iraqi threats.

The price of oil responded quickly to the invasion. By October 1990 oil prices had more than doubled from their levels three months earlier. Throughout the remainder of the year, the U.S. pursued diplomatic efforts and put together a coalition of forces to join in ousting Iraq from Kuwait.

In January 1991, the U.S. began military action against Iraq. In order to calm the oil markets, Bush ordered the first-ever emergency sale of crude oil from the Strategic Petroleum Reserve. The military campaign was over relatively quickly, and crude oil prices returned to their levels from before the war. But the precedent for U.S. military action in the Middle East to maintain stable oil supplies had been set.

The Gulf War was the defining energy event of Bush's administration, but there were other noteworthy developments. Due to environmental concerns, in 1990 Bush signed an executive moratorium banning offshore oil developments outside of the western Gulf of Mexico and certain parts of Alaska. The ban impacted the North Atlantic, Pacific Coast, New England, Mid-Atlantic, and the eastern Gulf of Mexico.[v]

▧ **Did you know?** The executive moratorium on drilling put in place by President George H. W. Bush in 1990 was lifted by his son, President George W. Bush, in 2008.

Bush also signed into law a comprehensive energy package—the Energy Policy Act of 1992 (EPAct). A wide range of energy issues was addressed in EPAct, including energy efficiency standards for buildings and appliances, energy conservation, and the promotion of use of alternative energy vehicles.

Bill Clinton

I am today concurring with the Department of Commerce's finding that the nation's growing reliance on imports of crude oil and refined petroleum products threaten the nation's security because they increase U.S. vulnerability to oil supply interruptions.

—President Clinton (February 16, 1995)

The year Bill Clinton became president, oil consumption was on the rise, oil imports were at an all-time high, and domestic production was at its lowest level since the 1950s. However, Clinton's two terms in office also corresponded with oil prices that were both lower and less volatile than those in the 1980s, and thus the idea of energy independence likely assumed a lower priority with the public than it had held in the 1970s and 1980s.

Still, there were some significant energy initiatives during the Clinton years. The Partnership for a New Generation of Vehicles (PNGV) was founded by the Clinton administration in 1993 as a venture between the U.S. government and major automobile makers including Chrysler, Ford, and General Motors. The purpose of the program was to develop vehicles with a fuel efficiency of up to 80 miles per gallon.

The PNGV identified several fruitful areas for increasing fuel economy, including lighter vehicles, higher engine efficiency, hybrid vehicles, and regenerative braking. The three major automakers—Chrysler, Ford, and GM—all built hybrid concept cars capable of achieving at least 72 mpg. However, the program was cancelled following Clinton's presidency by the George W. Bush administration.

As part of his deficit reduction plan in 1993, Clinton also pushed through a federal gasoline tax increase of 4.3 cents per gallon. The initial proposal had been for a 9-cent-per-gallon increase, but after fierce opposition in the Senate, the amount was reduced. There have been no federal increases in gas taxes in the U.S. since the 1993 increase.

The Clinton presidency marked the end of 12 years of Republican rule, and Clinton's priorities on energy and the environment sharply differed in some areas from those of Reagan and Bush. For example, Reagan was a proponent of developing the oil reserves in ANWR, but Clinton vetoed a bill from the Republican-majority House that would have allowed drilling in ANWR.

The Clinton administration also helped negotiate the Kyoto Protocol, which set targets for reducing greenhouse gas emissions. However, even though Clinton signed the protocol, the Senate voted 95-0 for a resolution to reject it on the grounds that developing countries were not being asked to make serious emissions cuts. So the administration decided not to send the Kyoto Protocol to the Senate for ratification.

In 1977, as the attorney general of Arkansas, Clinton had opposed the construction of a new nuclear power plant, arguing that increased efficiency was a cheaper route to meeting future energy needs. His opposition to nuclear power was still evident 20 years later, when nuclear power was conspicuously absent in his discussions regarding his administration's energy priorities. And in 2011, Clinton was critical of the Obama administration's loan guarantees for future nuclear power plants, arguing that the plants were too vulnerable to natural disasters and did not create many jobs.[vi]

In 2000, the last year of Clinton's second term, oil consumption was at an all-time high (the economy had been expanding for nearly a decade), oil imports were at an all-time high, and domestic production had fallen to a 50-year low. The situation seemed ripe for a rise in oil prices.

George W. Bush

Keeping America competitive requires affordable energy. And here we have a serious problem: America is addicted to oil, which is often imported from unstable parts of the world.

—President Bush (January 31, 2006)

The George W. Bush presidency was extremely eventful in terms of energy developments. Among the events occurring during his two terms in office were the September 11 terrorist attacks followed by a war with Afghanistan, another war in the Persian Gulf, major hurricanes that interrupted supplies and caused record gasoline price spikes, an almost uninterrupted increase in the price of oil, and passage of some major pieces of energy legislation that led to a massive expansion of biofuel production.

Like his father, George W. Bush had ties to the oil industry. Even Bush's vice president, Dick Cheney, was an ex-oilman, having served as the CEO of oil field–services company Halliburton. Thus, the administration would come under heavy criticism at times for being too cozy with the oil industry.

Within two weeks of taking office, Bush named Cheney as the chairman of the National Energy Policy Development Group (NEPDG).[1] The group's purpose was to "develop a national energy policy designed to help the private sector, and, as necessary and appropriate, state and local govern-

---

[1] Also commonly referred to as the Energy Task Force.

ments, promote dependable, affordable, and environmentally sound production and distribution of energy for the future."[vii]

The group's work culminated in the release of the National Energy Policy (NEP) in May of 2001. The report warned that in the years ahead, America would face the most serious energy shortages since the 1973 oil embargo. The report made specific recommendations designed to meet five goals:

- Modernize conservation

- Modernize U.S. energy infrastructure

- Increase energy supplies

- Accelerate the protection and improvement of the environment

- Increase U.S. energy security

The NEPDG came under criticism because its activities were not made public and critics charged that the oil industry heavily influenced the outcome. In fact, many of the report's recommendations were focused on increasing domestic oil supplies and ensuring that the U.S. maintained access to supplies abroad. However, continued access to oil was only one part of a comprehensive energy plan detailed in the report.

One area in which the group made specific recommendations was in the use of renewable and alternative energy. Among the recommendations were an expansion of a tax credit for landfill methane projects, acceleration of the permitting process for geothermal projects, expansion and extension of the tax credits for electricity produced from wind and biomass, a new tax credit for residential solar installations, a continuation of the ethanol tax exemption, an income tax credit for the purchase of hybrid or fuel-cell vehicles, and the development of hydrogen and fusion technologies.

President Bush aggressively pursued development of hydrogen power. In 2002, Bush replaced Clinton's PNGV with FreedomCAR,[2] which was a program designed to produce affordable cars powered by hydrogen fuel cells.

In his 2003 State of the Union address, Bush proposed $1.2 billion to develop hydrogen vehicles:

---

[2] CAR stood for Cooperative Automotive Research.

A simple chemical reaction between hydrogen and oxygen generates energy, which can be used to power a car, producing only water, not exhaust fumes. With a new national commitment, our scientists and engineers will overcome obstacles to taking these cars from laboratory to showroom, so that the first car driven by a child born today could be powered by hydrogen, and pollution-free.

Bush's hydrogen initiatives had numerous critics—myself included—on the basis that there were far too many major technical challenges to overcome and that this was not the best investment of tax dollars for alternative energy. The criticisms were seemingly validated in 2009. After nearly $2 billion had been spent on the program, Obama's new secretary of energy, Steven Chu, announced that funding for the program would be cut because, in the Obama administration's view, a hydrogen economy was unlikely within the next 20 years.

2003 also ushered in a new conflict in Iraq. The stated reason for the U.S. invasion was to prevent Iraqi president Saddam Hussein from obtaining and deploying weapons of mass destruction. However, the location of Iraq and its potential to disrupt the international oil markets certainly factored into the decision. After all, there are other dangerous dictators around the world who are largely ignored because they pose no real threat to the oil markets.

In 2005, Bush signed the Energy Policy Act of 2005 (EPAct2005). The act had numerous provisions across the energy space, including incentives for nuclear power, fossil fuel production, biofuels, wind power, geothermal power, solar power, and ocean power—and was arguably the most important piece of legislation ever passed for ethanol producers.

Ethanol production in the U.S. had been subsidized with tax credits for decades, but EPAct2005 for the first time established a Renewable Fuel Standard (RFS) that mandated specific volumes of ethanol that had to be blended into motor fuel. After the RFS was established (and expanded in 2007), the ethanol industry entered the fastest growth period in its existence. Thus, George Bush the oilman oversaw the largest expansion of biofuels in the nation's history.

In his 2006 State of the Union address, Bush famously stated that the U.S. was "addicted to oil" and that his administration had spent $10 billion to develop alternative energy since 2001. Yet during that time, consumption had increased and domestic production had fallen, leading to record-high oil imports.

In his 2007 State of the Union address, Bush called for reducing U.S. gasoline consumption by 20% in the next ten years, which became known as the "Twenty in Ten" goal. Later that year, Bush signed the Energy Independence and Security Act of 2007 (EISA), which was designed to meet those objectives. The EISA expanded the Renewable Fuel Standard program (RFS2) to accelerate and increase the volumes of ethanol that had to be blended into the fuel supply, and it established new categories of renewable fuel.

One of the biggest stories of the Bush administration was the volatility of oil prices when he was in office. During Bush's first week in office in 2001, the price of West Texas Intermediate crude was $31 a barrel. In 2004, the price breeched $50 a barrel, and then in the wake of Hurricane Katrina, in 2005, the price nearly reached $70 a barrel. In 2008, the price crossed the $100 threshold on the way to $147. But then a recession brought prices crashing back down, and during Bush's last week in office, in 2009, the price of WTI was back under $40/barrel (but not for long).

Barack Obama

> *We have known for decades that our survival depends on finding new sources of energy. Yet we import more oil today than ever before.*

> —President Obama (February 24, 2009)

Before President Obama was elected, he campaigned on familiar themes. He said that a major priority would be to end dependence on oil from the Middle East and Venezuela within ten years. The core of his energy policy would revolve around a $150 billion investment in renewable energy that he estimated would create 5 million new jobs. Domestic drilling, he said, would be a stop-gap measure.

Obama promised to help retool U.S. automakers to produce more fuel-efficient cars, to tap domestic natural gas resources, and to develop new clean coal technologies. He took a cautious approach with nuclear power, promising to find a way to safely harness it but never pushing it as a major piece of his platform.

Prior to being elected, candidate Obama took a hard stance against domestic oil producers, declaring that it was not fair that they were making record profits in tough economic times. He promised to implement a windfall profits tax that would be used to rebate $1,000 back to American families. He also said that he would take a "use it or lose it" approach to existing oil and gas leases, arguing that oil companies were leasing lands that they were not developing.

By the time Obama was inaugurated, the U.S. was in the midst of a recession and oil prices had plummeted from record prices of the summer of 2008. To facilitate his technology-centric energy policy, he tapped Nobel Prize–winning physicist Steven Chu as his energy secretary.

In February 2009, Obama signed the American Recovery and Reinvestment Act of 2009 (ARRA), and one of Secretary Chu's immediate priorities became disbursement of more than $70 billion in ARRA funds dedicated to energy efficiency, clean energy, and transportation initiatives.

In June 2009, Obama signed the Supplemental Appropriations Act of 2009, which contained within it the Car Allowance Rebate System (CARS), commonly known as "Cash for Clunkers." This program provided rebates for consumers who traded in their inefficient automobiles for more efficient models. The program proved extremely popular with consumers, and the initial $1 billion allocated for the program was quickly depleted. Congress then allocated an additional $2 billion, and ultimately a total of $2.9 billion in rebates was paid out under the program.

June 2009 also saw introduction of the American Clean Energy and Security Act of 2009 (ACES), which would have established a greenhouse gas emissions trading plan in the U.S. This bill was narrowly passed by the House of Representatives but failed to pass the Senate.

In February 2010, Obama announced over $8 billion in federal loan guarantees for the construction of the first new nuclear power plant in the U.S. in over 30 years. He noted that nuclear power has "serious drawbacks" but stressed that investing in nuclear power was a necessary step.

In March 2010, and in the face of oil prices that had recovered to above the $100/barrel mark, Obama announced that he would allow oil and natural gas drilling offshore along the Atlantic coastline, the eastern Gulf of Mexico, and the north coast of Alaska.

On April 20, 2010, the Deepwater Horizon drilling rig in the Gulf of Mexico suffered an explosion that killed 11 men. Over the next three months, millions of barrels of oil leaked from the sea floor into the Gulf of Mexico.

Some supporters of expanded drilling reversed course as a result of the accident, and the Obama administration announced the suspension of planned exploration in two Alaska locations. It also canceled a pending lease sale in the Gulf of Mexico and another offshore in Virginia, extended a moratorium on deepwater drilling permits for six months, and suspended activities on 33 deepwater exploration wells in the Gulf.[viii]

In December 2010, the administration announced a seven-year ban on drilling in the eastern Gulf of Mexico and off the Atlantic Coast because a "more stringent regulatory regime" was needed.

In March 2011, the disaster at the Fukushima Daiichi nuclear power plant in Japan altered the debate over nuclear power in the U.S. The incident was a setback for Obama's nuclear power plans as it hardened objections against nuclear power within Obama's own party.

THE KEYSTONE PIPELINE DEBATE

One of the ongoing major energy policy debates during the Obama administration concerns the Keystone pipeline project. In 2008, TransCanada proposed an extension to the existing Keystone pipeline system, which delivers crude oil from Canada to refineries in the U.S. The extension, designated Keystone XL, requires U.S. State Department approval because the pipeline crosses the U.S–Canadian border.

The State Department issued a favorable environmental impact statement, noting in it that if the pipeline was rejected, Canada would "seek alternative transportation systems to move oil to markets."

Growing indications that the pipeline would be approved by the Obama administration mobilized opposition against the pipeline. Huge protests against it were organized to occur outside the White House. The protesters demanded that President Obama live up to his campaign promises, because as a candidate Obama campaigned against the "tyranny of oil."

The protesters cited several objections against the pipeline, but ultimately the objections came down to a desire to slow development of Canada's oil sands, the source of the oil for the pipeline. NASA scientist and Keystone opponent Jim Hansen said that the pipeline would be the "fuse to the biggest carbon bomb on the planet" and that if it were built it would be "game over" for the climate.

Proponents of the pipeline argued that it would enhance the energy security of the U.S. by opening up greater oil supplies from a friendly nation. They argued that if the pipeline was not approved, then Canada would likely build a pipeline to its West

Coast and sell the oil to China. Or, they argued, Canada would simply keep moving the oil through existing pipelines, by truck, or by rail.

In the wake of the massive protests, the Obama administration blinked, announcing that it couldn't make a decision until early 2013—conveniently, after the 2012 presidential election. Opponents of the pipeline praised the decision. Pipeline proponents began to immediately use the (deferred) decision as a campaign issue against Obama, and they have made legislative attempts to authorize the pipeline despite the administration's decision.

My personal view is that it was not—as pipeline opponents have portrayed it—a courageous decision by the Obama administration. A courageous decision would have been to take a bold stand on one side of the issue or the other. This decision was not sound environmental or energy policy. Obama made a calculated political decision in order to try to appease the environmental constituency while still holding out the possibility for pipeline proponents that it may be ultimately approved.

In August 2011, Solyndra—a solar power company that had been a recipient of $535 million in loan guarantees under Obama's 2009 stimulus package— declared bankruptcy. As a result of the bankruptcy, taxpayers had to pay back the loan. The failure of Solyndra, as well as the failures of some other alternative energy companies that had received grants and loan guarantees, raised questions—especially among Obama's critics—about the efficacy of his clean energy initiatives.

In his 2012 State of the Union address, Obama announced that his administration would open more than 75 percent of potential offshore oil and gas resources to exploration and development. After noting that U.S. oil production was at an 8-year high and that dependence on foreign oil was at a 16-year low, he stressed his commitment to develop natural gas reserves in the U.S. He further said that the U.S. should stop subsidizing oil companies and direct the money instead to clean energy tax credits.

Some of Obama's initiatives will have a meaningful impact, some will have a modest impact—but at a very high cost—and some will have little impact or may even be counterproductive. But it will be several years before we can judge the impact of the entire Obama energy policy.

There is one great irony over oil production in the Obama administration. Obama is viewed as being not particularly friendly toward the oil-and-gas industry. Other than the concession to drilling that occurred prior to the Deepwater Horizon oil spill—which was later rescinded—few of his policies could be characterized as friendly to the industry. In fact, he criticized the oil industry in his 2011 State of the Union address and stated that it was in the business of producing "yesterday's energy."

But the irony is that U.S. oil production under George W. Bush—whom everyone knows as an oilman sympathetic to the needs of the oil industry— fell every year he was in office. During Obama's first three years in office, oil production rose every year (see Figure 14-2). Further, in 2011, oil refiners actually became net exporters of finished products[3] for the first time in decades, and fuel exports were the nation's highest-value export of the year.[ix]

U.S. Oil Production Under Bush and Obama

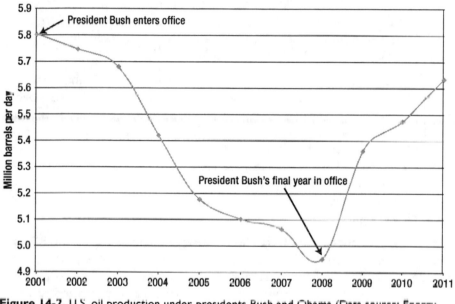

Figure 14-2. U.S. oil production under presidents Bush and Obama (Data source: Energy Information Administration)[x]

If this seems counterintuitive, that's not surprising. It is counterintuitive, but the explanation holds the key to why the past eight presidents have been unable to tame U.S. oil dependency.

---

[3] Note that this is very different from being a net exporter of oil. The U.S. is still heavily dependent on oil imports to produce the exports; it just means that the U.S. exported more finished fuel than it imported.

Why Presidents Fail to Tame Oil Dependence

So why did the past seven presidents—using many different initiatives and approaches—fail to rein in 40 years of growing dependence on foreign oil?[4] Why did they fail to rein in consumption, or reverse falling U.S. production?

The answer—in the simplest terms—is that presidents simply do not possess that kind of power in a democracy. Further, the fruits of the power they do wield will often not bear fruit for many years. Draconian measures may work to reduce oil imports or cut consumption, but draconian measures result in fierce opposition from political opponents and from the public. But even draconian measures will have a limited impact on a commodity that is global in nature and in high demand.

U.S. oil production didn't fall under Bush and rise under Obama based on the policies of these presidents. Production behaved according to policies that had been put in place years earlier, and in accordance with the behavior of oil prices in previous years. Jimmy Carter experienced a rise in oil production because the Alaska Pipeline—approved by Nixon—was completed while he was in office (see Figure 14-3). Obama experienced a rise in oil production following years of climbing oil prices, which increased the number of economically attractive oil projects and led to record capital expenditures by oil companies.

Ultimately, presidents don't have a lot of long-term influence on the oil markets for two reasons. First, although high prices are known to cut consumption and imports, consumers (a.k.a. voters) don't like to pay high prices, so any policy that a president puts in place that is perceived to cause oil prices to rise is a political liability.

---

[4] I omit President Obama from this list because it is too early to determine whether his policies will ultimately succeed where others have failed.

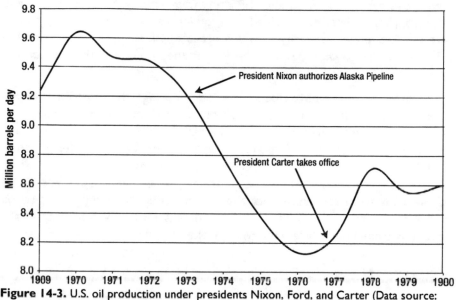

Figure 14-3. U.S. oil production under presidents Nixon, Ford, and Carter (Data source: Energy Information Administration)[xi]

The second reason is that the two major political parties in the U.S. have very different ideas about energy policy, and the policies of one administration are often overturned by the next administration. This results in an inconsistent energy policy, and uncertainty causes energy projects to be cancelled or delayed. Thus, passing new energy legislation every two to four years that sometimes changes the rules in the middle of the game has a detrimental impact on energy production—both fossil and renewable.

Summary

Four decades of presidents—from Nixon to Obama—all publicly fretted about the loss of energy independence for the U.S. They tried many different approaches to solving this problem—from serious intervention in the energy markets to letting the free market solve the problem. Many billions of dollars have been spent on programs with the intent of eliminating dependence on foreign oil. Yet in 1969, Americans depended on oil imports for 10% of their consumption, and in 2008 that number had risen to over 50% of consumption (but it has started to decline since then).

Presidents have underestimated the ability of domestic supplies to fill our needs, overestimated the ability of alternative energy to replace oil, and failed to pass policies that reined in growing consumption. These trends have put U.S. energy security at much greater risk than at the time of the OPEC oil embargo of 1973, and the longer they continue, the greater the threat to the U.S. economy.

Nevertheless, there have been periods during the previous seven administrations where the trends of declining domestic production and increasing consumption and imports reversed direction for a period of time. The U.S. is presently undergoing a reversal of years of declining oil production, and Goldman Sachs recently went so far as to project that by 2017 the U.S. would once more reign as the world's largest oil producer.[xii] To the contrary, I rather suspect the current situation is analogous to oil production during President Carter's administration, when the Alaska Pipeline provided but a brief respite from the annual production declines.

References

[i] Jon Stewart, "An Energy-Independent Future," *The Daily Show*, broadcast June 16, 2010 on Comedy Central, available at www.thedailyshow.com /watch/wed-june-16-2010/an-energy-independent-future.

[ii] International Energy Agency (IEA), *CO_2 Emissions from Fuel Combustion*, 2011 Edition (Paris: Organization for Economic Cooperation and Development, 2011).

[iii] David Frum, *How We Got Here: The '70s* (New York: Basic Books, 2000).

[iv] National Research Council, *Effectiveness and Impact of Corporate Average Fuel Economy (CAFE) Standards* (Washington D.C.: The National Academies Press, 2002), p. 9, electronic edition accessed January 1, 2012, http://books.nap.edu/openbook.php?record_id=10172&page=9.

[v] Energy Information Administration (EIA), "Moratorium on Offshore Drilling (1990)," accessed January 2, 2012, www.eia.gov/oil_gas /natural_gas/analysis_publications/ngmajorleg/moratorium.html.

[vi] Michiko Kakutani, "Bill Clinton Lays Out His Prescription for America's Future," *New York Times*, November 7, 2011, www.nytimes.com/2011/11 /08/books/back-to-work-has-bill-clintons-ideas-for-america-review.html.

vii National Energy Policy Development Group, *Report of the National Energy Policy Development Group*, May 16, 2001, available at http://wtrg.com /EnergyReport/National-Energy-Policy.pdf.

viii Ray Suarez, "Obama Extends Drilling Moratorium, Defends Administration's Spill Response," *PBS News Hour*, May 27, 2010, www.pbs.org/newshour/bb/environment/jan-june10/oil1_05-27.html.

ix Associated Press, "In a First, Gas and Other Fuels Are Top US Export," *USAToday.com*, December 31, 2011, www.usatoday.com/money/industries /energy/story/2011-12-31/united-states-export/52298812/1.

x EIA, *Crude Oil Production*, accessed January 30, 2011, www.eia.gov/dnav /pet/pet_crd_crpdn_adc_mbblpd_m.htm.

xi Ibid.

xii London Bureau, "Goldman Sees US as Top Oil Producer in 2017," Dow Jones Newswires, September 12, 2011, http://rigzone.com/news /article.asp?a_id=110840.

The Road Ahead

Planning and Preparation

Knowledge of what is does not open the door directly to what should be.

—Albert Einstein

The primary message that I hope readers take away from this book is this: When it comes to energy, there is no free lunch. There are always trade-offs. Politicians often end up dictating our energy policies based on the perceived desires of the electorate, but the electorate is often woefully uninformed about energy issues. This often leads to ineffective or counterproductive energy policies. Hence, the first step toward improving energy policies is ensuring that citizens are well versed in energy issues.

The second major message I want readers to take away is that, despite assurances from people that there will be adequate supplies of oil for the next 50 years, or warnings from others that peak oil will soon send the world back to the Stone Age, the future is uncertain. So we have to plan for various possibilities.

The Three Tenets

Here is what I want in an ideal world: access to clean and affordable energy for everyone. A push for simply affordable energy may result in exploiting the dirtiest energy options on the planet. This is the driver behind the huge increases in carbon dioxide emissions in the Asia Pacific region over the past decade. Affordable energy is energy that is often used frivolously, and this is a problem when the affordable energy source is polluting.

On the other hand, a rush to clean energy may result in energy that is too expensive for many people to afford and supplies that are inadequate. So there have to be compromises.

Those compromises are what this book is about. We make these compromises without even realizing it, and very often they are made for us. Oil may be one of the cheapest liquid fuel options, but it comes with a price, and with risks. Corn ethanol comes with a price and with risks. So do nuclear power, wind power, hydropower, coal, and natural gas. The trick is in balancing the risk-to-reward ratio. How do we provide affordable energy for people at the lowest possible economic and environmental risk?

There are three broad tenets that largely define the positions I take.

Tenet One

Because fossil fuels are a depleting resource that present special economic and environmental risks, we must plan for an orderly transition to more sustainable energy sources.

I think everyone would broadly agree that this transition must occur, but some believe it needn't occur for years or decades, and others believe that the market will take care of the transition. In other words, they believe that as fossil fuels deplete, oil prices will skyrocket and alternatives will become competitive.

The inherent risk in this view is that we have seen how quickly oil prices can change, and alternatives can't scale quickly enough to fill supply shortfalls and prevent those price spikes. Thus, it is imperative to manage this transition via policies such as those I have put forth in the book. These policies are designed to have features that people with opposing viewpoints can agree to, but they will require some level of compromise on certain points.

Tenet Two

As we make the transition to an economy built on more sustainable sources of energy, we need to ensure that we have adequate energy supplies during the transition, and carefully evaluate the trade-offs from our energy policy decisions.

We must be aware of—and be willing to have a civil debate about—the inherent trade-offs in our energy choices. For example, there is a legitimate debate to be had about the impact of biofuels on food prices—a debate that has been characterized as "food versus fuel." But it is important to keep in perspective that we need both food and fuel. Many things will increase the cost of food, including high oil prices. So while using arable land to produce biofuels could increase the price of food, it could also provide some competition to oil, potentially lowering overall energy costs. Thus, there are circumstances in which it is perfectly acceptable to use arable land to produce fuel, especially if the result is an overall lowering of the total cost of food plus fuel.

Of course, the reverse is true if the biofuel that is being produced is heavily dependent on fossil fuels for its production. In that case, it may take arable land out of food production and potentially even drive up the overall cost of energy. This is a worst-case scenario that we wish to avoid: higher food prices and higher energy prices without actually alleviating the dependence on fossil fuels. But we must be willing to have civil discussions on these issues in order to achieve the most desirable trade-offs.

Tenet Three

In the process of producing energy, we must take care of our air, water, and especially our topsoil to preserve our ability to feed the world's population.

Most people would likely agree that food security is as important—if not more so—than energy security. A country that is capable of feeding itself and providing for its own energy needs could weather a lot of global turmoil.

Areas that can produce food can also produce crops and byproducts that can be used to make fuel. Of course, this must be accomplished with sustainable agricultural practices. There are going to be a lot of people to feed in the future, and we can't afford to strip mine the soil and deplete fossil aquifers. We have to farm in a way that encourages good stewardship of the land, and we must not encourage unsustainable farming practices.

These three tenets explain why I have often been critical of corn ethanol policies in the U.S. Corn ethanol is heavily dependent on fossil fuels. Corn farming requires petroleum for herbicides, pesticides, diesel, and gasoline. It requires natural gas for fertilizer. Ethanol refineries rely almost exclusively on natural gas to produce steam for cooking mash and distilling ethanol, and their electricity supplies are often coal-based. So we have a fuel that is often characterized as renewable, but the majority of the energy content in ethanol can be traced directly to the fossil fuel inputs.

Further, corn farming has one of the higher environmental impacts among the crops we grow. It is a high fertilizer consumer, and we apply lots of fertilizer, pesticides, and herbicides that end up running off into our waterways.

These are the sorts of trade-offs we have to debate and discuss. But in my opinion, the answer is not to abandon corn ethanol, but rather to encourage it in the most sustainable way possible.

The Unpredictable Future

A 1999 article in *The Economist*, "Drowning in Oil,"[i] projected that oil might fall to $5 a barrel, noting that "the world is awash with the stuff, and it is likely to remain so." Instead, the price went on a decade-long run that increased oil prices by an order of magnitude.

On the flip side, in 2003, the late Matt Simmons, an energy investment banker, predicted an imminent natural gas crisis. He predicted, "Under the best of circumstances, if all prayers are answered there will be no crisis for maybe two years. After that it's a certainty."[ii] What happened? In 2005, advances in natural gas fracking resulted in the beginning of the largest expansion of natural gas production since the 1960s. Despite the prediction of the certainty of a U.S. natural gas crises, new all-time records were set for natural gas production and natural gas prices plummeted.

Contingency Planning

Because of the uncertainty of the future, what we must do is plan for contingencies, and not for calamity or business as usual. At different times, I have been asked for my opinion on whether someone should forgo college or having children because of the energy-related calamities that surely await us. I always respond to these sorts of queries in the same way: "We don't know for sure what the future holds, so don't put your life on hold waiting for a calamity. Go live your life, and if adversity lies ahead, we will work hard to deal with it."

Some people don't like this response, because they "know" that we are in for a disaster within a few short years. And they ask, "Why would you bring a child into a world that is going to be so terrible?"

Certainly there are challenges ahead. But some people have been awaiting imminent disaster for decades. Those who have read books like Rachel Carson's *Silent Spring*[iii] (1962), Paul Ehrlich's *The Population Bomb*[iv] (1968), or *The Limits to Growth*[v] (1972), a report for the Club of Rome, may have concluded that *Mad Max*[1] scenarios were all but assured by the year 2000.[2] So if you placed your life on hold in 1968 and began preparing for the end of civilization, you may have missed out on the joys (and challenges) of raising a family, or of advancing your education and working in exciting fields that were still in their infancy (e.g., computers and biotechnology).

On the other hand, it would be exceedingly foolish to dismiss risks simply because scenarios have not played out over a specific time line. I often hear the following type of criticism directed at people who express concern over the implications of peak oil: "Peak oil alarmists have wrongly forecasted imminent doom and gloom many times, and therefore their warnings can be dismissed."

To me, this is sort of like arguing that since my house has never burned down, it never will. This argument has two major flaws. The first is that it fails to recognize that one reason my house has never burned down is that I am aware of the many risks that could lead to my house burning down, and I have taken appropriate precautions. Therefore, educating people about the risks can cause changes in behavior that lessen the risks.

Concerns about the risks of future oil supplies have led to many policy changes—such as higher fuel economy standards and the implementation of the Strategic Petroleum Reserve—that have reduced the risks of future oil shocks.

The second flaw is that even when precautions are taken, homes can still burn down. Therefore, it is important not only to take precautions, but to have insurance and contingency plans in place in case the home does burn down.

With respect to peak oil, some precautions are being taken. Development of alternative fuels, increased mass transit options, and new enhanced oil recovery technologies all offer the potential to mitigate against declining global oil production.

---

[1] *Mad Max* (1979) and its sequels, *The Road Warrior* (1981) and *Beyond Thunderdome* (1985), are post-apocalyptic movies starring Mel Gibson.

[2] Note that this is not a criticism of the books themselves, but rather a commentary on how some people respond to such books.

Are the precautions enough? So far, they have not prevented record-high oil prices that have challenged economic growth. But we could imagine that the economic situation might be a lot worse if countries had not implemented tougher fuel economy standards, or if oil companies weren't developing unconventional sources of oil.

But what is it that we are trying to prevent? What is the peak oil equivalent of the house burning down? For me personally, it is persistent fuel shortages that disrupt lives and/or fuel prices that become unbearable for the average person and wreak economic havoc. But others have different ideas, to the extent that some believe the house *should* burn down.

I imagine that most of us would like to see the sort of continued technological and economic progress we enjoyed over the past century. Let's face it; most of us don't want to go back to an 18th century lifestyle. But there are plenty of people who believe that the world is heavily overpopulated, and who are ready for the end of growth (both economic and population). There are also those who want to see an entirely new paradigm. Then there are those who do want a return to simpler times. Some of these desires are mutually exclusive, and therefore some people are not going to get what they want.

Business As Usual?

So what can we expect? I don't claim to be able to predict the future either; instead, I try to view the future as a set of possibilities. I am sometimes asked if I believe a business as usual (BAU) scenario is possible, or whether my projections about the future make that assumption. When people mention BAU, they may be referring to a number of different things, but for purposes of this discussion, BAU generally means that the trends of the past 50 years—population growth, higher energy consumption, more economic growth—will continue in the future.

My opinion is that for the most part BAU will continue for at least the next decade or two (although economic growth will not necessarily be enjoyed by all countries or all industries), and political and business leaders will do everything they can to keep that paradigm going for as long as possible. But things will evolve over time. Is "business" in 2012 the same as it was in 1970? No, but many of the same aspects are there. We still drive to work, fly for business and pleasure, and enjoy affordable electricity. Our energy mixture has shifted, as has political power among oil importers and exporters, and we have become more energy efficient. But BAU continues.

I expect that the same will hold true for the next couple of decades. Business as usual will continue in some ways, and in other ways it will not. I believe we will continue to drive and fly, but I don't think we will do so as much as we do today. I don't believe that the U.S. can continue to consume 20 barrels of oil per person per year while China consumes 2 barrels per person. China—and many other developing countries—is on a growth trajectory that will see that figure go somewhat higher, and I believe that will come at the expense of the high oil consumers like the U.S.

Thus, it seems to be a prudent course of action to envision and plan for a world in which U.S. consumption of oil is ultimately a fraction of today's consumption. That will require planning, unless we are happy to let the market take care of that on its own. I personally believe that approach is too risky, which is why I proposed a set of energy policies in Chapter 9 to accomplish the objective of lessening dependence on oil while ensuring that oil is available during the transition. These policies are designed to satisfy multiple possible outcomes, as well as people of widely differing political beliefs.

Summary

There are few things that influence so many aspects of our lives as thoroughly as does energy. But we take energy for granted. We expect there to be fuel at the service station when we pull up, and we expect the lights to come on when we flip the switch. Yet the energy policy decisions that were made in years past determine how much we pay for that energy, its reliability, and all of the related externalities. Sometimes we observe those externalities firsthand, as in the case of oil spills that get major news coverage. Sometimes the externalities are largely hidden from view, because they take place half a world away. Other times, the externalities are merely an acceptance of a greater level of energy insecurity, as when oil is imported from unstable regions of the world.

But there is little doubt that the path we are on is unsustainable. Fossil fuels have sustained us for a very long time, and they will continue to sustain us in the future. But the price we pay is likely to get higher—in terms of physical price, the costs to the environment, and economic risks—and therefore we must proactively plan for a transition away from fossil fuels.

I believe the energy policies in place in many countries are inadequate given the risks we face. Improving our energy policies requires improving our understanding of energy issues. My sincere hope is that this book has helped your understanding in some small way.

References

i "Drowning in oil," *The Economist*, March 4, 1999, www.economist.com /node/188131.

ii Matthew Simmons, interview by Mike Ruppert, "Behind the Blackout," *From The Wilderness.com*, August 21, 2003, www.fromthewilderness.com /free/ww3/082103_blackout.html.

iii Rachel Carson, *Silent Spring* (Greenwich, CT: Fawcett, 1962).

iv Paul Ehrlich, *The Population Bomb* (New York: Ballantine Books, 1968).

v Donella Meadows and others, *The Limits to Growth: A Report for The Club of Rome's Project on the Predicament of Mankind* (New York: Universe Books, 1972).

Index

W, Z, Y, Z

CPSIA information can be obtained at www.ICGtesting.com
Printed in the USA
LVOW062118021012

301265LV00002B/115/P